The
Lifeboat
Baronet

JANET
GLEESON

The
Lifeboat
Baronet

Launching the
RNLI

The
History
Press

To Isabel

First published 2014

The History Press
The Mill, Brimscombe Port
Stroud, Gloucestershire, GL5 2QG
www.thehistorypress.co.uk

British Library Cataloguing in Publication Data.
A catalogue record for this book is available from the British Library.

ISBN 978 0 7524 9001 4

Typesetting and origination by The History Press
Printed in Great Britain

Contents

Portrait of Sir William Hillary. (Courtesy of RNLI Heritage Trust)

Foreword

We owe so much to Sir William Hillary – the man whose vision and sheer determination sparked the establishment of our lifesaving charity. Over 140,000 lives have been saved by the RNLI since this charity was conceived. It was an idea too far-fetched for some: the idea that a humanitarian organisation could save lives at sea through the generosity of donors and volunteers who would give their support and time to answer the call for help. But, today, 190 years on, a day doesn't go past without thousands of people showing that generosity.

At the entrance to the RNLI College in Dorset – where all our lifesavers and staff now carry out training – our memorial sculpture features Hillary's family motto: 'With Courage, Nothing is Impossible.' I believe we have proved him right.

But have we done enough in the past to fully understand Sir William Hillary – to appreciate his complex background and character? The answer is that we have not. And so, we are extremely grateful to Janet Gleeson, the author of this book. In the best traditions of the RNLI, she volunteered her time to help us archive our considerable historical records. Like so many people who learn of our heritage, Janet was fascinated and vowed to seek the answers to so many unanswered questions.

I was delighted to learn that she took her research to a new level, comprehensively exploring the history of a man who, in his own words, was somewhat 'chequered'. Janet's time and research has culminated in a significant work that undoubtedly adds to our understanding of our founder. It is a remarkable story in its own right – and a thoroughly enjoyable read.

Paul Boissier

Paul Boissier
RNLI Chief Executive

Acknowledgements

Many people generously shared their expertise and provided me with invaluable information and guidance during the research and writing of this book. Firstly, thank you to Dr Joanna Bellis, RNLI Heritage Curatorial Manager, who sparked my interest in Sir William Hillary when she gave me the task of transcribing the letters in the Institution's archive and happened to mention she thought a book about Hillary might be a good idea. Secondly, to Wendy Thirkettle, archivist at the Manx Heritage Library, who not only helped me dig out sources I might otherwise have missed, but took the time and trouble to wade through the manuscript in the early stages and offered her suggestions for illustrations. Thank you also to Adrian Corkill for help in sorting out the complexities of Manx wrecks and sending me accounts of them when I could not access them from Dorset. I am also immensely grateful to Dr Nick Draper, Rachel Lang and Katie Donington at UCL for sending me the references to Hillary in the Simon Taylor papers and helping me find out about Hillary's Jamaican connections; to Verity Owens, Carol Waterkeyn, Kevin Smith, Julie James and Liz Cook at the RNLI headquarters in Poole; to Christian Algar from the Rare Books Reference Team at the British Library; and to Nick Steele for putting me in touch with the team at UCL. Thank you also to my agent and old friend Christopher Little for having the faith in this project that helped me see it through to the bitter end.

Preface

Through the deep gloom the lurid lightning flies,
And, by its momentary livid blaze,
A scene of mortal agony displays!
'Reft of each anchor, shattered every sail,
The vessel drives before the raging gale;

'Lines on the first anniversary of the Royal Institution for the Preservation of
Life from Shipwreck', Mrs Henry Rolls (*née* Hillary), 1825

L
ate in the afternoon of 15 May 2009, coxswain Gary Fairbairn, on duty
at the Dunbar lifeboat station, launches the all-weather lifeboat. A gale is
blowing and 37 nautical miles north-east of Dunbar the *Ouhm*, a Swedish
yacht, has radioed the coastguard in difficulties. The yacht belongs to Jonas and
Ingrid Akerblom. It has capsized twice, there is no life raft on board, only one
buoyancy aid (which Ingrid is wearing), and they are drifting at a rate of five
knots towards the north shore of the Firth of Forth.

Ten minutes after the call comes in, Fairbairn and five crew members clear the
breakwater, heading north-east, for the position the yacht has given. The swell is
7m high, with limited visibility, and as the lifeboat ploughs into the storm, conditions worsen. The boat scales 10m-high peaks, plummets into vertiginous troughs,
before confronting another wall of wind-whipped water surging towards her. At
one point a wave of such ferocity hits the starboard side that she is submerged on
her beam, with the port-side wheel house windows under water. Then, as she is
designed to do, she rights herself and battles on.

By the time Fairbairn reaches the position given it is 7.45 p.m. and glimpses of the masthead light, shining between the troughs of the colossal waves, are the only signs the yacht is still afloat. In an attempt to hold the *Ouhm* steady and stern to sea, Jonas has thrown a drogue or makeshift sea anchor overboard. But under these extreme conditions the measure is hopelessly inadequate and she is drifting at the mercy of wind and waves.

Towing the yacht in such weather will be impossible, Fairbairn decides, but the couple's lives are in imminent danger and there is little option but to evacuate them – no easy task in a gale of such magnitude and the yacht beam on to the sea. The lifeboat makes her first approach on the windward side, only to be struck by a ferocious wave. Rapidly applying power astern, Fairbairn avoids collision, retreats, then swings back for a second try. This time he comes close enough for the crew to grab Ingrid and haul her to safety. Someone throws a life jacket to Jonas, but before he can climb aboard, the sea intervenes, forcing the two boats apart. Undaunted, Fairbairn comes back for a third attempt. This time, aided by the crew, Jonas clambers over the guard rail to the sanctuary of the lifeboat's deck.

With the lifeboat speeding her way back to Torness, in the shelter of the wheel house, the crew ply the rescued couple with first aid and hot drinks. They have only the few possessions they had time to pack and what they are wearing, but back at the station the crew donate dry clothing and money to pay for their overnight accommodation. The next day the *Ouhm* is found, drifting at sea but still intact, and is towed in to harbour by another lifeboat. Fairbairn's efforts in the rescue are later rewarded with a bronze gallantry medal presented by Princess Anne.

This is what the RNLI do, 24 hours a day every day of the year, all around the coast of the British Isles. In some ways it is a far cry from 1824, when an impecunious baronet with a shady past decided to take matters into his own hands and do something to prevent the needless loss of life and property by shipwreck. But the principles of the organisation he pioneered remain the same. The RNLI is still a voluntary institution, funded by charitable donation. It still saves lives and property, and recognises the gallantry of those who risk their own safety in so doing. This is not to say the organisation hasn't moved with the times. Some things have changed, and for the better. In the early days, Hillary struggled to raise the funds for fewer than a dozen boats. They now have a fleet of over 330 vessels, which covers the entire coast of the British Isles. They also run a lifeguard service and flood rescue team. Last year alone they gave assistance to more than 18,000 people.

Of course, most of this hardly needs stating. Nearly everyone knows more or less what the RNLI does – it is one of the nation's favourite charities, part of our national identity. We readily drop coins in their boat-shaped collection boxes when they are rattled under our noses, or rattle boxes under other people's noses. Or take our children to visit their stations on days out to coastal resorts and wonder what it feels like to career down the slipway in a gale to save a stranded vessel. Yet there is something much more deep-rooted than nostalgia to our affection for the RNLI. We still need it even though the sea is no longer the only highway to the world at large. Cars, trains and aeroplanes have made us less conscious of shipping, and many of us associate boats mainly with moments of leisure. Yet the sea remains an essential means of transport to our island nation and the world at large. Nowadays more cargo than ever before travels by sea, including nearly all freight to and from Britain and Ireland.[1] Modern shipping may have GPS navigation systems, radar, powerful engines and radios, so there are fewer problems when gales blow. But, as the story of the *Ouhm* and others like it testify, sometimes things still go wrong. And even if we are more likely to be rescued from a surfboard than an ocean-going schooner, the principles are the same. Knowing there are lifeboats standing by makes us feel safer about the world we inhabit. None of us wants to discover what it is to be alone and adrift without hope of assistance. Perhaps that is why the RNLI is awash with supporters; there are normally over 200,000 members and 40,000 volunteers at any given time.

But what do we know about the man who started the institution – its founder, Sir William Hillary? Given the iconic status of the charity in public affections, it seems oddly anomalous that the answer is really very little. This fact was brought home to me when I, like thousands of others, joined the ranks of the RNLI's volunteers. The heritage department, at their headquarters in Poole, asked me to transcribe a collection of letters written by Sir William Hillary – a name I didn't recognise. Beyond a typed list of dates and mysterious three-word subjects such as 'steam life boat' or 'Tower of Refuge', nobody seemed to know much about what they contained.

And so I began. One of the first letters I read was written just after Hillary's return to the Isle of Man from a trip to London in October 1825. He had written in a firm forward-sloping hand:

> I had only been arrived in this island a very few days when one of the most severe storms took place which has been known here for many years, in which the *City of Glasgow*, a steam vessel of the first class, with more than 50 persons on board, was stranded on our dangerous coast ...

I looked up from the creased pages of his letter, across a featureless 1970s office in the aptly named William Hillary House, to the ultra-modern RNLI College and the nautical paraphernalia of Poole Harbour beyond. It was a breezy day in late May. A group of volunteers were waiting at the door to the submersible chamber for a training session. Nearby, glinting in the sun, was the RNLI memorial to lost rescuers – a silvery storm-tossed lifeboat in which a man leans over the gunwales to retrieve a lost sailor from the waves. The inscription on the plinth is Hillary's family motto, 'With Courage Nothing is Impossible', and bears the names of those who have given their lives trying to save others. Beyond it, liveried orange, blue and white, lifeboats were moored along the quayside, bouncing on water ruffled by the gentle wind. The light was so clear that outside the breakwater you could see for miles. It wasn't the sort of weather in which boats get into trouble – nothing like the dark night in 1825 when Hillary had fearlessly set out to the *City of Glasgow*'s rescue. Then he had saved more than fifty lives, nearly drowning in the process, but was reticent to talk about his own efforts. 'The part it fell to my lot to take on this occasion has precluded me from making any report upon it to the committee …' he had written. What motivated him to take to the sea in a tempest, in an open rowing boat, in 1825, I wondered, and why not describe his actions? Did he have something to hide? But to capture the ghosts of history you need substance as well as a spirit of willing enquiry. Aside from the fifty-seven letters in the library in Poole, what else was there to find?

At first it seemed not much. I tracked Hillary through the National Archives, where there are some papers relating to his tangled financial dealings, and on to a few letters in the British Library and Metropolitan Archives. It was still slim pickings – even if reading the newspaper reports of his rescues and reversals of fortune surprised and held me gripped. Then I had an unexpected breakthrough. In the oak-panelled Council Chamber of the Order of the Knights of St John, at Clerkenwell, watched over by portraits of robed Grand Masters, a hefty red morocco-bound volume was placed before me. Full of anticipation, I opened it to find another hundred-odd letters written by Hillary to his friend and fellow knight Sir Richard Broun.

Put together with those from Poole, and the other material I had found, the man who had made it all happen began to emerge. Charismatic, amiable, improbably multi-faceted, yet in his flaws eminently human, he started life as a slave owner's son, became a Regency rake and social climber, then metamorphosed, improbably, into a Victorian philanthropist and reformer. More digging uncovered evidence of financial recklessness, as well as testimony of formidable energy and daring. There were letters referring to his early life and others written after his escape to live, like a Byronic hero, in an island exile. There were also reports of the story of the heartrending shipwreck that prompted his campaign and the foundation of today's RNLI.

Yet I discovered that even during his lifetime his achievements were only patchily acknowledged, and after his death his name was virtually forgotten. Obituaries

were scant and, oddly, in an age that loved heroes, his grave went unmarked for a
century. Which gave rise to more questions: why had he led such an unsettled life
– and why had he slipped through the mesh of historical memory?

I wondered whether part of the problem was his fondness for burying certain aspects of his life. He had, by his own admission, lived through a great deal,
witnessing history from the sidelines. Or as he chose to put it, with the florid
lyricism of the day:

> My life has indeed been exceedingly chequered – intermixed with a great vari-
> ety of scenes and during eventful times in many countries, amongst those who
> filled a much higher station than myself, and in days so remote as to have now
> become a matter of history, in which it has certainly at times been my lot to
> make great efforts accompanied with their share of peril.[2]

The friend to whom he wrote this urged Hillary to tell his own story, yet although
he loved writing, Hillary never did commit the details of his past to paper. He had
probably told his friend only part of his story, leaving out the shameful misdemeanours of his youth. Time had distanced his early life and his failures by then
– why resurrect them in his later years, when they might distract attention from
his greatest achievement – founding the RNLI?

Reading his correspondence I began to get a sense of a man of restless physi-
cality, who relished putting himself to the test. Rather than organise and watch
lifeboats go to the aid of stranded shipping, as most gentlemen without any obvious connection to the sea might have done, his approach was hands-on, leading
from the front, directing operations from inside the rescue boats. Those who
knew him said he could launch a lifeboat single-handed in a swell, and there are
numerous accounts of him guiding his crew through mountainous seas to assist
vessels in distress until he was more than 60 years old – all this despite the fact he
could not swim. More than once he was swept overboard, found himself pum-
melled by hostile seas and rocks, almost drowned, seriously injured. Yet hazards
and misadventures never seem to have deterred him. Rather the reverse. From
his descriptions I felt that confronting danger was what spurred him on – it made
him feel alive.

But something in these accounts also made me wonder if there was more
to his attachment to the sea than first appeared. Shipwrecks and storms are not
just physical phenomena; they are woven into our cultural past, founts of poetic
imagery, symbolising God's power or absence. Hillary lived in a time when the
sea's power – nature in its sublime untamed state – was layered with meanings.
In literature a sea voyage was a metaphor for man's journey through life. In the

newspapers shipwrecks aroused horror and fascination. To the romantic poets, the terrors of the sea in a storm represented an awe-inspiring beauty embodying God's power. As an educated man Hillary would have read Edmund Burke's essay *On the Sublime and Beautiful* and Defoe's *Robinson Crusoe*. Shelley's death by drowning off the Italian coast of Leghorn in 1822, the ultimate romantic death, cannot fail to have moved him. He had found himself in similar stormy seas as a young man in Italy but survived them. Like many men of his age, Hillary had a taste for romantic poetry and the tumultuous scenery it celebrated. He knew Wordsworth and his sister Dorothy, featuring in his poetry, and called the Isle of Man 'this romantic isle'. All of which raised the question, was there more to his affinity to the sea than first appeared? Had vanquishing storms and rescuing lost souls held some other significance? Maybe his life was fashioned to fit the romantic model – a noble social outcast, living in a wilderness, undertaking deeds of daring because confronting terror provided some form of release or gratification? Or was his courage tangled with more personal motives – was saving others a way of saving himself?

Certainly the changing currents of the age played their part in shaping his path. In 1770 George III was still on the throne, Britain still ruled America, France still had a king and queen and long-distance travel at sea relied on the power of the wind. In those days death – whether by drowning or by any other means – was seen as an act of Providence, something dreaded but inevitable. By 1847, when he died, a new mind set prevailed: Britain had emerged from the threat of Napoleon, three kings had been and gone and the young Queen Victoria ruled. By then you could travel across seas by steamer and death by drowning was no longer accepted as an act of divine will. Instead educated men were asking questions of the natural world around them, striding ahead in efforts to understand and conquer its vagaries.

Hillary was a man of his age, straddling the two centuries in which he lived. A side of him always clung to eighteenth-century traditions: a stratified society, each man in his place, life predestined. He wrote and published copiously: works partly inspired by his Quaker upbringing which had taught him writing was an effective way to reach an audience and change people's minds. But as the content of his pamphlets shows, he was also a modernist; a man enthralled by science and the technological progress of his age, someone at one with the new century's spirit of humanitarian endeavour, who believed shipwrecks were not God's will but something preventable.

Change has accelerated since those days. Thanks to scientific advances we comprehend and, mostly, master the elements. But this much remains unaltered: the sea can still be unpredictable and perilous. Lifeboats are still launched to rescue stricken sailors. Lives are still saved by their crews. And perhaps for this reason, if no other, 190 years after the birth of the RNLI, the forgotten story of the man who founded it, and in doing so made the sea a safer place, deserves to be explored.

Notes

1   I am grateful to Adrian Corkill for pointing this out to me.
2   Archive of the Order of St John, Hillary letters, 15 April 1844.

1

The *Vigilant* and the *Racehorse*

Cast on the rock, in vain are lights display'd,
In vain the frequent gun implores for aid;–
Another flash! – the lofty masts descend,
The hull divides, the crashing timbers rend!
One frantic cry resounds along the shore,
Soon lost amidst the closing billows' roar;

'Lines on the first anniversary of the Royal Institution for the Preservation of
Life from Shipwreck', Mrs Henry Rolls (*née* Hillary), 1825

At first there was no cause for alarm. With a brisk west-northwesterly gale blowing up on the afternoon of Sunday 6 October 1822, Douglas Bay, on the east coast of the Isle of Man, offered welcome shelter from the fickle Irish Sea. Several boats had taken refuge there, among them the HMS *Vigilant*, one of the navy's flagship revenue cutters, whose role was to intercept the trade in contraband that was rife in these waters. Launched the previous year, the *Vigilant* was a beacon of naval pride. Built to a state of the art design, with a diagonally timbered construction for resilience in extreme conditions, she was equipped with every attribute needed for snaring the wiliest of smugglers. Her slender lines provided swiftness and manoeuvrability under sail, and her ten guns and fifty-four man crew gave the muscle to apprehend those she discovered. But autumn storms are frequent in the Irish Sea and, like any good commander, Lieutenant Reid had no wish to place the safety of his crew at unnecessary risk. Douglas was a stopping-off point between Milford Haven and Liverpool, often used by revenue patrols. The *Vigilant* slid into the bay and dropped anchor the previous day, and her crew, resplendently uniformed, saluted the island's governor in a showy ceremony designed to attract the attention of malefactors as well as innocent spectators. When new boats arrived the harbour became a place of bustling activity, and a crowd, some doubtless hoping that their illicit trade would not be interrupted for long, congregated along the Red Pier to watch.

Before midnight, the wind shifted unexpectedly. Reid's thoughts were now no longer of ceremony or contraband. As he well knew, if the wind came from the east, Douglas Bay was exposed to the full onslaught of the waves. Under such conditions, moorings often failed or drifted and boats were easily washed onto the rocks or ran aground. True to form, with the wind now backing to the southeast, row upon row of swollen breakers streamed in and the cutter lurched and strained on her mooring. Taking stock of the situation, Reid decided he would be prudent to leave his anchorage and ride out the storm elsewhere. He summoned his crew and ordered them to weigh anchor.

Using oil lanterns to illuminate the darkness, the storm sails were raised and Reid set his course, heading for safer water. But he was not alone in doing so and without warning out of the gloom a heavily laden sloop materialised. There was little time to spare other than to register that the sloop's course cut across *Vigilant*'s bow, and that unless Reid took evasive action immediately he faced certain collision. He made a snap judgement and adjusted his wheel.

The murky night and sea stirred by the unruly wind, made Conister Rock – an unmarked, notoriously treacherous island reef that lurks like fangs in a serpent's mouth at the south of the bay – virtually invisible. Reid's navigational skills, in common with every ship's master of the day, were as reliant on his knowledge and observation of the local landscape as his ability to read charts. But the weather was hostile, the dark impenetrable and as misfortune would have it, the new course he had chosen took the cutter closer to the submerged rocks than it was safe to sail. The danger became clear when the *Vigilant* plunged into the trough of a wave, shuddered and came to a creaking halt.

With a cauldron sea swirling around the stricken vessel and a tide that would soon be on the turn, Reid tried everything he could think of – to no avail. The *Vigilant* remained immobile, her stern wedged between the rocks, the breakers threatening to roll her hull and split it open like an egg at any moment. Even if she held in the ebbing tide, Reid feared there was every chance she would be swamped by the rising level of the sea once it turned. In either case the ship would be lost, and with it, in all likelihood, his own life and those of the men in his charge. Outside assistance was now the only hope of survival. Ordering flares to be lit and distress signals fired, Reid must have prayed that help would arrive soon, and that his ship's innovative but now creaking construction would be strong enough to withstand the tempest until it did.

Above the wind, the crack of the cannonade reverberated across the town of Douglas in the early hours of the morning. The sound drifted towards the elegant villas on Prospect Hill on the outskirts of Douglas, where Sir William Hillary heard it and rushed from his bed to scan the moonless horizon. A Lancashire man by birth, he had settled in the town a decade earlier. During this time, storms, shipwrecks and frequent loss of life had become all too familiar and he recognised the danger signs as easily as any gale-hardened Manx sailor. 'Placed as the Isle of Man is, in the midst of a stormy sea ... with strong tides and a rocky and dangerous shore ... (which) the fatal experience of almost every succeeding winter contributes to confirm by the various shipwrecks on its coasts but too frequently attended with the loss of many valuable lives',[1] he would later write, recalling the many tragedies he had witnessed. The *Vigilant* was invisible in the darkness of the October night, but the gunfire and flares were enough for him to grasp the gravity of her situation.

A contemporary who knew Hillary described him as 'a man of military bearing, of more than medium height, with high forehead and ... kindly sympathy shown in every lineament of his face'.[2] The only surviving portrait of him shows a hawkish man with a well-defined jaw, patrician nose and luminous determination. His hair is neatly curled, his forehead broad, and the cut of his coat and glint in his eye suggestive of a dapper man with an appetite for adventure. Apart from the thin and world-weary set of his lips, little in the portrayal suggests the humiliating reversals of fortune he had suffered. But perhaps this isn't surprising – he had learned the art of bravado and, having settled in Douglas, distanced from his past misfortunes, in public, at least, the mask never slipped.

No longer in the first flush of youth, Hillary was in his fifties, affable and happily married but inwardly itching for more. The *Vigilant*'s distress signal in the dark of the night ignited his sense of purpose. The chance to demonstrate his physical strength and courageous character, to organise, cajole and do whatever was needed to save the lives now threatened, was not something to shirk. Rather the reverse, he embraced it.

Ignoring the lashing storm and the fact that, like most men of his day, he had never learned to swim, Hillary hurried down to the Douglas quayside and met up with three similarly doughty acquaintances. Mr Hanby was the owner of the York Hotel and several boats. Lieutenants Burbridge and Graves were both ex-naval officers, who had been drawn by the financial advantages of life in the Isle of Man (taxes a fraction of those in Britain and life far less costly) to settle in Douglas. The three had also heard the *Vigilant*'s distress signal and wanted to do whatever they could to help.[3]

Together the four set about galvanising assistance from local sailors and fishermen. This was no easy feat. The hazards of trying to rescue a stranded vessel in a gale were self-evident and few were keen to risk their necks. Their concrns were not only for their own well-being. There was no financial reward for such life-threatening work, and if they perished or were injured attempting a rescue, their families would suffer extreme hardship.

There was another, darker reason for their reluctance. On the island, as in many other coastal communities where livings were hard, wrecks were seen as fair game for supplementing livelihoods – and not just those of the poor. 'It is a matter of general belief that such nefarious practices are not confined to the ignorant and lower orders of society but that men in more respectable circumstances and far above the temptation of want are concerned therein, either as actual plunderers themselves, or recipients or partakers in the nefarious gains of others,'[4] the editors of a local journal complained, after a wrecked brig laden with cargo 'of immense value' was plundered, with the tacit connivance of the security guard appointed by Lloyd's underwriters.

Even so, faced with the galvanising energy of Hillary and the others, no one wanted to be seen standing by while lives were unnecessarily lost and resistance crumbled. Hanby solved the problem of finding suitable boats, offering three small vessels from his own fleet. His contribution was essential because despite the frequency of shipwrecks off the Manx coast, rescuing vessels in distress was still a hit and miss affair. Douglas, like many other coastal towns, had no coherent method for giving assistance, even when ships were stranded close to shore. It was a port where, in one way or another, the majority of residents earned a living from the sea, but it did not have a lifeboat.

Elsewhere in the British Isles, lifeboats were in similarly scant supply. Here and there sporadic attempts had been made to rectify the shortfall: Lloyd's had sponsored the building of lifeboats in Liverpool and donated funds to several other maritime communities around the coast of Britain. A handful of philanthropic individuals had also donated lifeboats for vulnerable stretches of coast, such as Bamburgh Castle in Northumberland and coastal towns such as Lowestoft, Liverpool and Rye. The Isle of Man's Governor, the Duke of Atholl, had paid for a purpose-built lifeboat for the island in 1802. But these were isolated gestures, in the Isle of Man's case made with no formal provision for the vessel's long-term deployment or maintenance. Over the following decade, the boat saved many lives but when not in use was left exposed to the elements on the shingle at Douglas Head. There it remained, slowly decaying, until a December storm in 1814, when the boat was swept away at high tide and smashed to matchstick wood on the unforgiving rocks.

Designs of lifeboats varied according to the terrain and were usually equipped with water-tight compartments containing air or cork helping to prevent capsize in heavy seas. But the boats that set off to assist the stranded *Vigilant* on that dark

October night were meant for fishing or unloading – not rescue in a gale. They were robustly made; broad of beam and deep of keel, designed to safely transport cargoes or hauls of herring and the nets that caught them. They had no cork-filled buoyancy chambers, no method of draining water should a wave swamp them, nor any other modifications to withstand the conditions they were about to confront.

Burbridge and his crew went first, with Hillary following close behind and Graves skippering the third boat. They forged their way into the wind and heaving sea with nothing more to power them than flimsy oars, a small lantern and determination. The force of the gale caught them as they emerged from the shelter of the harbour, sweeping them towards the serrated rocks of Conister. Ignoring the jarring motion of the boat and avoiding the danger of the reef, they navigated close enough to catch the heavy hawsers thrown from the deck by *Vigilant*'s stranded crew. Securing the ropes they drifted downwind, the fury of the sea's power adding strength to their oars as they strained to pull the cutter free.

Even with the aid of the now incoming tide, the men's efforts were futile. *Vigilant*'s stern remained clenched in the grip of the rocks. Reid recognised he would have to do more to assist the rescue boats' efforts. Reducing the weight of his ship was the obvious solution – increasing her buoyancy would help the rising tide work her free. Reid ordered the mast to be dropped and thrown overboard, and when this did not help, instructed the crew to jettison the heavy guns into the sea. One by one the eight expensive stern cannon were released from their mountings and hurled into the black waves.

When the three boats tried again to haul the *Vigilant* to safety they felt her hull yield and shift. Hillary and his fellow oarsmen were able to edge her loose and drag her to the safety of deeper water. Miraculously, although her stern post and rudder were lost – and, they would discover later by daylight, a gash had been ripped into the aft of her keel – she was still watertight. The damage was above the waterline. With lines securing her, the *Vigilant* was able to ride out the gale until the following morning. Then, 'with much difficulty', she was hauled into the narrow entrance of Douglas Harbour to undergo temporary repairs.

Reid, suffering from the strain of his ordeal, as well as the physical effects of battling the storm, was by now 'in a very ill state of health',[5] reported the *Rising Sun*, and his crew were exhausted. From Hillary's point of view, however, the night was an unqualified success. No lives had been lost, and despite considerable damage – later estimated at £1,500 – a valuable ship, not to mention naval pride, had been preserved.

Hillary had been up half the night and must have been physically exhausted. Yet the storm was not over, nor had danger passed for other shipping moored in the bay, and his determination remained unwavering. Returning to the harbour that Monday morning, he grew concerned for two schooners, three sloops and a brig, 'driven at their anchors considerably to leeward in the bay'.[6] One of them, The *Merchant*, a sloop en route from Dundalk to Liverpool with a cargo of oats, vividly illustrated the dangers of Douglas Bay in the grip of a south-easter. Forced to take refuge when the storm blew up and exposed to the fury of wind and sea, the *Merchant* had been 'driven from her anchorage and now run aground on the shore opposite Castle Mona', reported the *Rising Sun*. The imposing residence of the Duke of Atholl stood on the hillside towards the centre of the bay and marked the start of a ribbon of rock which unfurled in a northerly direction. Caught on the reef, the combined pounding of reef and waves 'soon knocked a hole in her bottom'. By the time Hillary became aware of the *Merchant*'s predicament five of her crew had drowned and most of her cargo had been disgorged, 'washed along the beach in all directions'.[7]

He enlisted the help of two eminent members of the town: Mr Quirk, Douglas's High Bailiff, and the harbour master, Mr Cox. With their support he intended to organise a rescue mission, but this time met apathy and stony-faced resistance. Those who had turned out to help with the *Vigilant* were now in need of rest; the other seamen and fishermen of the town were unwilling to help. Aside from the obvious dangers involved, their reluctance stemmed partly from self-interest. The vessels in question were all commercial ships, carrying cargoes that might provide useful additional income if they happened to fall into their hands – a distinct possibility if the storm was left to do its work.

Hillary chipped away the hostility with assurances of financial reward, reiterating his readiness to join them, regardless of his own safety. He was determined to provide aid to the stricken vessel. The risk involved was of little concern to him; what mattered was that something should be done for those who believed themselves lost. Fired up by the crisis, he was careless of his crew's safety safety. 'He never allows the men employed in this service to wear cork jackets, or to be lashed to the boat, deeming such precautions calculated to diminish their intrepidity: nor does he himself, though unable to swim, make use of them',[8] recorded a bemused contemporary.

We cannot but wonder what motivated such unflinching and, arguably, reckless courage. Perhaps outfacing a perilous sea brought an exhilaration that made him feel alive in a way he never did in his everyday life. Perhaps he believed so strongly in his own invincibility that he did not acknowledge the danger. Or maybe he remembered similar times when he had been saved. Whatever the motive, shattered though he was, while the *Merchant* and other boats needed assistance, he would not rest. His tenacity and conviction wore away misgivings and the reluctant seamen agreed to go with him into the turmoil of the storm. The remaining crew on *Merchant* were saved from drowning and the sloop *Eliza* and schooner *Content* were towed into the safety of the harbour with no lives lost.

Still the wind continued to blow, the following day, Tuesday, strengthening again and shifting to the south. Gazing out across the bay and seeing every remaining vessel flying a distress signal, Hillary, who had barely slept for two days, felt as compelled to help as he had when first roused from his bed by the crippled *Vigilant*. 'Hillary and other gentlemen were indefatigable in their exertions to urge the boatmen to get them into harbour',[9] reported the *Rising Sun*. The first vessel to demand immediate attention was the brig *Two Sisters*, which had sought refuge in the bay after a night of tragedy at sea. Twenty miles off the Calf of Man, 'a wild and romantic' treeless rocky outcrop off the south-western tip of the Isle of Man, the *Two Sisters* had been swamped by a freak wave that had washed her master and four members of her crew overboard and seriously damaged her deck. Three of those swept into the sea had managed to scramble back on board – including the master – but 'the other two men were seen no more'. Having limped into Douglas Bay to undertake repairs before continuing on her way, the *Two Sisters* was now dragging her mooring and being blown downwind.

Assisted by Quirk and Cox and volunteer crews in three small boats, Hillary again set out into the swollen waves and helped drag the brig to the safety of the harbour, saving the lives of her remaining seventeen crew. He performed similar services for the schooner *Fame*, the sloop *Dove* and three other vessels. The following day the wind died and the sea grew calm. By then Sir William Hillary had offered assistance to ten vessels and in all helped save 106 lives.

The storm passed over the horizon but a further episode in the story was yet to unfold. When word of the *Vigilant*'s fate reached the Admiralty, an escort was dispatched to bring her back to Plymouth for proper repairs. The vessel chosen for the task was *Racehorse*, an eighteen-gun naval brig that had seen action off Madagascar and the Cape of Good Hope during the Napoleonic Wars. Since then she had been stationed for several years in the Mediterranean. Recently returned to Britain, she was now under the command of Captain Suckling.

Racehorse set sail on a fine winter's morning, with a crew of one hundred officers and men, intending to be back in Plymouth in convoy with the *Vigilant* in time for Christmas. Progress was steady and she made stops along the way at Milford Haven and then Holyhead, where a pilot, William Edwards, was taken on board. Early on Saturday 14 December, 'in gallant trim and gay',[10] according to the *Liverpool Mercury*, *Racehorse* left the coast of Anglesey on the final leg of her voyage to Douglas. The passage was uneventful, and as darkness fell the following evening at 5 p.m., the lookout spotted the twin lighthouses of the Calf of Man. By now the weather was looking distinctly less favourable. The wind was stiffening and a choppy sea deepening to an ominous swell. In view of the deteriorating conditions Edwards, the pilot, suggested a north-easterly heading, taking the *Racehorse* closer to land to help him pinpoint his position. At about 5.30 p.m. he spotted a beacon shining in the dark. Assuming it to be the light marking Douglas pier-head, he told Suckling he could now alter his course and enter the bay. Without questioning the pilot's judgement, Suckling ordered the crew to haul the sails to windward and reef the top sails. He realised his dreadful mistake minutes later, when, with the menacing sound of splintering wood, the ship struck rocks.

Edwards had miscalculated his position by over 10 miles. The light he had spotted was in fact that of Scarlett House, a building on Langness Point. In changing course, *Racehorse* had struck Skerranes – a gnarled finger of rock that juts two miles out into the sea between Castletown and Douglas, the latter lying about seven nautical miles further to the north-east. No sooner had she struck than *Racehorse* began shipping water. Suckling hurriedly ordered the pumps to be manned, but the damage to her keel was too great; nothing could keep her afloat. Soon the water was lifting the lower deck and, as *The Times*[11] later put it, 'all hopes of saving her was at once given up'.

Caught on an isolated stretch of coast, miles from the nearest town, in a churning sea and the black of night, Suckling frantically instructed the men to set off 'guns of distress, with rockets, false fires and other signals'.[12] He was going through the motions. Stranded so far from habitation, he presumed that the chances of the signals being noticed were remote and his best chance of saving his crew now lay with the two auxiliary vessels carried on board: a small cutter (an open sailing boat) and a galley (a rowing boat). He ordered the cutter to be launched first, hoping that if she was brought alongside with a stream anchor she might provide protection and stabilise the sinking sloop. Again things did not go as he hoped. With breakers crashing over and an incoming flood tide, even getting the vessel safely into the water proved far more difficult than expected and it was impossible to hold her steady alongside. Fearing that the *Racehorse* might break up at any time, Suckling ordered as many crew as the cutter could safely carry to board and directed his second Lieutenant to head for Castletown to summon assistance. Then the galley was launched, loaded with seventeen more men, and sent on her way, 'to land if possible among the rocks of which there appeared but little hopes as the sea was beating over them with great violence'.[13]

It would be several hours before either of these vessels made landfall, but fortunately, the *Racehorse*'s distress flares had been heard in Derbyhaven. J. Quirk, the

Douglas Water Bailiff, one of those roused, vividly recounted the night's events: 'I went down to the pier and from the light which the rockets and blue lights afforded I could see a loom of the land within the ship and that she was ashore upon the most dangerous part of the coast',[14] he reported. Three small fishing boats 'with lanterns at their bows' went by sea to help the stricken vessel, while Quirk and several custom-house officers and others hurried overland. At the headland they were joined by a small crowd of curious townspeople, perhaps hopeful of salvage as well as of saving lives. Although the presence of custom-house men curtailed overt criminality, there was an unpredictable expectancy among the clusters of onlookers strung like cormorants along the rocks. 'It was an extreme dark night … the tide of flood had commenced and the sea was very heavy', Quirk recalled, describing how some men scrambled over rocks and lit straw fires among the jagged rocks to help the rescue boats find their way safely to shore.

So violent was the sea that of the three vessels that set sail from Derbyhaven, two were almost swamped as they rounded the point and turned back; only one managing to reach the *Racehorse*. This boat, valiantly skippered by its owner, a fisherman by the name of Quayle, made five consecutive trips, taking the crew off the stricken ship in orderly groups and navigating through a narrow channel in the rocks to land them on shore. 'Such was the excellent discipline on board … that not a man attempted to quit her without orders',[15] *The Times* related.

Suckling, his first lieutenant and the young ship's mate, Mr Bone, a popular young officer who had recently passed his naval exams to become a lieutenant, waited until the last boat, which was loaded more heavily than the rest, with seventeen men. On shore, meanwhile, conscious that the rising tide and angry sea were making conditions increasingly perilous, Quirk, two officers and five or six boatmen waited on the rocks, ready to assist the boat to land. 'There was occasionally a high surf, and the tide had flowed over some flat rocks, making the narrow inlet to shore appear wider',[16] he recorded. He was watching the heavily laden fishing boat's progress when, still some distance from the shore, she was caught by a freak wave, hurled against the rocky ledge and capsized. 'It was a most dreadful spectacle, and the cries were most appalling … two of the boat's crew only were saved (three others) … were not seen at all – they must have been confined under the water by the boat. The boat was righted when she reached the rock, but a hat only floated out of her',[17] wrote a shocked Quirk, who watched in horror as the tragedy unfolded. Suckling, a strong swimmer, made it to the shore, as did the lieutenant, who was dragged from the waves unconscious. Six other members of the *Racehorse*'s crew and several Manx sailors also survived. The rest were not so lucky.

Mr Bone, the young ship's mate, 'beloved by all,' was among the nine unfortunate victims of the storm. He had at first clung to an oar, but two other members of the crew were holding on to him, and eventually, finding it 'impossible to support their weight', he had let go and attempted to swim to shore without aid. He was no match for the brutal force of the sea and 'was seen no more, having most probably been dashed to pieces amongst the rocks',[18] surmised the *Morning Post*. Among the three Manx fishermen who drowned was Mr Quayle, the fisherman owner of the boat that had saved so many lives.

Shipwreck stories always exerted a terrifying hold on public imagination. The sea was the only route to the world beyond British shores and the nation took pride in her maritime past. Everyone knew that naval power had played a key role in saving the country from Napoleon's armies and mercantile shipping underpinned her place as an increasingly prosperous, outward-looking trading power. But alongside the benefits of Britain's maritime prowess there were perils that could never be forgotten. 'Melancholy' shipwrecks had featured in fiction from before Shakespeare's time, while factual accounts of marine disasters made frequent headlines in newspapers and told a grimly repetitive tale.

In the case of the *Racehorse*, when the news broke, it was mainly the plight of Quayle and his family that struck at people's hearts. 'So persevering had this poor fellow been in his endeavours ... in making the fifth and last trip ... he fell sacrifice to his humanity',[19] declared the *Morning Post*. As if that were not poignant enough, Quayle had left a widow and family who were entirely dependent on him for their well-being. 'She had just been delivered of her eighth child and has by these means been deprived of all her hopes in this life which depended solely on her husband's exertion,'[20] reported the paper.

The family circumstances of the other two fishermen were only slightly less disturbing. One left a wife and two infants; the other provided for his sister and her children. In addition, sympathy was felt for the predicament of the survivors of the *Racehorse*, who 'by this sudden catastrophe' had lost everything except for the clothes they were wearing when rescued'.[21] Reliant on the goodwill of the local community for food and shelter, the officers were installed at the George Inn, Castletown and the men put up in barracks where beds, blankets and cooking apparatus were provided. Until the Admiralty decided what to do, 'a temporary subscription is raising for them',[22] reported a local paper. Meanwhile Quirk did his best to help. 'My principle object in writing is to ask if some provision cannot be procured from the British Government for the widows and children of the boatmen – voluntary subscription will be merely a temporary relief.'[23]

In the event what happened was as follows. The Admiralty, concerned by the loss of a ship that had cost them nearly £18,000, announced a court martial of the crew. In early January, HMS *Brazen*, a naval sloop was sent to bring the *Racehorse*'s crew back to Plymouth. The hearing took place on 8 February, on board HMS *Superb*. In a statement of defence, Edwards asserted he had never been involved in an accident in his seventeen years as a pilot; the watch had been removed and 'sent aloft' without his knowledge. As further mitigation he claimed 'the light which deceived me was right over Langness Point and is called Scarlett House – the gentleman who occupied it (a Captain Thompson) died on that day, so the house was well lighted up, which occasioned me to take it for Douglas Pier Light ... that light has before ... been the occasion of several vessels being lost.'[24]

Those on the examining board were familiar enough with maritime reality to recognise this as the unsavoury truth. Navigating a stormy sea at night was never easy. Many had found themselves in similarly uncertain predicaments. After brief deliberation Suckling was subjected to a 'gentle' reprimand for failing to ensure depth soundings were regularly taken, while Edwards was 'severely reprimanded' and his pay suspended for negligence. The rest of the crew were acquitted.

If the incident was viewed as a sad inevitability, the plight of those who depended on the casualties was not. During the course of the enquiry, the role played by Quayle and his crew in saving so many lives was gratefully acknowledged. The widows concerned were awarded pensions totalling £84; public subscription topped up the fund, with a donation of another £100. Formal thanks were also made to Sir William Hillary, Lieutenants Burbridge and Graves and the others who had offered assistance to the *Vigilant*. A reward of £20 was distributed to the men involved. And then a line was drawn under the matter.

Hillary had not actively participated in the rescue of the *Racehorse*. He lived 12 miles away and was unlikely even to have been one of those who congregated on the shore when word of the unfolding tragedy spread. Although he tracked events with interest, he knew of plenty of other shipwrecks where the toll of lives had been higher. Nevertheless his involvement in the *Vigilant*'s rescue gave these losses an especially disturbing resonance. He was struck by the thought that if the unfortunate victims of the *Racehorse* were added to those who had died in other storms and other wrecks throughout the year, the numbers were truly catastrophic. Had more assistance or better craft been available to the *Racehorse*, how many of the pitiful casualties might have been spared? What would become of the bereaved families? Would the gallant men who had gone to the aid of the stricken brig willingly do so again when they realised the predicament in which their families might be left? The questions haunted Hillary and stirred his desire to act. He could no longer sit on the sidelines of life, while in the treacherous

seas around the Isle of Man people drowned. He wanted to do something to put
right the injustice of lives needlessly lost; his dilemma was simply how to realise
his aim. And so, as the New Year turned to spring, an idea took shape in his mind.

Notes

1 RNLI Archive, WH to Captain Foulerton (Brethren of Trinity House) 12 June 1824.
2 Samuel Norris, *Manx Memories and Movements*, (1938), p. 46.
3 Account based on report in *Rising Sun*, 12 October 1822.
4 PRO ho98/77.
5 Rising Sun, 12 October 1822.
6 *Rising Sun*, 12 October 1822.
7 Ibid.
8 Charles John Shore, *Sketches of the Coasts and Islands of Scotland and of the Isle of Man*, 1836.
9 *Rising Sun*, 12 October 1822.
10 *Liverpool Mercury*, 27 December 1822.
11 *The Times*, 24 December 1822.
12 *Morning Post*, 24 December 1822.
13 *Liverpool Mercury*, 27 December 1822.
14 Manx National Heritage Archive, AP 110 (2nd) 25; Quirk to James.
15 *The Times*, 24 December 1822.
16 Manx Heritage Archive, AP 110 (2nd) 25.
17 Ibid.
18 *Morning Post*, 24 December 1822.
19 Ibid.
20 Ibid.
21 *Liverpool Mercury*, 27 December 1822.
22 *Rising Sun*, 27 December 1822.
23 Manx Heritage Archive, AP 110 (2nd) 25.
24 A. Corkhill, *Shipwrecks of the Isle of Man* (2001).

2

The Merchant of Liverpool

Hail, ye enlighten'd sons of British sires,
Who, as Philanthropy's pure flame aspires,
Were first to quicken by its rising rays,
And through your country pour its glorious blaze!
Boldly go on! Yours is a noble strife.
The prize ye seek, not less than human life!
Bound by no party, to no clime confin'd

'Lines on the first anniversary of the Royal Institution for the Preservation of
Life from Shipwreck', Mrs Henry Rolls (*née* Hillary), 1825

The sea recurs, sweeping through William Hillary's life, at times sparkling, smooth or stormy, bringing coherence to the oddly disparate chapters of his story. Fittingly for a man who would make the sea a safer place, he was born in Liverpool on 4 January 1770.[1] According to the records, the day was one of boisterous wind with large white clouds and showers that buffeted the riggings of the hundreds of ships moored nearby.

The Liverpool of his birth was a city of contrasts – a port on the rise where men of enterprise were growing fabulously rich, yet a place where prosperity relied on a dark and shameful trade. Many of the ships moored two and three-deep all along the newly built docks had made their way there from the West Indies. Laden with sugar, rum, tobacco, cotton, coffee and timber, they had navigated Atlantic storms and braved the perilous currents of the Irish Sea, avoiding privateers and the treacherous shoals guarding the entrance to the River Mersey. Safely moored at the wharf and sheltered from the ebbing tide, their cargoes were unloaded into a warren of cavernous warehouses. Then emptied holds were replenished with locally made products: guns, metal wares, woven cotton, pottery and glass beads. And when high water came they would again set sail, some heading back to the West Indies via Europe, others navigating south for the west African coasts of Ghana, Togo, Benin or Calabar. In these far-flung outposts cargoes would be discharged, traded for slaves and, with a new human cargo manacled and stowed, the ships sailed on to the West Indies to begin the cycle again. So the triangular trade would turn small merchants into international entrepreneurs and transform their once insignificant home port into a flourishing financial centre.

Hillary was raised against a backdrop of sails and storm-rattled riggings, and warehouses crammed with hogsheads of sugar, yet this world of traffic and trade seems never to have fired his imagination or penetrated his heart. He would always be a reluctant merchant, his sense of belonging captured early on by a place where commerce and crowds played little part. As a small boy his father took him to north Yorkshire, where he had been born into a yeoman farming community and where family members and old friends still lived. They went to Wensleydale, to a remote, rugged and sparsely populated valley near the border with Cumberland. In the seventeenth century, another William Hillary (our Hillary's great-grandfather) had married Anne Metcalfe and settled here, after her family bequeathed her two farms at the northern end of Wensleydale.

The landscape was one of clean air and stirring open panoramas – of steep crags and ridges, tumbling streams and grey stone bridges, overshadowed by Mossdale Fell, which was carpeted in purple heather in late summer and snow-clad for the winter months. It is hard to imagine anywhere more different from the shrill, salt-rimed streets of eighteenth-century Liverpool.

William Hillary's great-grandparents lived in Birkrigg, a modest sheep and dairy farm that still crouches amid a mosaic of sheep-mown pasture and dry stone walls. His grandfather, John, was born here but, finding the remoteness daunting, in the early years of his marriage to Mary Robinson, he moved to a more comfortable house nearby, now known as Hillary Hall. From the front porch of this new grander residence John could gaze over the sweep of the fells and the rock-strewn River Ure, but he also had a local community in the village of Burtersett to alleviate his isolation.

The family farmed some of the best land in the region; pasture that lay low down in the valley, where the grazing had been sought after since Norse settlers first brought their animals here in ancient times. Added to this they owned a thousand acres of moorland; steep, exposed terrain where livestock perished in the blistering winters, and even in summer crops would not flourish. You couldn't make money from this land but with grouse on the moor and streams filled with trout, both as a young boy and as a young gentleman keen on sporting pursuits, William Hillary revelled in it. In his youth he befriended the children of local farmers, rambling the countryside in their company. As a young man, he would continue to visit, turning Rigg House into his holiday sporting lodge and allowing this rugged unpopulated landscape to become engrained in his soul.

For his grandparents John and Mary, however, life revolved around work rather than play. They had nine children, of whom seven survived to adulthood. Hillary's father Richard, born in 1703, was the youngest of the boys. Isaac, the eldest, was born in 1694, then another William, born in 1697.[2] Although the family were comparatively well to do – their sister Rachel is described as 'blessed with affluence'[3] in a testament of the times – idleness was something their parents deplored. In any case, as younger sons, Richard and William knew they stood to enjoy little in the way of family inheritance and needed to find their own way to earn a living. William was studious by nature and there was enough money for him to go to Leiden to study medicine under the leading teacher of the day.[4] Richard took a more direct approach to providing for his future, deciding on a career in trade.

And so he came to Liverpool – the obvious place for him to try his chances. During the century that his life nearly spans, its population would burgeon from under 10,000 in 1700, to reach 78,000 in 1801. After London and Bristol it was the third largest city and third port in the country, a source of admiration and astonishment to those who witnessed its rapid growth. 'The town has now an opulent flourishing and increasing trade... so that in a word they are almost become like the Londoners, universal merchants',[5] wrote an awestruck Daniel Defoe after visiting the city in the early 1700s. 'Some merchants are certainly far wealthier than many sovereign princes of Germany or Italy', wrote an incredulous Cesare de Saussure in 1727, mesmerised by those who had already made fortunes from the lucrative trade with the West Indies.[6]

Money wasn't Liverpool's sole attraction. The city was a Quaker stronghold and Richard Hillary was a member of the faith, schooled in the Quakers' strict moral code, with prudence, piety and industry at its core. Life in the city may have been a jolt after his quiet and remote Wensleydale upbringing. But with other Quakers around, ready to teach, trade and perhaps one day marry him, the transition held few fears. He had every expectation his new life would be brimful of opportunity.

With his nephew John Scott, he formed a partnership, based in Old Hall Street, one of the city's most ancient thoroughfares. The street was only a rutted track, in parts barely wide enough for a single wagon to pass, but it was conveniently close to the docks. From shabby premises they followed the model of many others;

setting themselves up as 'merchants in commerce', they began to trade with the West Indies. Opportunities were plentiful and Hillary and Scott soon had a flourishing trade importing exotic mahogany, bales of linen and cotton, and hogs heads of sugar, rum and coffee.

Family connections helped. After practising medicine in Ripon and fashionable Bath, Richard's physician brother William moved to Barbados for several years. His medical research led him to write *The Diseases of Barbados*, one of the first books on tropical maladies to be written by a British physician. Having a well-known brother *in situ* in the colonies aided Richard's business interests, and he cannily invested in ships and property in Tortola and Jamaica, where there were established Quaker communities. By mid-century Richard Hillary was listed as one of Liverpool's principal ship owners.[7]

When Richard allowed himself moments of leisure, he would stride north, to a fashionable park called Ladies Walk, promenading the tree-lined avenues with his Quaker friends, talking business and glimpsing views of the estuary and open fields beyond. 'These walks used to be thronged with the townsfolk, who sported their bravery in broad-skirted coats, satin breeches, gold-laced waistcoats, silk stockings, square-toed large-buckled shoes, and three-cornered hats; while the ladies exhibited high toupees hooped dresses, and high-heeled shoes', recalled one observer. As a Quaker, Richard avoided such showiness. Nor did he approve of the, 'disgraceful conduct ... without the least regard for decency' that went on nearby on an area of foreshore where 'people used to take their plunge, leaving their clothes with little urchins who made a livelihood by taking charge of them'.[8] The passing years did little to soften his wariness of Liverpool life outside the society of his Quaker friends. He took satisfaction from seeing his business grow and spread across the sea, but for the important things in life he never ventured into wider social circles.

Outwardly the family was prospering but at home they were swamped by a succession of misfortunes. First Isaac, the eldest brother, died, unmarried; then William, the eminent doctor, returned from Barbados famous and rich but also unwed and childless, and in 1763 he too fell prey to a sudden and virulent fever. Preoccupied with his business, Richard had until now pushed thoughts of a family of his own to one side. He was 60 at the time of his second brother's death, yet still a single man. Presumably the realisation that after him there was no male Hillary to inherit the family estates spurred him into action. Predictably, he turned to his Quaker acquaintances to search for a suitable bride. A year after his brother's death his sights settled on Hannah Winn-Lascelles.[9] Perhaps he courted her along the shady avenues of Ladies' Walk, pointing out his ships' comings and goings. She was only 26 – young enough to pass for his daughter, but she promised all he required in a wife. Hannah's family, like his, were devout Quakers, and had useful links in the West Indies. Her uncle Isaac was a sea captain trading between Europe, Jamaica and America and, it is possible, had sailed Hillary ships. Marriage thus brought Richard multiple advantages: useful links with the colonies, and five longed-for children in rapid succession. The baby destined to become Sir William Hillary was their second surviving son, named after his famous doctor uncle who had died eight years earlier. Two years before him came a boy named Richard after his father, then Mary, five years his junior. The marriage was not immune to sorrow. Two other children died in infancy; John was the first-born child but died aged five months; another baby, also called William, was born nine months later, but died, aged two, in November 1766.

Under the watchful eye of their parents William and his siblings grew. Frustratingly, we have no records of these early days. Where did the children go to school? What were they taught? How did they progress? Knowing that the Quakers placed great emphasis on education for both sexes, we can surmise all three were well-educated, the boys groomed to take over the family business and, inevitably, their sister taught that her future lay in marriage. Their later lives show that William and Mary were articulate, well-read and good at arguing a point. Mary would marry a clergyman and became an acclaimed poet – Mrs Henry Rolls. Her work, heavily influenced by Byron and Wordsworth, sometimes drew on her brother's peripatetic life for inspiration. Richard and William, meanwhile, were keen to acquire a gloss of cultured sophistication. As young men they subscribed to the Atheneum, a gentleman's club in Liverpool boasting an impressive library, where the well-to-do gathered to discuss books and news. At home, even though Quaker convention disapproved of luxury, they lived comfortably, with books to read, paintings on the walls, silver and china on the table.[10]

Soon there was also money enough to allow them to move round the corner to a more prestigious house in Dale Street, one of Liverpool's showiest roads. Their neighbours were Liverpool's newly rich merchants, whose ranks Richard had now joined. Even in these luxurious surroundings commerce was never far from their daily existence. Scattered between the flashy facades of Dale Street's mansions were coaching inns – the Golden Lion, the Golden Fleece, and the Wool Pack, to name but three. These establishments may have disturbed the tranquility of the well-to-do residents, but they were a cornerstone of the prosperity they enjoyed. From busy coach yards strings of pack horses, some fifty and sixty strong; and eight-horse wagons, with harness bells jangling, shuttled West Indian imports to the rest of the country, returning laden with merchandise for export from the docks.

Growing up in such an environment, waiting for news of ships' comings and goings, watching the wagons clatter into the distance with the goods brought in from the West Indian plantations and lumber back to the yards with merchandise for the export trade, William Hillary was conscious from an early age of the profits and perils of the sea. We can imagine him standing with his brother searching out his father's ships as they manoeuvred their way into the docks or clambering among cargoes of cotton, molasses and rum, full of excitement yet, to begin with at least, oblivious to the injustice that lay behind it. Even so he learned early on that a ship's safe arrival with a lucrative cargo on board was a matter for celebration, while a loss represented human and commercial tragedy. Both occurrences were routine, and Liverpool's civic authorities, sensitive to the repercussions of maritime dangers, were making efforts to reduce losses.

When a pilot service was installed, Richard Hillary joined as a member of the regulatory commission. Young William Hillary must have heard talk of how the city had improved its lighthouses and introduced a lifeboat station and (even more unusually) a system of awards for those who helped save stranded vessels.[11] The Liverpool Institution for Recovering Drowned Persons was founded in 1775 to rescue and resuscitate people using trained medical assistants and offered rewards in much the same way as the London-based Royal Humane Society. Yet the recurring tragedies listed in the newspapers bore witness to the limitations of a solitary lifeboat powered solely by oars. If a ship foundered further afield, it did so with little hope of assistance.

Somehow Richard's ships must in great part have survived the perils of the sea, and he found time to take his children to Wensleydale for family holidays. Breathing clean sweet air, exploring the empty vales, making friends with other Quaker children in the sparsely populated villages, Hillary had a taste of freedom and peace he would always cherish. In later life, when things went badly wrong, he would draw strength from these memories, writing nostalgically of 'my old friends in a place where in earlier life I had passed so many happy days and which often has a place in my mind mixed with many feelings of regret'.[12]

Perhaps it was during these holidays that his father told his children memorable stories about their forebears, sowing the seeds of Hillary's later fascination with his lineage. The family proudly traced their origins to an illustrious French cleric who had come to Britain and served under Henry II as Bishop of Chichester. According to a chronicler of the time, this Hillary 'was in great favour with that monarch, and had charge of the shire of Surrey.' The children must have drunk such tales in and for the rest of his life Hillary would love to discuss his illustrious ancestry. 'He is descended from the real Lord Marmion's daughter, whose family tree he showed me',[13] wrote Tom Scott to his brother, Sir Walter, after spending an evening with Hillary on the Isle of Man.

The stories served not just as treats to while away the hours; they were wrapped up with a moral message. Throughout the generations, the children learned that the Hillary family had striven to improve their position in society; often through royal service, patronage and advantageous marriage. His father's choice of Hannah was no exception. Hannah's mother was a Lascelles, a member of an eminent Quaker family, with property in Jamaica and links to the Earls of Harewood. The young Hillary would have gathered that such a shrewd choice of a wife could facilitate an ambitious man's ascent up the social ladder.

In other ways too Hillary's cultural heritage shaped the man he became. The Quakers valued moral consciousness, self-improvement and servitude. Hillary's desire to contribute to wider society, his ambivalent attitude towards money, his fondness for cliques and societies, his sense of honour are all echoes of Quaker teaching. When, in later life, he had a cause to champion, he invariably turned to pamphlet writing, as the Quakers had always done. Distanced from the brethren, he would one day also recall the Quakers' comforting patronage network, their loyalty, the way they shared business with one another. Nurturing alliances, in one way or another, would serve him on many future occasions.

Money may have been secondary to altruism in Quaker eyes, but that didn't prevent members of the Brethren becoming canny businessmen as well. To many it seemed no more than an awkward paradox that Liverpool's wealth was inseparable from slavery. 'Methinks I everywhere smell the blood of slaves', the artist Fuseli famously declared. The Quakers did not claim to be untainted by slavery. Some squared troubled consciences, telling themselves that if they avoided trading directly in slaves, owning them to produce or deal in sugar and cotton, and providing them with Christian teaching was necessary and justifiable. Others actively promoted abolition or salved qualms by sponsoring charity schools, alms houses, gardens, hospitals and dispensaries.

Where did Hillary's sympathies lie in what became one of the great debates of his age? There is nothing in his writing to confirm that he sided with the abolitionists and circumstantial evidence doesn't help. We know that William Wilberforce supported Hillary's earliest efforts in founding the Shipwreck Institution, and that he had business dealings with William Roscoe, a Liverpool banker and politician and vocal abolitionist. But he also had friends such as George Hibbert and John Vincent Purrier, whose enterprises were enmeshed in the slave trade and who were vehement anti-abolitionists. As a small boy the rights and wrongs of his father's business were not something Hillary would have thought to question, accepting as a given that plantations relied on slaves. But we cannot be sure to what extent he began to listen to the rising crescendo of anti-slavery voices, and to what extent he dismissed them. The family property, valued at £120,000 at the time, equated to a workforce of some 900 slaves, and as we will see, even in the 1840s, when the industry was in terminal decline, he would accept government compensation payments for more than 230 slaves. Whether he did so comfortably or not remains open to conjecture.

The first chill wind to blight the Hillary fortunes arrived with the onset of war with America. The West Indian colonies relied on America as a market for their rum and molasses and as a source of staples to feed workers and maintain estates. During the hostilities, trade embargoes and rising costs led to slaves becoming malnourished and dying by the thousand, while sugar prices slumped. For many plantation owners the only way to survive was to take out loans. Over the last quarter of the eighteenth century the price of sugar would fall by almost 20 per cent in fits and starts, while costs of production rose steadily. 'We sincerely wish it was in our power to inform you of some favourable change in the prices of sugar, but the market still continues in the same dull state and the demand very small – nor is there any appearance of its soon turning more considerable', [14] wrote one disappointed trader. 'I am really tired of laying out money on an estate that makes no returns – the estate having cleared me nothing for these six years past', [5] grumbled another. The close of the war brought little respite. Running costs remained high, investment dwindled, debts swelled. Then, worse still, a succession of hurricanes hit the island of Jamaica in the 1780s, leading to more hardship and the deaths of over 15,000 slaves.

When Richard Hillary senior died in 1789, at the grand old age of 86, the family business was probably already in difficulty. To salvage the situation, Richard junior, aged barely 20, was dispatched to Jamaica and placed in the care of his uncle, Isaac Lascelles-Winn. A well-respected figure on the island, Isaac was the owner of the Adelphi estate near Montego Bay, one of the largest on the island. Before buying his plantation he had been a sea captain plying his trade with American ports, where he had many friends among the Quaker community. Richard would later be sent to visit one of his closest friends, the congressman Pierce Butler, in Philadelphia. 'The arrival of your nephew in this city has brought me a satisfaction that I have been long and reluctantly deprived of – that of hearing from you ... I have asked Mr Hillery [*sic*] a thousand questions concerning your health, spirits etc, his answers to which gave me pleasure', [16] his friend enthused. On his return to Jamaica, Richard would join the ruling elite as a member of the House of Assembly, presumably trying to improve the trade restrictions driving so many plantation owners into penury.

Meanwhile William Hillary, two years younger, aged 19 and left at home, must have said his farewells to his brother with a mingling of admiration and envy, perhaps yearning for the moment when his time to leave home and explore the wider world would come. Already there were signs he would not turn out to be the man his father expected him to be. Like many young men raised in new affluence, intellectual ideals and artistic interests held more allure than the nitty-gritty of commercial enterprise. But he was not a wayward son and nor did he ignore his familial duty. Until the climate changed, he resigned himself to helping his mother with the running of the Liverpool side of the business.

Any hopes Hillary harboured of escape from this sugar-dominated world were continually hampered by declining prices. More loans had to be taken out and, rather than launching into the young gentleman's life he had expected, he and his mother moved again, down-sizing from prestigious Dale Street to a smaller house next to the docks in Springfield Street. The limitations chafed.

He would wait seven years before the financial situation eased and, with an upturn in sugar prices, his chance finally arrived. By then he was aged 26, a physically strong young man of adventurous inclination and keen social ambition. The years of waiting had convinced him of the direction he would steer his life. He would rise above his associations with trade; forget Quaker prudence and piety and live life to the full. All of which meant leaving Liverpool.

Notes

1 The date and place are recorded in the Quaker record books. His birth is sometimes mistakenly put a year later in 1771 in Birkrigg and sometimes a year earlier in 1769.
2 There is a phalanx of Williams in the Hillary family – for clarity's sake, where there is a risk of confusion, I refer to the subject of this book as 'Sir William Hillary' even though he was not awarded his baronetcy until 1804.
3 Quaker Library, Temp MSS 745/hr3/p. 11.
4 C. Booth, *The Friends Journal.*
5 Daniel Defoe, *A Tour Throughout the Whole Island of Great Britain* (1724).
6 Roy Porter, *English Society in the 18th Century*, p. 93.
7 Thomas Baines, *History of the Commerce and town of Liverpool*, vol. I, p. 606.
8 *Liverpool Table Talk a Hundred Years Ago* (1882) pp. 22-3.
9 Name is variously spelled Winn, Wynn and Wynne.
10 Hannah Hillary's will lists all these luxuries and more.
11 Oliver Warner, *The Lifeboat Service* (1974), p. 3.
12 Quaker Library, MS vol. 338 f 193, William Hillary to William Thompson, Haws 22 February 1825.
13 *Letters of Walter Scott 1821-1823* (1932), p. 461.
14 Figures and quote taken from S.H.H. Carrington, *The Sugar Industry and the Abolition of the Slave Trade* (2002), p. 126.
15 Ibid. p. 129.
16 Pierce Butler to Isaac Lacelles Winn, 13 March 1793, *Letters of Pierce Butler 1790-1797*, p. 241.

3

The Royal Servant

I like the women too (forgive my folly!),
From the rich peasant cheek of ruddy bronze,
And large black eyes that flash on you a volley
Of rays that say a thousand things at once,
To the high Dama's brow, more melancholy,
But clear, and with a wild and liquid glance,
Heart on her lips, and soul within her eyes,
Soft as her clime, and sunny as her skies.

'Italy versus England', George Lord Byron

William Hillary had set his heart on travel – on a jaunt that would lead him across the sea to explore the continent of Europe. The trip would be a rite of passage, adding polish to his education, allowing him to soak up the culture, and with luck, to mingle with the upper echelons of society. Embarking on such an adventure would also give him access to more risqué entertainments – a taste of the dissipation denied him in Quaker Liverpool, under his mother's shadow.

Hillary's plans mirrored those of many other young men of the eighteenth century, but he set off at an inauspicious moment for an extended trip abroad. Britain was in the throes of war and the French, victorious in Holland, Austria and the Rhineland, were sweeping into northern Italy. In these turbulent times, travel abroad had become more risky than usual. Hillary however turned a blind eye to the alarming political situation, perhaps reminding himself that there were bonuses as well as hindrances to travel at such a time. To a gregarious thrill-seeker the cultural experience might gain an added frisson from the threat of Napoleon's advancing armies, plus the scarcity of travellers might work to his advantage. The British abroad invariably mixed with one another. Fewer tourists would make it easier to infiltrate circles from which a Liverpool merchant might otherwise be excluded.

He headed for Italy and gravitated to Rome, a city that had so far escaped Napoleon's attentions and where English travellers still congregated. Here he went sight-seeing and started to network. Forgetting his Quaker upbringing, which condemned all forms of gratuitous display, he began by imitating many young aristocrats during their travels – commissioning a portrait of himself as a souvenir.[1] Sitting to William Artaud, an established second division artist, brought him into contact with fellow visitors. And so, following a well-trodden path, Hillary manoeuvred his way to the fun-filled and glamorous circle of Prince Augustus.

George III's sixth son had earned a reputation as a party-lover among British tourists. 'One of the houses we have found most agreeable here is our own Prince Augustus's ... who does the honours to Englishmen *on ne peut pas mieux*, and has a general conversazione every Sunday',[2] confided John Morritt, a fellow British traveller. The prince was two years William's junior. Tall and good-looking, his carefree manner belied a life that was not all it seemed. From an early age he had suffered from frequent 'spasmodic constrictions of the chest' – asthmatic attacks that were treated in a similar way to most ailments at the time, with blisters, purging, and bleeding.

At the time William Hillary entered the stage, it was not the prince's ailments but his love life that had drawn the public's attention. Three years earlier, he had embroiled himself in a romantic liaison that still supplied the sightseers of Rome plenty to spice up their letters home. Shortly before his 21st birthday, the prince had fallen deeply in love with Lady Augusta Murray, a well-born lady ten years his senior. Ignoring the Royal Marriage Act, which prohibited royal children from marrying without the king's consent, the pair had undergone a clandestine wedding ceremony that was splashed across the newspapers in Britain within weeks.

Summoning his son back to London, an incandescent George III made it clear that since the prince was under the age of consent at the time of his marriage, the union was invalid. Augusta was by now expecting his child, so the prince held firm. Naively telling himself that the king would eventually back down, he organised a second secret ceremony in London, to ensure there was no question over the marriage's legality.

The prince soon realised how drastically he had misjudged his father's resolve. Rather than acknowledging Augusta as his daughter-in-law, an unbending king ordered Augustus to return to Italy on the day his 'wife' gave birth to a son, and issued instructions to have the marriage officially nullified. He also announced that any attempts the couple made to defy his ruling and reunite in Italy would be blocked. Should the prince attempt to contravene this order he would forfeit his allowance and be cut off without a penny.

Terrified of incurring the king's wrath, many of his friends evaporated at this point, especially those embroiled in a secret scheme to spirit Augusta back to Rome. Meanwhile, in Italy, fan-twitching English society began to tut unkindly. Had he been bewitched by a designing woman rather than fallen passionately in love? Shouldn't Augusta have known better than to encourage his pursuit? Why wasn't it enough for her simply to accept her role as his mistress? 'I must own I felt for the honour of our laws and the feelings of his parents, which his creatures tried to set him against. He said that at our house he and his friends were talked against, the reply was that at every house in Rome he was talked of ... All Rome is on our part and all the good of the English. I do very truly pity him for the bad way his is in, being surrounded with such wretches as he has picked up',[3] censured Lady Knight.

It was while the debate continued that the young William Hillary infiltrated the prince's orbit. He was just what the prince needed – attractive, fun to be with, eager to please and the ladies loved him. It is easy to see why the much-scrutinised prince might have wished to befriend someone new and undemanding who was willing to say what he wanted to hear and do what he wanted to do.

Before long Prince Augustus asked William to become his equerry – an invitation a flattered William accepted without a moment's hesitation. From his point of view, a place in a prince's household – even an ostracised one – was a shortcut to elite circles in British society, one of the reasons he had left Liverpool. Here was his ticket to an intoxicating world, where there would be new adventures to sample, and new experiences to savour. Added to which, the prince was a genuinely likeable character. 'He appears to have a fund of conversation and fluency. His vanity is so undisguised he wears it as a form of frankness', swooned Mrs Trent after meeting the prince and chatting for two hours.[4]

Not all the British visitors were so smitten; the prince's choice of friends and especially his penchant for artists and musicians, drew criticism in some circles. 'He is as familiar with them as a lady's lap-dog is with her fan', an outraged Lady Knight told her friend Mrs Drake of an evening during which Prince Augustus invited members of the Roman opera to his house for a rehearsal and sang with them; 'Even a Grub Street journal would be contaminated with all the tales that are told'.[5] But the prince's detractors did not hamper his penchant for the artistic set. As well as socialising with musicians, he was on friendly terms with many of the British painters working in the city, and Hillary may have joined him at the funeral of James Durno, 'an ingenious artist and ... a man of a most benevolent disposition', when he died suddenly of 'putrid fever'. 'All his brother artists, I mean British artists attended, and his funeral had the peculiar honour of having the presence of Prince Augustus who carried a torch as did his two gentlemen and Lord Wycombe, Mr Amherst and Mr Disney Fytche',[6] wrote one attendant. Hillary learned that the last gentleman in that cortege was travelling with his two attractive young daughters, Frances and Sophia. When, before long, he met the young ladies he was charmed; their presence added further to the enchantment of Italy.

At some stage Hillary learned of the cloud hanging over the Disney-Fytche name but, swayed by the prince's morally permissive milieu, chose to ignore it. Fytche was a wealthy banker whose canny marriage had brought him Danbury Place in Essex, a large house 'handsomely furnished with rooms and convenient offices of every description ... the whole surrounded by a fine park of about 200 acres, abounding with rich and extensive prospects'.[7] As the incumbent of Danbury, Fytche had once enjoyed life as a pillar of Essex society. But, Hillary discovered, this world had been shattered when he was indicted by the Chelmsford Assizes for assaulting William Ford, a waiter at the Cock and Bell at Rumford. The charge in itself wasn't too bad. Eighteenth-century society could take a physical assault in its stride – especially when it took place in a tavern rather than a ballroom. What gave the accusation an unacceptable dimension was the accusation that Fytche had also attempted a serious sexual attack on the waiter. The press reflected general outrage, deeming this 'an unnatural crime' and deciding the evidence produced in court could not be reported, because it included 'a detail too indelicate to mention'.[8]

Fytche's defence relied upon his being able to summon 'a number of most respectable gentlemen' to vouch for his character. After two hours' deliberation, the jury, 'who were special and consisted of the first men of the county' (in other words came from the same social strata as Fytche), found him guilty of common assault but acquitted him of the sexual offence. It was fortunate for him they did so – homosexual crimes were treated with little tolerance. The accused were liable to be lynched and severely beaten, and those found guilty punished by death, imprisonment or the pillory. Often this was the worst punishment of all, since it allowed the mob to vent their anger, usually by pelting the prisoner with stones, mud, dead cats, rotten vegetables and whatever else lay to hand, and leaving him so severely injured he never recovered. As a result, convictions for homosexual crimes were uncommon and few laboured under the illusion that an acquittal signified innocence.

The Fytche case was referred to the King's Bench for sentencing. Here, because of the disturbing nature of the evidence, the judge refused to have the trial reread.

Nevertheless, he ruled Fytche's behaviour 'extremely indecent and unaccountable' and fined him £100 – an inordinate sum for a common assault.[9]

Stigmatised by public outrage, Fytche decided to put some distance between himself and his peers and move his family abroad. He bought two mansions in Paris and a jewel-like estate at Chambourcy. Known as the *Désert de Retz*, the estate adjoined the royal forest of Marly. A *désert* was a carefully manufactured Arcadian wilderness in the manner favoured by Marie Antionette. The queen loved to promenade here and admired the artfully placed grotto, pyramid, Chinese pavilion, temple and colossal shattered column, swathed in moss and foliage.[10] But during the French Revolution, the paradise was blighted by political turmoil. The estate and the Parisian properties were seized, and Disney-Fytche and his daughters were lucky to escape to Switzerland unscathed, only 'a few days before the cruel decree of the National Convention passed against the English'.[11]

And so it was that William Hillary of Liverpool, royal equerry to Prince Augustus, entered the life of Frances, Lewis's eldest daughter. Love accelerates in unfamiliar settings when there is nothing to constrain it. The Fytches were busily art buying with their friends, acquiring, among other things, cameos at the studio of one of Rome's leading makers. Years later, Hillary would present an Italian cameo of himself to a close friend. It shows him in profile, with feather fronds of hair wisping over his noble brow, a long shapely nose and well-defined chin.[12] Perhaps Frances, watching admiringly as his handsome features were sketched in the dazzling light, was dazzled too. Perhaps the heated political situation, and the prince's intense yet thwarted love for Augusta, heightened the attraction. Imagine them strolling the piazzas and palazzos of Rome, descending the Spanish steps, sightseeing on the Capitoline Hill. By then almost a decade had passed since the scandalous case that had tainted the family name. To Hillary, freshly liberated from Quaker decorousness, immersed in the perfections of classical architecture and youth, the blemish was no deterrent to a friendship that might ripen to something more.

Political events must have heightened the sense that convention could be ignored, for they were living in extraordinary times. By the New Year of 1797, France's inexorable advance made remaining in Rome unsafe and, like many other British travellers, the prince and his household moved to Naples. 'This morning after having been to church, we had the visit of Col Drinkwater and Mr Hillary who were both introduced by Freemantle', Eugenia Wynne, another recent arrival, recorded in her diary.[13] Eugenia had noticed Prince Augustus the previous day, waspishly remarking, 'I saw him on the *balcon* and found him grown very fat since the time I saw his RH at Venice.'[14]

If Rome relied on its artistic heritage to enthral its visitors, in Naples sex of all varieties was the chief attraction. It was a city where everyone let their hair down.

'In all our stay we have only known one or two good fellows among the men, and not one woman of character, or scarce common decency, among the ladies ... At Naples ... I would just as soon send my wife … to improve (her) morals in the upper boxes of Drury Lane,'[15] wrote a frowning John Morritt. British visitors invariably gravitated towards the residence of venerable British consul Sir William Hamilton (whose wife Emma was soon to catch Nelson's eye). Hamilton was a passionate collector of antiquities and convivial host, and guests were often riveted by an increasingly stout but revealingly clad Lady Hamilton posing in alluring 'attitudes' and miming famous subjects from classical history. The idea was to guess the identity of characters such as Medea or Cleopatra from her display – a sort of eighteenth-century charades. 'She takes almost every attitude of the finest antique figures successively, and varying in a moment the fold of her shawls, the flow of her hair; and her wonderful countenance is at one instant a Sibyl, then a Fury, a Niobe, a Sophonisba drinking poison, ... she sometimes does above two hundred, one after the other',[16] wrote one mesmerised audience member.

An equerry's duties were those of a glorified companion; someone to smooth the way and organise the practicalities of the prince's daily life, but also to join in the fun. In Naples liaisons flourished over hands of cards, or at musical recitals, or while driving in the countryside, or attending balls, or admiring works of art. 'One or two of the set always decide the rest whether they shall follow the Arts, gaming, whoring, or drinking',[17] wrote a weary Hamilton, who had seen it all before. The prince fell for the captivating singer Guisseppina Grassini, who advertised her conquest by touring the streets in the prince's liveried carriage - to the dismay of Edward Livingston, the tutor the king had sent to keep his son out of trouble. 'I found matters here as bad as possible ... the prince surrounded by a very bad society indeed, and living with a woman whose interest it was to keep up a division in his family,'[18] he seethed.

Perhaps the Fytches joined the prince's excursions to Herculaneum or Pompei along with Hillary. And then, as the sightseers clustered in the shade, to blush at ancient frescos of provocative nymphs and priapic satyrs, Hillary was seduced into believing Frances would make an equally enticing partner. Perhaps she went with him on a daring ascent of Vesuvius. Hamilton had studied the volcano's eruptions closely, scaling it countless times, and always recommended that visitors see it in action. It is easy to imagine them picnicking together on the upper slopes, surrounded by plumes of ash-filled smoke and fountains of lava; the thrill of danger turning to desire.

Along with love there was art. Hillary's eyes had already been opened to the joys of art-buying in Rome and as before he began to mingle with other collectors. Acting as a go-between for artists and well-heeled friends in the prince's circle, he organised commissions and met other like-minded collectors. Many were beguiled by his self-assured charisma and well-mannered charm and remained friendly with him long after their return to Britain. One of them was John Rushout (later Lord Northwick), attaché to the Neapolitan court, who like Hamilton was a keen collector with a fondness for Roman medals. 'His collection is upwards of twelve thousand, and he gives up his whole time to it from morning to night he is a most excellent antiquarian',[19] an awestruck visitor declared.

As part of the hard-playing prince's entourage Hillary also threw himself, indefatigably, into partying on a grand scale. With Napoleon's troops advancing inexorably south, it was the best way to forget the impending peril. 'The nobility and gentry of Naples are now at Portici and twice a week the Royal Gardens at the Favorita are opened to the public. There is a band of music and all sorts of rural diversions such as swings and wooden horses … or firing pistols at a Turks head. Last week there was a magnificent ball at the Favorita … there is also a temporary theatre here where either an opera or a play is performed every night', recorded Hamilton, describing one of the various late spring entertainments to which the prince and his entourage were invited.

A month later Hillary accompanied the prince to Caserta. The King and Queen of Naples installed themselves in their Versailles-inspired baroque palace for the winter months. Lavish hunting parties with the king and his entourage were the order of the day. Visitors strolled in the 'English-style' gardens Hamilton had helped design, and visited a working silk factory in a pavilion in the grounds. 'We met a large party of English, the Prince, the Lambtons, Ct. Hillary, Ct Greaves … and others',[20] recalled Eugenia Wynne, a guest at a dinner given by the Hamiltons' in their retreat nearby.

After the grey restraint and drudgery of Quaker life in Liverpool, Hillary was enthralled by the glamour of the world that now unfurled. The pleasure was made all the more piquant because he, like everyone else enjoying themselves in Naples, knew it would be short-lived. Each day brought ominous reports of the French advance. 'Neither His Royal Highness (Prince Augustus) nor any of His Majesty's subjects are perfectly at ease with the idea of a faithless enemy being so near – and particularly as they come like Hamlet's ghost in such a questionable shape',[21] wrote Hamilton with anxious prescience after the prince's birthday celebrations.

For Hillary the approaching threat acted as a catalyst. He had never been politically motivated, but his role in the prince's entourage had fired him with patriotism and the desire to prove himself. He enjoyed being part of the royal hierarchy, working within a social structure, being the focus of attention and respect. The prince's patronage made opportunity easy to engineer and in conversation with Hamilton, Hillary expressed an interest in a diplomatic career. Hamilton, anxious for reports of what was happening in the south of the country, needed little persuasion to send him on an unofficial mission. 'I undertook at that time rather a hazardous excursion to Calabria, Sicily and Malta and took with me letters of introduction from the Duke of Sussex [Prince Augustus] and William Hamilton,'[22] he proudly later related.

Even today, arriving at the entrance to the harbour of Valletta, guarded with its sentinel stone fortifications, is an awe-inspiring experience. Over two hundred years ago its gargantuan ramparts, battlements and arsenals were unrivalled anywhere in Europe and Hillary was overwhelmed: 'I was struck with the strength and magnitude of the works of that impregnable fortress',[23] he would recall many years later. Situated in the narrowest part of the Mediterranean, between Africa and Italy, the island had always held great strategic importance in Europe, offering a vantage point over Mediterranean traffic. Ostensibly part of the kingdom of Naples, since the 1530s Malta had been under the control of the Knights of St John, a chivalric military order whose origins went back to the early crusades to the Holy Land. The knights ran the island as benign despots, giving few privileges to the local inhabitants, but installing a variety of magnificent civic and commercial facilities, including a hospital, library, churches, dockyards and a quarantine service regarded as the most efficient in Europe.[24]

Hillary had not known what to expect from his mission, but brandishing newly polished social skills and freshly penned introductions, he found that doors opened effortlessly. Having manoeuvred his way into Valletta's elite, he was intrigued and impressed by a society in which the wealth accumulated by the knights was used to benefit the wider Maltese population. 'On presenting my letters I was most graciously received, and honoured … with seeing everything the island contained and by being introduced to the dignitaries and knights.'[25]

Ceremony was central to the Order of St John – the means by which power was displayed and hierarchy preserved. Hillary watched the inauguration of the new Grand Master of the order, Baron Ferdinand Hompesch, and was dazzled. Perhaps there were echoes in the enclosed nature of the order and its strict code of conduct with his Quaker brethren, but this was where similarity began and ended. What stirred his imagination and would stay with him for the rest of his life were the colour and the romance of the ceremony: the trappings of chivalry, the reminders of the noble ancestry of each knight, the sense of continuity and grandeur.

Entering the cathedral, he was confronted by heraldic devices at every turn: marble floors inlaid with insignia, armorial banners and flags fluttering over tombs to past knights. Processions of present-day knights, resplendent in ermine-trimmed robes embroidered with the Cross of St John, participated in the ceremony. 'I witnessed I may say the last ray of splendour of that dignified order, whose lustre had shone for so many centuries and then on the eve of being extinguished ... I heard all the romantic details, saw all the brilliant trophies of times long past',[26] he wrote, the memory of it all still vivid many decades later.

Spellbound though he was, Hillary observed the shabbiness amid the splendour. The knights who were supposedly bound by their code to live a life of altruism and chastity were open to corruption. Far from being freely elected, Hompesch had bribed his way to being elected as Grand Master. The resentment felt by the Maltese, who were oppressed by the ruling knights and largely excluded from positions of power, did not escape the young William Hillary. 'I saw the seeds of discord and treason already sown,'[27] he would record.

At the best of times Malta had been a bustling international entrepôt that[28] encouraged any shipping from a Christian country to use Valletta's docks, warehouses, quarantine facilities and hospital. By the time of Hillary's visit things had changed for the worse. The order's wealth was drastically reduced, since their French possessions had been seized at the outset of the Revolution. Conscious of the crippling shortage of money and encroaching threat from France, Hompesch had made overtures to Russia for financial assistance and was desperate for British aid. He could not have guessed that Napoleon's sights were set on Egypt but, sensing an invasion of Malta was imminent, he pressed Hillary to warn Hamilton that naval support was urgently needed. 'I was even at that time made the medium of overtures to the British government to call in to Sir Wm Hamilton, and I believe he as faithfully sent home – had these been promptly acted upon I firmly believe the catastrophe might have been averted.'[29]

Whether or not the message was ever relayed back to London remains debatable. What seems more certain is that the reports Hillary gave of the situation in Malta only added to Hamilton's mounting anxiety for the safety of the prince. His dispatches warned, 'we cannot count upon a moment's security, indeed the circumstance of His Royal Highness Prince Augustus's residence here at so very critical moment is truly alarming, although we are sure of every assistance from this court and government in the case of necessity. But should the French Venetian ships that are at Corfu come to Naples as they probably would ... all means of escape would be entirely cut off'.[30] Hamilton's hope that a British convoy would be sent to escort the prince home was disappointed and further news compounded his worry. 'An additional army of 30,000 French being on its march to reinforce that already in Italy,' he reported in March 1798. Then still worse intelligence arrived. 'We have reports that a portion of the French fleet at

Corfu endeavoured to get into the port of Malta, but that the master being well prepared would only suffer a limited number of ships to enter.'[31] Hamilton was under no illusions that the prince's safety as well as his own were now in serious jeopardy. 'When they can they will take all they can in <u>this</u> and every part of the world… is as clear as daylight.'[32]

In April, still holding on for instruction from London, in desperation Hamilton, accepted the King of Naples' offer of help. Preparations were set in train to take the prince to Manfredonia, a small coastal town on Italy's south-eastern coast. From there an armed warship – the seventy-four-gun *Archimedes* – would escort him to Trieste. A few days later the prince and his entourage set sail in an open fishing boat. 'I thought it high time that Augustus should be removed to a place of more security. Trieste (is) the only door now open for his retreat,'[33] Hamilton reported with a sigh of relief.

The choice of such an ill-equipped vessel was presumably to ensure the prince's departure was as swift and inconspicuous as possible. There was ever-present danger from stray French privateers patrolling the waters around the Italian coast. Had Hamilton known what the journey would entail, he might have felt less comfortable in bidding farewell to the prince and his companions. The voyage took over three weeks, involving several close encounters with storms and privateers. At the end of it the exhausted prince disembarked in Trieste and once again lapsed into illness.

Hillary, meanwhile, returned to Naples in May with another new friend, George (Beau) Brummell, to find the prince already on his way home and his own servants nowhere to be found. The two men lodged an official complaint at the disappearance of their staff, only to be informed by Hamilton that this was part of an evacuation order, as French invasion was now so perilously imminent.[34] Hillary left Naples immediately afterwards and rejoined the prince. From Trieste they travelled overland, stopping for four months in Vienna, then continuing on to Dresden and Berlin, the home of the Prussian court. During his travels across Europe, to avoid unwanted attention, the Prince travelled incognito under the assumed name of Count Diepholtz.[35] Even so, Hillary later recalled the various military duties carried out by the prince. 'I visited almost all the great armies and the contending powers of Europe there in the field.'[36]

We have no way of knowing when exactly Hillary learned that his role in attempting to protect Malta had failed, and that in early June the island had fallen into the hands of the French. He would later discover that the French fleet of twenty-five war ships and transports carrying 40,000 troops, among them Napoleon, had gathered off the coast of Valletta and demanded entry to Malta's harbour. When Hompesch cited the statutes of the order and refused entry to more than four ships at a time, Napoleon retaliated by declaring war. Two days later Hompesch surrendered with scarcely a shot being fired. 'The Maltese surrendered on the 12th inst and is now in the possession of the French Republic. Little or no resistance was made and treachery was everywhere evident … They have landed … from 10 to 15 thousand men',[37] wrote a weary Hamilton to England. Hillary was shattered to hear of a humiliation he would later describe as 'the disgraceful loss without a blow of what no common force could have conquered.'[38]

Dismay faded in Berlin, with plenty to distract him. Prince Augustus lived quietly under his assumed name – but was paid 'the most marked attentions by the King of Prussia,' who invited him to dine with him at Potsdam whenever he visited. But after the sunlit days of Italy, the chilly climes of northern Europe, coupled with the rigours of travelling the rutted roads of Europe had over-taxed Augustus's strength, and he was once again taken ill with a severe bout of asthma. Reports of his symptoms were serious enough to be dispatched to England, where they reached his erstwhile love, Augusta. Almost six years had now passed since the couple had seen one another, but despite the prince's Neapolitan lapses, their affection remained strong. Augusta, genuinely terrified the prince might die without seeing her again, decided to brave the king's edict banning her from contacting him and began planning a secret reunion. To avoid apprehension by royal henchmen she travelled under an assumed identity. In August 1799, a Mrs Ford arrived at Berlin.

Far from being on his death bed, Augustus was by then much recovered. He greeted Augusta warmly, torn by delight at seeing her and terror of alienating his father. Jittery though he was, he made no attempt to keep her presence a secret. Instead the couple lived openly together, making excursions around Berlin and visiting the king's palaces at Potsdam, Sans Souci and Spandau, often taking Hillary along as companion. Hillary would later testify that they 'lived in great harmony together at that time as man and wife.'[39] But it was a whirlwind reconciliation and after the initial euphoria, Augusta's common sense prevailed. For her own future as well as the prince's, she was anxious not to muddy the waters further with the king, and six weeks later decided to return to England. Before she boarded her carriage, the prince demonstrated his continued loyalty to her. A new will testifying that they had been 'solemnly and duly married' twice, and making her the main beneficiary of his estate, was drawn up. When the prince signed this document, the only member of his staff entrusted to act as witness was his equerry, William Hillary of Liverpool, Lancaster.[40]

By this time Hillary's thoughts had also turned to love and to leaving Berlin. In the weeks immediately after Augusta's departure he gave up his post with the prince and followed her to London. The reason for his early return was his continuing attachment to Frances Disney-Fytche and his determination to marry her. Aside from her father's disgrace, she seemed to have every attribute he looked for in a wife: she was young; six years his junior, aged only 24 at the time of their marriage. She was rich; heir to the Danbury estate with her sister. Her maternal grandfather had been a wealthy nabob and Governor of Bengal and the estate had come into the Fytche family from her mother's side. And she was impeccably well-connected, with an illustrious ancestor, Sir Walter Mildmay, a Chancellor of the Exchequer whom James I had knighted.

Fytche, by contrast, must have viewed Hillary's pursuit of his daughter with less enthusiastic feelings. His position with the prince gave him a certain respectability, but how had he acquired it? Probably not through family connection, but good manners and good luck. Granted, he was undeniably personable, attractive and ambitious, but in terms of his wealth and family status, he was hardly an eligible catch. He claimed the Jamaican properties his family owned were worth over £100,000, but these belonged in part to his brother Richard, who was still a bachelor and might marry. His family wealth in England was diminishing and founded on trade – which placed him several rungs down the social ladder. But if Fytche hoped for better for his elder daughter, he could not avoid the truth; his reputation had hindered her matrimonial chances. There is nothing to show he actively discouraged the courtship.

And so they were married in London on 21 February 1800, shortly after Hillary's return from Berlin. The ceremony was held at one of London's most fashionable venues, St George's Hanover Square;[41] the same church used by Prince Augustus for his second clandestine union with Augusta. The marriage took place by special licence. This was not a sign (as has been suggested) that they were eloping, but a discreet and speedy way to marry, favoured by the higher ranks, since the banns did not have to be read.

Afterwards the newly married couple travelled to Liverpool and moved into the family home in Springfields, St Anne's. If this seemed something of a comedown after the palazzos and mansions in which their courtship had been conducted, the couple consoled themselves with the thought that Liverpool was only a temporary home, and that grander surroundings awaited them. Nine months later, on 19 November, Frances gave birth to twins, a boy and a girl. A month after her 'lying in', on 19 December, the children were baptised. Tellingly, Hillary now felt the direction of his life had changed and the twins were not baptised as Quakers, as he had been. Instead the ceremony took place round the corner from their home and the docks, at St Nicholas' Church, which had strong links to the maritime community of Liverpool. His daughter was christened Elizabeth Mary after her grandmothers, and his son Augustus William, after the prince he had served and who, much to Hillary's pride, had consented to stand as godfather.

Notes

1 John Ingamells, *A Dictionary of British and Irish Travellers to Italy 1701-1800* (1997), p. 499. The portrait was painted by the artist William Artaud, who described William as 'a gentleman from Liverpool'.
2 Mollie Gillen, *Royal Duke: Augustus Frederick, Duke of Sussex (1773-1843)* (1976), p. 95.
3 Lady Elliot-Drake, (ed.), *Lady Knight's Letters from France and Italy 1776-1795* (1905), p. 206.
4 *The Remains of the Late Mrs Richard Trench: being selections from her journals, letters, & other papers* (1862), p. 55.
5 *Lady Knight's Letters*, 26 December 1895, p. 210.
6 *True Briton*, 27 January 1796.
7 *St James's Chronicle*, 31 October 1793; *The World*, 9 October 1793; *Morning Chronicle*, 12 March 1795.
8 *The World*, 27 July 1789.
9 *The Times*, 20 November 1789.
10 Patricia Taylor, *Thomas Blaikie (1751-1838): the Capability Brown of France* (2001), pp. 144-45.
11 *St James's Chronicle*, 14 November 1793. Disney-Fytche bought the property back in 1816 and it was inherited by his grandson Augustus William Hillary on his death in 1824.
12 Samuel Norris, *Manx Memeories and Movements* (1938), pp. 54-5.
13 Anne Freemantle (ed.), *The Wynne Diaries (1935-40)*, p. 149, Sunday, 9 January 1797.
14 PRO, HO98/77.
15 John Morritt, *Letters of John B Morritt (1914)*, 8 March 1796, pp. 283-4.
16 Morritt, *Letters*, pp. 281-2.
17 Ingamells, *Dictionary*, p. 455.
18 Gillen, *Royal Duke*, p. 98.
19 Morritt, *Letters*, p. 277.
20 Wynne, *Diaries*, p. 157, 9 February 1797.
21 PRO FO 70/11-12, Hamilton correspondence.
22 Hillary Letters, WH to Richard Broun, 13 June 1838.
23 Ibid.
24 J. Riley-Smith, *Hospitallers, the History of the Order of St John (1999)*, pp. 113-14.
25 Archive of Order of St John, Hillary Letters, 13 June 1838.
26 Ibid.
27 Ibid.
28 Provided they were not at war with Naples.
29 Archive of Order of St John, Hillary Letters, 13 June 1838.
30 PRO FO 70/11-12, Hamilton dispatches, March 1798.
31 PRO FO 70/11-12, Hamilton dispatches, March 1798, f55.
32 Ibid. April 1798, f3.61.
33 PRO FO 70/11-12, Hamilton 17 April 1798.
34 Ingamells, *Dictionary*.
35 *Observer*, 18 November 1798.
36 Hillary Letters, 13 June 1838.
37 PRO FO 70/11-12, Hamilton dispatches, f160.
38 Archive of Order of St John, Hillary Letters, 13 June 1838.
39 Gillen, *Royal Duke*, p. 106.
40 There were two other witnesses, both members of the Prussian court.
41 The wedding was listed in the press, including Jackson's Oxford Journal, 1 March 1800 and the *Ipswich Journal*, 1 March 1800.

4

Danbury Place

Broken in fortune, but in mind entire
And sound in principle, I seek repose
Where ancient trees this convent-pile enclose,
In ruin beautiful. When vain desire
Intrudes on peace, I pray the eternal Sire
To cast a soul-subduing shade on me,

'At Bala-Sala, Isle of Man', William Wordsworth, 1833

At Danbury Park, Essex, mid-morning on the first Monday in June 1803, the trudge of heavy boots heralded the arrival of a column of eleven hundred men. The First East Essex Legion of Volunteers, carefully drilled by their commanding officer, Lieutenant Colonel Hillary, marched through the avenue of leafy chestnut trees to the courtyard in front of the house, and reported for ceremonial duty. Dressed in new uniforms supplied by Mr Fisher of Castle Street in his 'best military style', they were already feeling the effects of the sweltering heat. Hillary allowed them time to recover in the shade while the invited dignitaries took their ring-side seats for the ceremony they had come to watch. He bowed and saluted Lord Paget, the Reverend Dudley, Major Generals Beckwith and Finch, and Colonel Watson – the inspecting officer of the district; and welcomed a phalanx of important ladies and gentlemen of the county.

When all were settled, the regiment formed a long line with the cavalry falling in on the right. At a signal they trooped in unison to form three sides of a square, standing to attention while the colours were ceremonially brought out, the chaplain stepped forward, consecrated the standards and delivered them into the waiting hands of Frances Hillary. Then, with stately formality, Frances passed each banner to her husband, raising her voice to address him publicly. 'With the greatest satisfaction, Sir, I present, through you these colours and standards to the First Essex Legion. I have the fullest confidence that they will be received by that corps as a bond of their union, and at all times be gallantly defended by their valour.'¹ Hillary accepted the standards before responding in similar vein: 'Madam, I return you the best acknowledgements in the name of the legion, for the honour you have conferred upon us. From the experience that I have had of their zeal and attachment to the cause in which they have embarked, I rest assured, that you will not be disappointed in the expectations which you have formed of their exemplary conduct.'²

As the band struck up 'God Save the King', the regiment trooped past the inspecting officers and the ceremony ended with a volley of gunfire in honour of the day. Afterwards, higher-ranking visitors were invited to enter the house. During the 'elegant cold collation and ball'³ that followed, Hillary was flattered by a shower of accolades. This was the recognition he had hoped for, a sign his efforts were worthwhile. It was nine months – a surprisingly short time – since he had begun to assemble the regiment – but speed was necessary in these perilous times. He was serving his country, performing his duty – at considerable cost to himself. But his mark had been made and he held every expectation he would soon be rewarded.

By then he and Frances had settled into comfortable married life, leaving Liverpool, city of his birth, with scarcely a backward glance, to move into her ancestral home, Danbury Place. Privately his devotion to his mother was unchanged, but he felt few qualms in leaving her on the other side of the country to run the family business. From now on it no longer mattered how many hogs heads of molasses and bales of cotton filled a ship's hold. He would reshape himself into a man whose surroundings matched his rising prospects, concentrating his efforts on infiltrating elite county circles and turning Danbury into a suitably impressive seat.

The house had fallen into a state of disrepair during the Disney-Fytches' long exile in Europe. Even so, it retained an atmospheric allure that suited Hillary's objectives and matched the romantic streak in his soul. Built on the traditional Elizabethan plan, its soaring mullioned windows, the grand entrance that seemed lofty enough to dwarf a tall man, and the crenulated parapets, which reminded him of the battlements on a crusader's castle, enthralled him. Rather than classical symmetry, in architectural style Danbury embodied gothic idiosyncrasy, which Hillary would always prefer.

The estate provided him with the trappings of a quintessential English country seat: a large deer park, three shrubbery-fringed lakes, a walled kitchen garden, formal parterres, stabling for twenty horses and outbuildings that included a laundry, ice house and backhouse. He was also enchanted to learn that in the church at Danbury there was the ancient tomb and effigy of a Knight Templar in his medieval armour. Surveying the vista from the great bay windows of his salon, he felt liberated from the docksides of Liverpool and the need to be a business man. He had arrived at a long-coveted destination.

Ensconced in his new house, with a new, rich wife by his side, Hillary gave rein to his passion for art. He bought on a large scale and not just for the fun of it, but as a way of staking claim to refinement – a badge of belonging to the upper echelons. Travel had honed his eye and made him appreciate the Old Masters. Hamilton and Lord Northwick (Rushout had now inherited the family title) had taught him that classical antiquities were intrinsic to any collection worth the name. His his own inclinations, in keeping with his character, were showier. He loved dramatic paintings and anything that smacked of medievalism. And so he filled Danbury's rooms with fine bronzes, antique busts on marble columns, ornamental vases on tripods and urns carved from porphyry, which mirrored the sophisticated classical taste of his friends.

Alongside these were paintings and objects that illustrate to his extravagant side: picturesque landscapes by Salvator Rosa that conjured the wilderness of Wensleydale; emotive religious scenes by Carlo Dolce, redolent of his time in Rome; stormy Dutch seascapes that recalled perilous journeys in the Mediterranean; and 'a curious assemblage of ancient armour',[4] crossbows, shields, spears, swords and chain-mail suits, evoking the glorious pageantry of the Knights of St John. He was tempted too by the unashamedly opulent, treating himself to examples of exquisite French craftsmanship finding its way to the British market after the Revolution. Soon the rooms of Danbury were resplendent with Boulle tables made in Louis XVI's royal workshops, intricately inlaid with tortoiseshell, brass and mother-of-pearl; exquisitely painted and gilded porcelain from Sèvres; and a brilliant Savonnerie carpet that had been made as a diplomatic gift.[5]

He was living in an age of turmoil and did not have long to enjoy these trappings in peace. In May 1803, the short-lived Treaty of Amiens[6] disintegrated, and Britain was again exposed to the threat of invasion. According to the reports that reached London, 100,000 French troops and a vast flotilla were poised to cross the channel and invade Britain at any moment. The danger gave rise to a growing sense of British nationalism – a sentiment always latent in Hillary. Naturally, when a flurry of new volunteering swept the nation (by the end of the year there were 380,000 new volunteers under arms[7]) he felt compelled to join in.

Conventional wisdom held that any invasion attempt would be close to London – probably either in Sussex or Kent - and military effort was concen-

trated there. Hillary believed, the Essex coast – exposed, undefended and a stone's
throw from Danbury – was also a possibility which should not be overlooked. In
times of national threat, aristocrats and lords lieutenant of counties were expected
to step forward and raise and train a regiment of volunteers. Hillary was neither,
but as the master of Danbury he felt entitled to act like one. Until this moment
he had never felt any inclination to pursue a military career; for one thing, his
Quaker upbringing forbade it. His military experience had been limited to
reviewing troops with Prince Augustus during their travels through Europe. But
the patriotism kindled through his royal service combined with his desire for
official status. He mustered a huge private militia and unhesitatingly took command of it himself.

During the earlier war with France there had been an army camp at Danbury,
with tents set up on the common and a watch kept from the church tower. The
posting was not a popular one. The surrounding terrain was low-lying and boggy.
There had been outbreaks of disease and unusually high fatalities among the forces
billeted there. None of this deterred Hillary. 'I availed myself of considerable influence upon an exposed and important coast of the county of Essex, part of it is so
unhealthy that the king's troops could not be stationed there without great injury
and yet where a considerable force seemed requisite',[8] he later proudly recalled.

His determination was adamantine and it is testimony to his ability to bring
others round to his way of thinking that, within a matter of months, the force he
assembled was the largest in the country. 'I brought forward almost the whole
population of a large district to take arms in the general cause and was enabled
to offer to the king the actual signature of more than seventeen hundred men to
serve under my command in any part of Great Britain, out of which, two battal-
ions, together 1,200 men and a corps of cavalry were accepted by the name of the
First Essex Legion, of which I was appointed to the command.'[9]

The government granted arms, equipment and a small payment to each volunteer. But with a shortage of supplies, it was up to each commander to ensure the
troops were trained, resources properly used and any outstanding bills paid. 'I have
written for 1,000 stand of arms to be consigned immediately to you at Danbury
Place,' assured Lord Braybrooke. Explaining the difficulties, he continued, 'I fear
it will be impossible to procure others at present than Prussian muskets (for they
have not yet others to issue from the Tower) but you may depend upon my using
my best endeavours to promote this or any other object you may have in view.'[10]

Setting aside the logistical difficulties and costs involved, Hillary found his
command surprisingly enjoyable. He relished the hierarchy and the structure of
army life. Being an officer in control of men, a focus of their respect, gave him
a sense of purpose and fulfilment that reinforced his status. He was grateful and

proud when his strenuous efforts made him stand out from the throng and his name was mentioned in the highest circles. 'Flattering testimonials (came) from Lord Braybrooke, Lord Lieutenant of Essex. Mr Pitt favoured me with his support and protection and the king personally thanked me ... in very marked terms for what His Majesty was graciously pleased to call *a noble service*.'[11]

Commanding the regiment had a further advantage: it brought him into frequent contact with the royal family. That summer, Hillary greeted his old friend Augustus, now ennobled to the Duke of Sussex, and his brother, the Duke of York. They came to inspect his troops and the military fortifications built to defend the county. Lord Braybrooke, who escorted them, was impressed by the discipline of Hillary's men. 'I cannot again write upon this subject without testifying the sense I entertain of your spirited efforts to bring to perfection the largest force not only within our county but I believe within the kingdom at large offered by one individual',[12] he praised.

Part of the reason for the government's gratitude was Hillary's willingness to fund any shortfall in his regiment's expenses. Then and later, he claimed, he did not expect financial reward; his prime motive was to protect and serve his country. Besides, he was confident he had the means to fund his militia because in November 1803, his brother Richard had died suddenly in Jamaica of a fever. 'We had a quiet dinner party to-day, and we rejoiced at it, for we heard, just before we sat down, of the death of poor Mr Hillary, after a very short illness. It is indeed shocking to hear of the many deaths that occur every day', wrote a sad Lady Nugent, the Governor's wife, in her diary on 17 November.[13] As his brother's chief beneficiary, Hillary now believed himself to be the owner of property that included the Adelphi Estate, a Jamaican sugar plantation he estimated to be worth £120,000.

With financial substance buttressing patriotic fervour, in January 1805, he and Frances headed to court for the queen's birthday celebrations. The event took place at St James's Palace, to the accompaniment of the music of Handel. It had always been a highlight of the royal calendar, attended by prominent members of the aristocracy, court and Parliament. New clothes were *de rigueur* on such occasions and a subject of comment in the press. Queen Charlotte wore a robe of white satin embellished with purple embroidery, silk flowers and tassels and diamond bows. We do not know how William Hillary or Frances were clad when they made their bows and curtseys to the king and queen, but they both must have looked the part, with Hillary glowingly confident that the coming year would be an auspicious one.

He had already been given an inkling of the honour in store: 'I cannot but think that you merit as much notice from government as any gentleman can and then it is also considered that from family connections the distinction of a baronet may be serviceable to you',[14] Braybrooke had promised. The formal announcement of the baronetcy as a recognition of Hillary's patriotic efforts to protect his nation, came the following autumn and was widely reported. Then one long-awaited afternoon in early October 1805, William Hillary of Danbury Place and Rigg House, Wensleydale, knelt before his monarch George III, arising minutes later as a baronet. No one at court knew William Hillary, merchant of Liverpool; he had faded into oblivion.

Yet behind the glory all was not quite as it seemed. Even before the announcement of the baronetcy, there were warning signs that Hillary's activities were the subject of criticism. 'Notwithstanding the immense sums which I know you have expended in the formation and equipment of your legion you have experienced unfounded calumnies from some invidious quarters',[15] wrote a sympathetic Braybrooke, who went on to commend him for having '(the) spirit and address to rescue your honour so as to confound your aspersers'.[16]

At the root of the problem lay the cost of maintaining his regiment, unforeseen delays in receiving the Jamaican inheritance and perhaps the excessive sums he had spent on art. Until the money from Jamaica arrived the regiment's expenses far exceeded his income. To bridge the shortfall, and in the belief that he would soon have the means to reimburse them, Hillary borrowed money from his friends. He did so assuring them his embarrassment was only temporary; as soon as his inheritance arrived they would be speedily repaid. But when time passed and the money came due, Hillary was unable to meet his obligations and forced to borrow more. Before long even friends like Northwick lost patience, pressing him with increasing urgency for repayment. Hillary owed Northwick nearly £3,000 and there were many others to whom he was similarly endebted. Yet he was too embarrassed to provide any clear explanation for the cause of his difficulties and invariably avoided confrontation with one excuse after another:

I do assure you that not only now but whenever I reflect on the very long delay which has taken place in the settlement of our affairs it has caused me the utmost uneasiness.

For some days past my time has been divided between a continued exertion to procure cash and making appointments with those who promise me means but in the end do not find them. I have been harassed the whole week without one hour of my own, indeed I never was more engaged or I should have called upon your lordship e'er this. Today I was promised money to pay you the £100. I have now an assurance I shall have it late tonight or early in the morning.

Tomorrow I will just go after it and then call upon you certainly before two o'clock. I do expect with that money, but in regard to a sum equal to your pressing occasion for the Harrow bill I really know not what to do – all in my power I most readily will. If when we meet any plan can be devised, and I see we ought to meet upon this affair...I have every day thought to call upon you but I will confess I really could not make up my mind to do it until I had some success in my endeavours, and for that cause have I deferred it from one day to another.[17]

By now he knew that his inheritance was ensnared in legal dispute but, terrified of finding himself incarcerated for debt, could not face telling his creditors the truth. Compounding his woes, the cost of financing the regiment increased when government-paid subsidies were reduced. The mounting anxiety of it all took a toll on his health. 'I have again been in town and at difficult times very unwell. I have had a bilious attack which has been very troublesome to me and perhaps in a great measure owing to my duty with my regiment having harassed me very much',[18] he told Northwick, hoping for sympathy – and more time in paying off his loans.

His spiralling difficulties did not prevent him from keeping up appearances. '(I) expect the Duke of Sussex at Danbury Place to stay for a week or ten days. Some of our other friends propose being with us and it would give us much pleasure to add your lordship to the number of our guest on this occasion ... Pray do come ... on Sunday a large brigade are to exercise in this park and my own regiment on Wednesday,'[19] he implored Northwick – having fobbed him off with yet another explanation for why he could not pay the money he owed.

The truth of Hillary's financial embarrassment was made clear to the world at large when, with no more friends willing to lend him money, he was forced to sell his possessions. 'The amateurs and cognoscenti will find infinite amusement and gratification in viewing the late collection of Sir William Hillary now at Squibbs Room; we are in doubt which ought most to claim our admiration, the valuable pictures, the rare antique busts, the magnificent inlaid tables or the very curious assemblage of ancient armour',[20] wrote the *Morning Chronicle* unkindly, regaling readers with the news that some of the most prized items in his art collection were to go under the hammer. In all, the catalogue informed would-be buyers, there would be some 125 lots, all taken from Hillary's London residence or country seat, Danbury Place, all to be sold without reserve.

Although there is more than a touch of *Schadenfreude* about the many newspaper announcements of the sale, they tell only half the story. The extent of Hillary's humiliation was far worse. Brought to a near nervous collapse by the financial strain, his integrity buckled and he resorted to shabby measures to try to make ends meet. Lord Radstock was aghast to discover that some of the paintings consigned as Hillary's property had in fact belonged to him. 'You will be sorry to hear that your old friend Sir W Hi(llary) has left me <u>minus</u> £2,900 – what is no small aggravation in this business is that I have but too much reason I believe that when he gave me his bond for a lot of my pictures that he did it with a view to pledge them, for instead of going to his own house they were lodged with Squibbs the auctioneer – you probably know that they were afterwards sold by auction and that too without giving be the slightest hint although I had called upon Sir WH full a week or ten days before. In short a more thorough swindling trick never sent a starving miserable creature to Botany Bay,'[21] he wrote, fulminating with rage, to Northwick.

It was not the only shameful act to which Hillary stooped. He borrowed and failed to repay money from some of his trusting old Quaker friends in Yorkshire, something which, years later, he would endeavour to excuse. 'You have my full authority to apply any funds of mine in your hands in discharge of that amount, which I deeply regret ever was in arrears and had the most specific orders which I gave to those who acted for me, been attended to in my absence, nothing of the kind could have taken place in Wensleydale',[22] he wrote in a long-overdue attempt to redress the wrong.

He had also alienated fellow West Indian merchants, taking out hefty mortgages and failing to repay the interest due. George Hibbert, one of the most powerful and prosperous London-based West Indian merchant financiers, had advanced him £20,000 and recognised the signs of what would probably now be diagnosed as a psychotic breakdown. 'That we hold on the Hillarys is a thing of mere consequence, for William Hillary is gone to pieces and has absconded and his brother, who was of no better character, is dead … William Hillary has scandalously treated and deceived us and we have therefore no obligation to him, but indeed his most sanguine creditor cannot look for any eventual advantage to his estate from the demand or right in Adelphi after our demand should be paid upon it',[23] he fumed to Simon Taylor, his factor and attorney in Jamaica.

As well as alienating old friends, Hillary's financial embarrassment and depression had disastrous repercussions on his relationship with Frances. It is easy to see why, when throughout his unravelling he continued to spend extravagantly on the regiment, dining with his cronies in the Neapolitan Club, reliving the heady Italian days, all the while glibly claiming to be 'activated only by an ardent zeal in a period of peril to render every aid in my power to my sovereign'.[24] Meanwhile, at Danbury, ashamed, terrified and infuriated in equal measure, Frances was left, increasingly disillusioned with married life and prey to other temptations.

Hillary would one day acknowledge that his obsessive dedication to the regiment had destroyed his marriage, confessing to 'the great augmentation of expense which, for years it made in every branch of my domestic establishment and the injury my private affairs sustained, by being deprived of so large a sum'.[25] Adding to his burden, his mother died, leaving him to mourn and untangle her estate, which included 'property inherited from my brother Charles Winn merchant of Jamaica',[26] along with another swathe of debt.

He would recognise this episode as the most testing of his life, yet never accept responsibility for his part in it. 'Through no part of my own, I have experienced unforeseen losses of West Indian property to a very great amount, which I had inherited from my family and am at present kept out of ... by a protracted suit in chancery',[27] he later claimed. Whether pride or the delusion of psychological strain froze the logic that ought to have made him disband his regiment we will never know. What is certain, however, is that even years later, whenever he reflected on this unhappy chapter of his life, he did so in the way survivors of a traumatic event often do, skirting over the surface without delving too deep:

> I married the heiress of the ancient houses of Disney and of Fytche, and soon after raised the First Essex Legion, consisting of more than 1,400 men, on the most exposed parts of that coast, then threatened with immediate invasion, and of which I continued in command until the close of the war, at an expenditure of fully £20,000 – and at the head of the largest force at that time raised by any one subject. – His late Majesty George III thanked me in the most gracious manner for what he was pleased to term 'a noble service' and conferred the baronetage upon me.
>
> Beyond this I never received any honour, emolument, profit or reward, nor did I ever receive a single day's pay – though a royal equerry I never sacrificed my independence to politics or party. My efforts have been for my country and mankind ...[28]

He was always vague about the precisely what happened to his inheritance. 'By one sudden stroke – an insurmountable defect in a mortgage which I had inherited – I was deprived of an ample fortune. In fact by one single blow I lost £120,000',[29] he confided to an old friend, as usual dodging the details of the issue. Whatever the truth, the discovery that his money was the subject of a case in Chancery must have disconcerted his numerous creditors. The court dealt with civil matters, especially disputes over wills and property. By the early nineteenth century, the labyrinthine complexity, inordinate cost and protracted time cases took to resolve was legendary and would later form the theme for Charles Dickens's great novel *Bleak House*.

Part of the problem was that depositions had to be made in writing rather than orally, and entire estates were often absorbed by the costs incurred. Hillary's case was further complicated in that it was dealt with by the Jamaican courts – making it even harder for him to control. His experience was far from unusual in that three decades after his brother's death, the case rumbled on unresolved, and he had yet to receive much if anything in the way of his inheritance. A large proportion of the money eventually credited to him would come through government allowances for the slaves he owned at the Adelphi and Marley estates. As part of the abolition of slavery, the government instigated a compensation scheme whereby slaves on every estate were categorised and owners paid to free them. The slaves on Hillary's disputed estates were valued at almost £4,400. By then, however, he had been forced to sell the possessions closest to his heart, including 'that eligible and very desirable sporting residence called Rigg House, built twenty-two years ago with very extensive plantations'. Also disposed of were 'the capital dairy sheep farm called Birkrigg,' and 1,600 acres of moorland rich with grouse and other game and latticed by trout streams.[30] In other words, he had lost the entire property that his family had carefully tended throughout more than two centuries, where he had happily played as a child and felt spiritually at home.

Adding to these bitter blows, his marriage reached crisis point. On 2 July 1810, Frances gave birth to a third child – a daughter named Wilhelmina. There is nothing very remarkable here, except to note that a decade earlier, when the twins were born, their birth had been widely announced in all the leading newspapers. This time things were very different. The baby's arrival went unmarked and two years would pass before she was christened in Hillary's absence. The choice of name was presumably a sop to Hillary, the man named as her father in the baptismal register. The truth of the matter, carefully hushed up to spare the reputations of all concerned, was that Hillary had parted from Frances well before Wilhelmina's birth, knowing (he later confessed to a friend) that his unhappy wife had 'dubbed him a cuckold.'[31] Despite what was written on her baptismal records, Wilhelmina was not his child.

Frances had found solace away from her husband, but she was far from liberated from his financial problems. In an age in which a married woman had few rights over her own property, she stood as guarantor for some of Hillary's debts. Worse still, several of his creditors were pursuing her for settlements that ,if enforced, would leave her penniless. Fearful for her own future security, as well as that of her children, she employed a solicitor, Francis Fladgate, to field the barrage of claims. Fladgate candidly conveyed the miserable truth of the situation to the creditors lining up for redress, telling Lord Northwick:

I am acting ministerially only, for Lady Hillary and her children ... it is among the many painful situations in which professional men are constantly placed, one of the most painful to know the perfect justice of a claim without enjoying the liberty of doing what his feelings and his wishes must dictate. Of the strong and obligatory nature of your lordship's claim, no one can bear better testimony than myself...but the fund which is under the responsibilities of the court of Chancery to be administered by Lady Hillary's trustees arises exclusively from the property of Lady Hillary and is by settlement (subject to the charges created by herself in conjunction with Hillary to relieve his receiptees amounting to about £40,000) secured to her and the children.

The amount of William Hillary's debts, many of them I am sorry to say very deeply founded in justice, would exhaust Lady Hillary's property altogether and leave her destitute. Two sets of creditors having judgements against Hillary have filed bills in chancery and it remains ... still a question to be decided by the chancellor whether their judgments give them any lean on the property. Whatever shall be the result, I fear the honourable creditors of Hillary will profit little by it ...[32]

For Hillary life was equally bleak. With a wife who had strayed, family estates sold, his inheritance lost, all he had striven for and so proudly accumulated seemed less substantial than a ship in the haze. There were, he knew, avenues of redress open to him. According to nineteenth-century marital laws, he could insist that Frances pay his debts and punish her infidelity by depriving her of their children. He could shame her by prosecuting her for 'criminal conversion' – divorce on the grounds of her adultery – and declare to the world at large that Wilhelmina was not his child. But to do so would be prohibitively costly and add prurient publicity to private misery, ruining her reputation and that of her children.

Even in the worst moments of his anguish, action of this kind conflicted with Hillary's high-principled core. Neither the depths to which he had sunk in his financial dealings, nor his mental torment, had transformed him into a vindictive man. At heart he would always be an idealist, albeit one with a weakness whenever it came to money. But this was a defining moment in his life. With debts still unresolved, his marriage in ruins, his psychological constitution shaky, the obvious way to resolve matters, he concluded, was to escape. Telling himself that misguided principle had led him astray and in time he would salvage his reputation, he left Danbury and London.

Notes

1 *Morning Post*, 6 June 1804.
2 *Morning Post*, 6 June 1804.
3 *Morning Post*, 6 June 1804.
4 *Leeds Mercury*, 31 March 1810.
5 The list is based on the items from his collection he would later sell to raise money to pay his debts.
6 It had begun in March 1802.
7 Mark Philip (ed,), *Resisting Napoleon*, pp. 91–110.
8 BL Add 38379 f126, 27 July 1814.
9 Ibid.
10 BL add 38379 f126, 7 December 1803.
11 BL Add 38379 f126, 27 July 1814.
12 Ibid.
13 P. Wright (ed.), *Lady Nugent's Journal 1801-1805* (1966), p. 182.
14 Ibid.
15 BL Add 38379 f126, Extracts of letters from Lord Braybrooke to WH, 4 September 1804.
16 Ibid.
17 Metropolitan Archives, acc 76/1098b, 1 February 1805.
18 Metropolitan Archives, acc 76/1098b, 19 October 1807.
19 Ibid.
20 *Morning Chronicle*, 21 June 1808.
21 Metropolitan Archives, Acc76/1098m, Lord Radstock to Lord Northwick 20 April 1809.
22 Quaker Library, MS vol. 338 f193, William Hillary to William Thompson, 22 February 1825.
23 Simon Taylor Papers, George Hibbert to Simon Taylor (reel 17), 7 July 1808.
24 BL Add 38379 f126, 27 July 1814.
25 BL Add 38379 f126, WH to HM Ministers, 27 July 1814.
26 National Archives, Hannah Hillary's will.
27 BL Add 38379 f126, 27 July 1814.
28 Archive of Order of St John, Hillary letters, 13 June 1838.
29 Ibid, 8 March 1841.
30 *Leeds Mercury*, 31 March 1810.
31 Ibid.
32 Metropolitan Archives, Acc 76/10980.

5

Appealing to the Nation

Another winter has scarcely yet commenced, and our coasts are spread over
with the shattered fragments of more than two hundred vessels, which, in
one fatal tempest, have been stranded on the British shores, attended with
an appalling havoc of human life, beyond all present means to ascertain its
tremendous extent … and shall this fearful warning also be without avail? …
With the most ample means for the rescue of thousands of human beings
from a watery grave, shall we still leave them to their fate?

'An Appeal to the British Nation on the Humanity and Policy of forming a National Institution for the Preservation of Lives and Property from
Shipwreck', Sir William Hillary, 1823

Twice a week in summer, a packet sailing ship made the crossing from
Liverpool to the Isle of Man, disgorging passengers and mail at the port
of Douglas. For those seeing the island for the first time, the arrival
– usually early in the evening – was always a memorable one. The great cres-
cent of Douglas Bay came into view as the boat swept past the headland. If the
weather was fine they would glimpse Castle Mona, the Duke of Atholl's palatial
residence in the centre of the bay, its pale facade emerging from a swathe of lush
gardens and gorse-covered hills. Close to the harbour a treacherous reef, known
as Conister Rock, lay half hidden beneath the waves. Unaware of the peril it represented, passengers gazed beyond its seaweed fringes to terraces of new villas and
a beach dotted with wheeled bathing machines, where children played on yellow
sand and gulls wheeled and mewed overhead.

Douglas was the Isle of Man's largest port, named after two converging rivers, the Dhoo and Glass, that flowed through the inner harbour and emptied into the bay. In Hillary's day a crowd always congregated on the Red Pier when the packet was due, for the quayside was the hub of the town, a place of comings and goings where elegantly dressed ladies threaded their way through clutches of Manx women in pepper-pot hats and straw-boatered sailors and fishermen unloading baskets of herring and pilchards. But beyond the bustle and buzz of the sunlit waterfront, visitors were ensnared by a less salubrious side of town: labyrinthine lanes lined with squat cottages, lodging houses, storehouses, smoke houses and noisy inns, all squeezed into the crease of the hillside like a tangled fishing net.

What did Sir William Hillary make of his new home when he abandoned his life as a ruined gentleman of Essex and decided to settle here? What made him choose this wind-blown island in the middle of the Irish Sea? He may have visited as a boy. The Isle of Man was fashionable as a summer holiday destination and easily accessible from Liverpool. Over previous decades Douglas had been transformed from a bustling fishing port and haven for smuggling, to become a busy trading post. Hillary's father's ships probably stopped and traded here. Mercantile connections were long established and the island depended on manufactured goods imported from the city and, in turn, exported herrings and other commodities through the port of Liverpool. There was also a murkier side to the trade between the island and Liverpool that may have influenced Hillary's choice of exile. Earlier in the eighteenth century, the Isle of Man acted as a warehouse for 'Guinea goods'; cargo collected by Liverpool slavers to be exchanged for West African slaves.

The Isle of Man also suited Hillary's character and present frame of mind. He had always admired unspoiled, rugged landscapes and there was a strand in him that loved ancient tradition and craved connection to his past. With its Celtic links and echoes of his beloved Wensleydale, this setting suited his vision of himself as a Byronic hero in search of a place to restore his reputation and assuage his guilt. The same thought may have struck his sister Mary when she wrote *The Fugitive* – heavily influenced by Byron and surely with her brother in mind:

O'er oceans ever heaving wave,
I go to hide guilt – my shame;
Dear tenants of that honoured grave,
Forgive this blot upon your name,
That but by me has known no stain.

There were further practical reasons for him to seek refuge here. The island was a crown dependency, constitutionally distinct from the mainland and governed by the Tynwald, one of the oldest legislatures in the world. Thanks to its unusual administration, taxes were low and living was cheap. Since the end of the Napoleonic Wars the Isle of Man had become known as 'a place where moderate people may be moderately happy at moderate expense'.[1] It was a well-known haven for men who were long on social standing but short on cash: retired officers on half pay, Regency rakes fallen on hard times. It was also a place where fugitive debtors were safe from British law.

For all these reasons, a recent influx of residents had settled in Douglas, and beyond its dilapidated core, newly built suburbs had sprung up: terraces of villas, a library, an assembly room, and even a billiard room where gentlemen might congregate. Despite his financial embarrassment, Hillary had means enough to rent a house towards the top of Prospect Hill, one of the newly built enclaves on the edge of town. The house had a flower court that reminded him of the parterres of Danbury and an excellent view of the bay.

The brush with ruin had devastated him, and Douglas's isolation and the healing power of the rugged Manx scenery helped him recover his mental well-being. As the months passed and unhappy memories and emotional disarray retreated, his need for company returned and he set about making new friends. Cornelius Smelt, the Lieutenant Governor of the Island, lived in Castle Rushen, a towering medieval castle which was the administrative hub of the Isle of Man in the centre of Castletown, the island's capital. Hillary, with his penchant for anything Gothic, must have loved visiting him there. But it wasn't only Smelt's drawbridge and tapestry-draped dining hall that appealed. Smelt's family came from the North Riding of Yorkshire, not far from the Hillarys' base in Wensleydale. He had served as a Lieutenant Colonel during the war – achieving the same rank as Hillary. Through his uncle, a tutor to two of George III's sons, he, like Hillary, had connections to the royal family. The friendship between the two men, founded on so much common ground, would last until the end of Smelt's life. Hillary was always admiring of his 'ability, justice and disinterestedness which ... greatly advanced the prosperity of the island placed under his charge'.[2] After his death, as we will see, he would raise a memorial to Smelt's memory, as well as petitioning Lord Melbourne for his job.

Friendship of another sort flourished at Lieutenant Colonel Ambrose St John's quayside home in Douglas. Once an MP for Callington in Cornwall and member of the militia during the war, St John was now living on a small pension in circumstances that were even more stretched than those of Hillary. St John had several attractive daughters, among them Sarah, who was in her late teens and became a devoted admirer of the debonair Hillary. It is not hard to see that her besotted attention must have lifted his bruised self-esteem. He did nothing to discourage her infatuation, but nor did he behave improperly, instead adopting the role of a brotherly guardian and, as we will see, eventually providing her with a permanent place in his household.

Then there was Sir Walter Scott's brother Tom, who had left Edinburgh to escape his creditors, briefly joined the local militia, the Manx Fencibles, and was largely occupied with research into the island's history for his brother. The Isle of Man would provide a setting for *Peveril Peak*, one of Scott's popular *Waverly* novels. Hillary regaled Tom with stories of his family history, as well as letting slip details of his more recent chequered past (as we will see), trustingly revealing his romantic aspirations to him.

Of all his new friends, Hillary was most drawn to Caesar Tobin. His family came from Irish stock, but had made their money in Liverpool from shipping and the West Indian trade. John Tobin, Caesar's uncle, had been the mayor of the city and Hillary may have known him during his childhood. The two men also shared military interests, since Caesar was a Major in the Manx Fencibles. As the friendship developed, something else drew Hillary to Caesar's door. He had several charming sisters, one of whom, Emma (also called Amelia), was regarded as a beauty.

Hiallry, still legally married to Frances and ten years Emma's senior, was quickly charmed and began to woo her. He was good with women – adept at flattery, full of sparkling stories of past adventures – and she was smitten. Tradition has it that her brother was, unsurprisingly, less enamoured at the burgeoning romance, even though he and Hillary were friends. A married man with a shady past and little in the way of financial provision wasn't quite what he had envisaged for his lovely sister. But if Caesar warned off Hillary, nothing he said hindered the blossoming liaison. Hillary placated him with assurances that he too wanted the respectability of marriage, rather than the subterfuge of an affair. It was simply a question of finding a way to make it possible.

In March 1811, a distinguished gentleman with a young female companion arrived in Edinburgh. The couple lodged a hotel under the names of Mr and Mrs Hastings.[3] Over the next few weeks the pair moved around the city from hotel to hotel. During their stay they were 'discovered' by representatives of Frances Hillary, who identified them as her estranged husband, travelling under an assumed name, with a woman who was fraudulently claiming to be his wife. After the confrontation the couple took refuge in rooms in Holyrood House and confessed their identities to be those of Sir William Hillary and Mrs Hastings.

If all this sounds like a scene from a Victorian melodrama, it isn't surprising. There was more than a dash of contrivance in the episode. Mrs Hastings was probably hired for the role she had performed. The scheme, including the discovery, had been carefully engineered by Hillary, with Frances's cooperation. In England, a husband could divorce his wife for adultery, but a wife could not do likewise unless there were further mitigating circumstances such as cruelty or desertion. In Scotland marital laws were less costly and more egalitarian. Frances only needed evidence of an adulterous husband who had deserted her four years earlier. Hillary's decision to spare her the public embarrassment of a divorce on the grounds of her infidelity had never wavered. The only difference now was that, having fallen for Emma, he wanted to extricate himself as quietly as possible from his former unhappy union. The engineered 'discovery' facilitated things all round. Frances was in a position to divorce him, the children avoided the dishonour and distress of their mother's infidelity becoming public knowledge and he would be free to remarry.

Frances compliantly lodged her testimony with the court: 'Notwithstanding the said marriage, the defendant had deserted the pursuer and withdrawn his affections from her; and having unfortunately contracted a load of debt, he left England about four years ago and took up his residence in the Isle of Man. From thence he came to Scotland and in March, 1811, he was discovered residing in an hotel in Edinburgh, under the fictitious name of Hastings and in company with a young woman calling herself Mrs Hastings',[4] reported *The Times*.

In defence, Hillary claimed to object to the jurisdiction of the court. Neither he nor Frances should be subject to Scottish law since they had not been married or lived there, he said. When he was 'discovered', he was living in the city temporarily, because of his financial difficulties. Given the fact that Hillary was the secret instigator of the divorce, it seems odd he raised an objection. Presumably this was all part of the charade – the divorce of British subjects in Scotland was unusual, and having witnessed Prince Augustus's legal wrangles over marital status, he wanted to be certain the legal process was validated at the highest level. It was a wily move: the matter was referred to the Supreme Court which, as he hoped, concluded that there were precedents for such a case in Scottish legal history. To the relief of all concerned, the Hillary vs. Hillary divorce was granted.

Hillary did not succeed in keeping the case out of the newspapers,[5] but everyone emerged with their dignity relatively unscathed. An unfaithful wife was a humiliation no man would wish to suffer, while a married man who strayed was a common enough reality. Many would have seen it as a transgression that underlined aristocratic status and masculinity. Hillary also benefited financially from the arrangement. As part of the agreement, Frances's father settled his outstanding debts and made generous provision for him in his will. Even before the case

came to court, Hillary candidly confided the truth of the matter to his new friend
Thomas Scott, who immediately reported the revelation to his brother, Sir Walter:

> There is a probability of William Hillary of Denby Park [*sic*] paying a visit
> this summer upon a most curious piece of business. He married a wife who
> dubbed him a cuckold – and to preserve the character of his children, daughters
> – and upon having all settlements made good by my lady's father – he goes to
> Scotland to commit fornication there in order that Lady Hillary <u>may divorce</u>
> <u>him</u> – I cannot help laughing at the scheme but it seems the first English coun-
> cil <u>think it will do</u>.[6]

Sir Walter was amused by the scheme, responding flippantly: '(Hillary) is not quite
singular in his choice of Scotland as a fitting place to break the seventh com-
mandment. Lord Paget did the same in order that the now Duchess of Argyll
might get rid of him. Being in love and in debt, your worthy Bart only wants to
be in drink also to complete the situation of the man in the old catch.'[7]

Liberated from his unhappy first marriage, Hillary was now free to propose
to Emma. They married a year later, at the end of September 1813, travelling to
Whitehorn, an ancient settlement in Dumfries, where the first Christian church
in Scotland was built in the fourth century by St Ninian. A large priory had
flourished here in the medieval period, when pilgrimages were popular, and the
crumbling ruins and ancient associations must have appealed to Hillary's sense of
romance and fascination for antiquity. Emma, compliant, young and in love, was
content to humour him.

His second marriage brought him immediate happiness and would ripen to
long-lasting affection, but could not entirely erase the scars of his past life. The
litigation in which he was embroiled would drag on for years and even if what
he had told Tom Scott was partly true, and Disney-Fytche settled his outstanding
debts, his income was small and money would always be a worry. Mostly he was
happy to live in Douglas with Emma, but there were times when matrimonial
contentment wasn't enough; the allure of his reclusive existence paled and long-
ing for a meaningful occupation pressed in.

News of his estranged children cannot have helped. Having moved to France
for the same financial reasons that took Hillary to the Isle of Man, the twins,
Wilhelmina and Frances were enjoying a sophisticated life in Paris under her
father's protection. According to Fanny Burney, Frances had taken an apartment
that belonged to Madame de Grandmaison prior to 'defraying expenses by start-
ing a voyage ... through the Low Countries, Switzerland or even Italy, before
coming to Paris'.[8]

In Douglas, meanwhile, with too much time to reflect and not enough to do, Hillary fell prey to gloom. Despite the knighthood he had received, he felt aggrieved that his efforts and expenditure during the war had not been fully acknowledged. Over and above government grants to maintain his regiment, he had spent £20,000 of his own money and never asked for or received any form of recompense. Even now, during his darkest moments, he did not seek financial redress, rather something that seemed infinitely more precious, a useful role; something that would give his life the purpose it once had but now lacked.

A year after his marriage, in July 1814, he wrote to Charles Broughton, secretary at the Foreign Office, 'laying a brief statement of circumstances before His Majesty's Ministers'. His letter summarised all he had done during the war and did not skirt over his reduced circumstances. 'I have experienced unforeseen losses of West Indian property to a very great amount, which I had inherited from my family ... my income is in consequence exceedingly impaired and I am compelled to live in complete retirement, upon less than the interest of the money I have expended.' What he wanted, he went on to explain, was 'future employ in an appointment compatible with my situation ... an appointment to one of the consular situations at present vacant'.

In putting himself forward for a diplomatic post he must have recalled his visits to William Hamilton's residence, Lady Hamilton's enchanting attitudes, the life he had enjoyed at the German courts and his unofficial expedition to Malta. His experience as equerry and military commander qualified him for such a role and Emma, his lovely young wife, would grace his arm wherever they were sent. 'I have stated to his lordship [he had written to Viscount Castlereagh, Foreign Secretary] that I have already passed some years on the continent of Europe ... but it is not for me to do more than to lay a simple statement of facts before His Majesty's Ministers, leaving it to them to decide whether this, or any other mode may be more eligible through which the favour of government could be expressed',[9] he continued.

It was not to be. Those in government office probably knew about his flawed past and, unsurprisingly, did not consider him appropriate material for a consular post. Over the coming weeks and months, Hillary watched the packet ships arrive from his terrace on Prospect Hill with an increasing sense of despondency. The diplomatic places were gradually filled; meanwhile his longed-for letter of appointment never materialised.

He would wait another eight years until he found the sense of purpose he needed. Caught up in the shipwrecks of the *Vigilant* and *Racehorse* he witnessed over the autumn of 1822, his life changed; a new role presented itself. here was a cause providing something worthwhile he could do.

Musing on what he had witnessed during those stormy nights, he analysed the lessons learned. The tragedy of shipwrecks was often preventable, provided there were rescue boats and crews willing to man them. Yet all around Britain's coast there were towns and villages without lifeboats, where rescue depended on the goodwill of local men and boats built for a variety of commercial purposes (fishing, unloading and transporting) but not to withstand extreme weather conditions. Granted, there was a scattering of lifeboats stationed in various coastal towns and ports. However, these were individually funded and while some functioned efficiently, many were poorly manned and maintained. As a further injustice, those brave enough to go to the aid of a stricken vessel could expect no regular method of reward. When rescuers died trying to aid stricken ships, their bereaved families were reliant on the shipowner or insurer for assistance, support which might or might not be forthcoming. Furthermore there were clear incentives for men to withhold aid; they might profit from the salvage of a stricken vessel.

Hillary realised that the problem was entirely soluble; a nationally coordinated organisation supplying, supervising and maintaining lifeboats, not just in a particular town or village, but around the entire coast of Great Britain. The institution would have a clearly defined mission. It would offer rewards, acknowledge bravery and take care of bereaved families. It would be an organisation worthy of Britain, the leading maritime nation of the world. It would ignite a spirit of humanity and demolish the venal incentives that presently encouraged men to withhold their assistance.

His own experience added weight to his idea. As the zigzag course of his life now seemed imbued with meaningful purpose, he recollected:

> Having in my early years resided much on the sea coast I acquired a strong bias for maritime affairs, though ... afterwards in the course of my travels as a young man I made several voyages in which I witnesses several disastrous shipwrecks more than once narrowly escaping when numbers around me perished.[10]

Thanks to his Liverpool connections he knew ship owners, sugar merchants, members of the banking and insurance fraternity, all with vested interests in improving safety at sea. Through royal service he had established links with the royal family. His role as military commander had taught him how to motivate and manage men and, above all, how to operate fearlessly on a grand scale. So the design took shape.

The scheme he settled upon would be a wake-up call to the nation at large – a pamphlet rather cumbersomely entitled *An Appeal to the British Nation on the Humanity and Policy of Forming a National Institution for the Preservation of Life from*

Shipwreck. In choosing this method to promote his idea Hillary, consciously or not, drew on his Quaker heritage. As a child he had read pamphlets and broadsides written by George Fox and other prominent members of the faith to promote their beliefs. Lapsed Quaker though he was, following their tradition seemed an obvious way to reach an audience and gain the support he needed.

The argument he composed echoes his character, intertwining cool logic with stirring force, idealism with practicality. Shipwrecks were at the forefront of public consciousness, he wrote, because they were a subject of national relevance that 'in a peculiar manner appeals to the British people'. The issue of shipwrecks was also bound up with patriotism: no one could contest the importance of the sea to British history and trade. So unless steps were taken to reduce the perennial tragedies that befell vessels in distress, 'we shall be wanting in our best duties to them, to our country and to ourselves'. The loss of life and property was costly both in human and commercial terms. Everyone agreed that Britain's prosperity and status among civilized nations relied on her maritime ascendancy. For all these reasons, inertia would represent a failure of common humanity and common sense. In other words, failure to do something now, while more vessels foundered and more lives were lost, would simply not be British.

Visionary and of its moment, it was an argument guaranteed to raise a cheer; a rallying cry for a cause that tapped into the spirit of the age. Since the end of the war, a mood of benevolence and a refusal to accept social injustice had swept the nation. This was a time of petitions and pressure groups, never mind upsetting the old status quo; if you wanted to put wrongs right, making a noise was justified. So causes connected to slavery, government corruption, Catholic emancipation, animal cruelty, the poor, children and even the absence of a memorial to Nelson roused vociferous fury and energetic support. Now, with Sir William Hillary at the helm, the light was to be shone upon the subject of shipwreck.

Notes

1   Belcham J.A., *New History of the Isle of Man*, vol. V (2000), p. 19.
2   PRO, HO 98/77.
3   *The Times*, 20 August 1812.
4   In some reports the coule are called Wilson
5   *The Times*, 20 August 1812.
6   *Letters of Sir Walter Scott 1821-1823*, (1932) note p. 461.
7   Ibid.
8   Joyce Hemlow (ed.), *Letters of Fanny Burney*, p. 525, 3–9 July 1817.
9   BL add 38379 f126, William Hillary to ministers, 27 July 1814.
10 William Hillary, *An Appeal to the British Nation on the Humanity and Policy of forming a National Institution for the Preservation of Lives and Property from Shipwreck* (1823).

Founding the Institution

The Helmsman steered, the ship moved on[ ]
Yet never a breeze up-blew;
The mariners all 'gan work the ropes,
Where they were wont to do

The Rime of the Ancient Mariner, Samuel Taylor Coleridge

He was not the first man to turn his attention to the subject. Since 1774, the Royal Humane Society had paved the way, tackling the subject of drowning with educational publications with instructions on saving people from the water. The society also set up stations where bodies could be brought for resuscitation and rewarded those involved in successful rescues. In 1799, Dr Fothergill of Bath wrote a prizewinning essay on the subject of shipwrecks. In it he recommended that ships be equipped with lifeboats and life-jackets; learning to swim be seen as an essential part of education; lifeboats be stationed in coastal towns; and ships foundering close to land be protected by an officer of the law from blatant plunder.[1] Then there was Captain Marryat (1792–1848), a man after Hillary's own heart with a hands-on approach to preventing deaths at sea, whose life had odd parallels with Hillary's. Now best known for his novels – especially *The Children of the New Forest* – Marryat, like Hillary, had lost a West Indian inheritance. He had also been recognised for his gallantry at sea during the war. During his naval career Marryat jumped overboard on numerous occasions, famously saving more than a dozen people from drowning. He also designed a lifeboat and perfected a method of maritime signalling.

George Manby (1765–1854), perhaps the most famous maritime paragon of Hillary's day, had approached the problem of shipwreck in a different way.

Witnessing the horrific wreck of the *Snipe*, a naval ship on which more than two hundred crew and French prisoners of war drowned within 60 yards of the coast of Yarmouth in 1807, inspired him to invent 'Manby's Apparatus', a line fired from the shore to the stricken boat by a mortar rocket, promoted in *An Essay on the preservation of shipwrecked persons with descriptive account of the apparatus and the manner of using it.* His invention had been championed in Parliament by William Wilberforce, who in 1811 recommended that coastal stations should be equipped with the apparatus and that government should meet the costs. By the time Sir William Hillary sat down to put his thoughts into words, Manby was regarded as a national hero. His apparatus had saved 229 lives and he had received more than £2,000 for his efforts. Hillary fervently hoped his own scheme would find an equally appreciative audience.

The aims he went on to outline in broad strokes remain unchanged to this day: to fund, by private subscription, a voluntary association equipped with the most advanced technology, including 'lifeboats, anchors, cables, hawsers, and the beneficial inventions of those enlightened and highly patriotic officers Captains Marryat and Manby'. The organisation would be run by a London-based central committee which would coordinate lifeboat stations around Britain's coast. The aim was to preserve life, assist vessels in distress, aid those rescued and reward those who risked their lives to help others. The stations' locations were to be decided by drawing on the advice of such bodies as Trinity House, Lloyd's and coastal city corporations. The most remote, wild and exposed areas should not be overlooked and should be provided with the means to assist ships in distress, even if this was only a set of Manby's apparatus, a rope fired by a rocket.

Barely a month after he began to write, the pamphlet was complete. Fired with determination, he scraped together enough money to pay for the printing of 700 copies and the real work began – attracting the attention of 'the most eminent characters in the country', most of whom were besieged by countless other good causes. A dozen pamphlets went to the Admiralty board, others to the merchants of Liverpool, the East and West India Merchants and Trinity House, all of whom had vested interests in improving safety at sea. Drawing on his eminent connections, he sent copies to members of the royal family and government ministers, among them Sir Robert Peel, Home Secretary. In early April, Peel was one of the first to offer moral support (but no money) and promised to forward a pamphlet to the king. By then Hillary's conviction had strengthened and he was already planning a second edition of his pamphlet. Even so, Peel's kind words provided a boost. Speedily he wrote back, enclosing the additional sheets he had penned.

The press also responded kindly, impressed by Hillary's willingness to spend his own money on promoting a charitable scheme. 'The object of this pamphlet is so thoroughly praiseworthy, the suggestions which it offers are so judicious and the subject altogether is so deserving of public attention, that we cheerfully yield our assistance ...' wrote the *Monthly Censor* in May. But it wasn't all good news. After much delay the Admiralty's verdict board crushingly declared they thought the scheme impractical, and while 'they wish success to any undertaking which has for its objects the saving of the lives of mariners they do not see they can at present take any steps in this matter'.[2] The rejection came as a bitter setback but did little to suppress Hillary's conviction. He had struck on a subject close to everyone's heart, and, with a second edition published, the campaign had gathered too much momentum to fail.

Compared with the first pamphlet, the second approaches the subject more emotively, speaking to hearts first, heads second. His melodramatic language resounding with moral certainty, Hillary described:

> ... the conflicting fury of the elements, the darkness of night, the disasters of the sea and the dangers of the adjacent shores, but too frequently combine to place the unhappy mariner beyond the power of human aid...While we pause they continue to perish; whilst we procrastinate, the work of destruction pursues its course.

Pleading and determination were not enough to turn the tables in his favour. Offers of support were scant. Lloyd's Insurance pledged a donation of £50 towards a lifeboat for Douglas. Others, including Mr Montefiore, a ship owner whose vessel had been given assistance during a storm off the Isle of Man, followed suit. This was all very well, but what use was a lifeboat in the Isle of Man to a ship foundering off Land's End or Rye or Skegness or Brighton? Almost a year had passed and Hillary had to face the disappointing truth. Despite his energetic letter-writing and relentless petitioning of old friends, little real progress had been made. Which raises the question: was the lacklustre response connected to Hillary's past misdemeanours? There is nothing to prove it was, although, in the closed circles of London and Liverpool society, Hillary's financial disgrace was still recent enough to be common knowledge. Even those who believed in his cause might be forgiven for feeling reluctant to hand over cash to a man who, judging by past behaviour, might not be entirely trustworthy.

A reviewer in *Blackwood's Magazine* of January 1824 recognised the financial impasse but attributed it to Hillary's isolation on the Isle of Man, rather than his chequered reputation. The reviewer offered a workable solution. 'The pamphlet will perish like its objects, if the benevolent pamphleteer should limit himself to pamphleteering,' he suggested, before going on to offer his candid advice:

This well-meaning and human man (should) add a little city exertion to his remote and sea shore philanthropy – let him come up to town, put advertisements in the papers, calling a meeting at some city tavern ... offer a set of intelligible resolutions and boldly demand a committee and a subscription. There can be no doubt then of his success sooner or later..

Happy to act rather than wait, Hillary took the hint and dashed back to London.

The first person he enlisted was an unlikely ally – an erstwhile creditor, who had once viewed him in a far from friendly light. A decade and a half earlier, as we have seen, George Hibbert, a wealthy financier of the West Indian trade, had lent him £20,000. Infuriated by Hillary's dubious financial dealings, and despairing of ever recovering what he was owed, Hibbert confided his damning judgment of Hillary to his attorney: 'We have so bad an opinion of his personal responsibility that we would willingly make a sacrifice of some part of the amount of our demand.'[3] The court case between them was ongoing and yet some form of settlement must have been reached, for now Hillary managed to persuade Hibbert to promote the lifeboat cause.

His allegiance marked a pivotal moment. As director of the West India Dock Company and government agent to Jamaica, Hibbert had a network of useful friends among the political and mercantile elite. With their support and patronage, others, Hillary trusted, would follow. Then came another stroke of good fortune that gave further desperately needed momentum to the campaign. A second champion joined the cause.

Thomas Wilson, the energetic MP for Southwark, was brimming with ideas on how best to get the institution founded and had invaluable connections in Parliament and within royal circles. The three agreed that a public meeting should be the next step. They would hold it on 4 February 1824, and where better than the Tavern in Bishopsgate, a favourite haunt 'of noblemen and gentlemen', in which many other successful charities had been launched.

When the day came Hillary must have been crestfallen to find only fifteen people had stirred themselves to attend the meeting. Even so, he noticed among the audience several influential faces: Samuel Gurney, the Quaker banker and philanthropist; Samuel Hoare, Quaker founder of the abolitionist society; John Vincent Purrier, a business colleague of Hibbert's and, ironically, the son of the receiver in the dispute between Hillary and Hibbert and Lord Amelius Beauclerk, an illustrious naval officer. With Wilson in the chair, Hillary, exuding a quiet confidence, began to describe the plan as he had outlined it in his pamphlet: 'Taking into consideration the frequent loss of life by shipwreck, and believing that by the pre concerted exertion of practical men, and the adoption of practicable means, such calamities might often be averted.'[4] The fifteen listened intently before responding with suggestions of their own. Together they agreed another meeting should be held – but before that they would need to attract sponsors, 'of the nobility, gentry, merchants traders and others'. Illustrious names were crucial if the plan – the foundation of the National Shipwreck Institution, Hillary's long-cherished dream – was to be realised. But how should they secure the support they needed from men of prominence? In the convivial atmosphere of the tavern, as the fire blazed and burned low and bottles of wine were emptied, a plan was carefully worked out. Announcements of the impending meeting were placed in the leading newspapers. Meanwhile, behind the scenes, Wilson drew on his connections within the establishment to try to persuade the king to act as patron and worked on the Earl of Liverpool (the Prime Minister of the day) to become president. Everyone agreed that securing the allegiance of these two was crucial. With their endorsement other members of the royal family would be persuaded to take posts as vice patrons, then 'noblemen and persons of distinction' would become vice presidents. And where such elevated members of society led, the rest would follow.

With a sense of eager anticipation the meeting was closed with a final vote of thanks to Hillary, 'for his exertions in bringing this interesting subject before the meeting, and his assistance in its deliberations'. Hillary left the tavern warmed with pride as well as wine, and elated by the hope that after all his disappointments, something positive was about to happen.

The long awaited moment arrived on 4 March 1824.[5] The Archbishop of Canterbury presided over an audience of illustrious aristocrats, clerics, politicians, naval officers, insurance brokers, merchants and shipowners – including, Hillary was gratified to see, William Wilberforce and Captain Manby. Before these eminent men the Royal National Institution for the Preservation of Life from Shipwreck was formally founded. The 'Royal' in the title was the ultimate accolade for which Hillary had hoped; a signal of the impressive support Wilson, Hibbert and he had successfully secured. George IV had agreed to serve as the institution's patron. The Dukes of York, Clarence, Sussex, Cambridge and Gloucester and Prince Leopold, would be vice-patrons. And – as a final plume in the institution's cap – the Prime Minister, the Earl of Liverpool, had consented to become president.

The meeting did not pass without a moment of drama. Feeling his place as hero of the shipwrecked mariner was being usurped, Manby had grown jealous of Hillary's role in the newly founded institution. His rancour bubbled over when Wilson made a vote of thanks to Hillary 'as father of the institution'. A verbal fencing match ensued in which an infuriated Manby prompted his brother-in-law, Thomas Gooch, to rudely interrupt. 'However great might be William Hillary's merits, the formation of such a society as the present had been recommended long ago by Captain Manby.'[6] This was far from true – Manby's efforts had always been firmly focused on installing his apparatus at coastal stations, not on establishing a national lifeboat institution. Even so, no one wanted a row that would reflect badly all round, and to mollify Manby before the situation escalated further, the Archbishop of Canterbury swiftly intervened. 'This was a very honourable competition and he had no doubt the thanks of the meeting would be given to both men.'[7] The altercation was reported in the press, but revealingly, no mention of it was included in the official minutes of the meeting.

Manby's resentment may have created a hiatus in the euphoria of the moment, but he could do nothing to overshadow Hillary's joy. His happiness reverberates from the appendix he added to the second edition of his pamphlet two months later:

> A year had scarcely elapsed after the first edition of the preceding pamphlet was committed to the press, when the great object it recommended was accomplished ... honoured as this institution has been, by the high patronage of the King and of his illustrious family ... sanctioned by many of the most distinguished characters in the church and state, and sustained by the bounty of a generous nation ... it only remains for me to express the heartfelt satisfaction which I experience in witnessing the attainment of this object of my most earnest solicitude, and in the firm conviction ... that this institution is now established on principles which will extend it beneficial effects to the most distant shores, and to generations yet unborn.[8]

There was much to do in the early days and committee meetings took place almost weekly. The quest for funds was pressing. Letters enclosing Hillary's now famous appeal were dispatched to lobby for financial support from directors of the East and West India Company, government departments, the Bank of England, the Royal Exchange, the London Insurance company, the Hudson's Bay Company, the Levant Company, the Russia Company. Others were addressed to Lord Lieutenants of counties, to Oxford and Cambridge Colleges – and so it went on.

As well as seeking funds, the committee sought advice. They asked Trinity House and Lloyd's where stations should be positioned and which areas of the coast were most treacherous. They wrote letters to find new offices, to agree what equipment should be bought and even to ask if all costs of postage could be waived – a request the treasury office refused.

Within weeks, a cascade of brave rescue stories and accompanying requests for rewards were delivered to the institution's offices. Among them was the report of Captain Freemantle, who had saved the lives of the crew of a Swedish brig near Christchurch, Dorset, during a tempest on 8 March. As soon as he was notified of the ship's distress, Freemantle had gone to help and discovered a crowd gathered on the shore, watching the ship founder yet unwilling to assist. With no boat available Freemantle stripped off and, with a line attached, swam out to the stricken brig. The vessel began breaking up as he arrived. Freemantle saw the crew washed overboard before he could assist them and had then to be 'dragged to the shore senseless'. Fortuitously the crew were also washed close enough to the shore to be plucked from the waves without any fatalities.

Then there was the tale of the *Olive*, a brig lost in a gale en route from Tenby to Littlehampton at Gunwalloe, in Mount's Bay, Cornwall. Seven people had been saved but Lloyd's had refused to reward the rescuers on the grounds that no boats had set out from shore. In Brighton, Charley Watts claimed that he had saved three people's lives when a pleasure boat had been swamped off the coast in an incident in which three other passengers had drowned. Further afield, J. Mornay of Mexico and an officer from the American schooner *Shark* informed the institution that an English vessel had got into difficulty at Vera Cruz and the assistance provided by the *Shark*'s crew had resulted in the deaths of fourteen Americans.

Conscious of the importance of careful investigation to avoid fraudulent claims, inquiries were made via local coastguards and other officials. How much money had been subscribed locally to the institution in Helston? What had been raised from the salvage of anchors and cables or any other property that may have been preserved? Charley Watts would be given £5 and both he and Freemantle were awarded a medal. The men who helped the *Olive* would get £30 to be shared among them. But the crew of the *Shark* would receive nothing, on the grounds that 'The case does not come within the principle of the institution which extends only to cases of shipwreck that occur on the coast of the United Kingdom.'[9]

The rush of early applications only underlined what everyone already knew – the frightening statistics of shipwreck. One of the committee members, Captain Bowles, had been asked to establish precise figures since no comprehensive records existed. The task was not an easy one but his report found that over the past three years, 'it appeared that 438 vessels had been wrecked and stranded, out of which no less than 341 lives had been lost besides the whole of the crews of sixty-six other vessels which had also been wrecked or stranded ... and there have also been many cases where lives have been lost when the number could not be ascertained.'[10]

Given this horrifying toll, it was essential new boats and apparatus should be supplied, as a matter of urgency, to areas most in need. But the question of what type of boat or equipment should be used was not straightforward, and in the early weeks the numerous petitions from boat builders and others eager to promote their designs led to the formation of a 'Committee of Inventions' to decide where money would be best spent.

Boats built expressly for the purpose of rescue had been made in Britain from the late eighteenth century. Designs varied, but key features were buoyancy chambers – usually watertight metal or cork-filled compartments and the ability to drain water ingress by a system of plug holes and valves. Manoeuvrability, stability and strength were also vital. A lifeboat needed to be easy to power into a storm, able to withstand collision with ships or sandbanks and roomy enough to transport as many rescued passengers as possible.

In Britain, an early prototype patented in 1785, made by Lionel Lukin, a fashionable London coach builder, transformed a Norway yawl into an 'unsubmergible boat'. One of Lukin's boats was used at Bamburgh, a notoriously treacherous stretch of coast home to one of the earliest lifeboat stations. Newspaper reports of trials at Lowestoft claimed his boats could hold 'fifty persons with safety, when quite full of water'.[11] Lukin's rival for the title of 'inventor of lifeboats' was Henry Greathead, who had turned his attention to the problem after a ship named *Adventure* sank off Tynemouth with the loss of many of her crew. A group of local businessmen sponsored a competition for a design for a rescue boat. Greathead's lifeboat, named *Original*, the winner of the two guinea prize, was 28½ft long and 9½ft wide with a shallow cork-lined hull powered by ten oars, and could carry twenty people. After his first boat was launched in 1790, Greathead went on to supply over thirty more. Lloyds chairman Julius Angerstein paid him £2,000 for fourteen boats. He also won 50 guineas and a gold medal from the Royal Humane Society, £1,200 from the government, 100 guineas from Trinity House and the same from Lloyd's.

Sifting through a steady flow of alternative lifeboat designs, the Committee of Inventions considered recommendations from John Bennett of Lloyds for lifeboat designs that were smaller and more manageable than Henry Greathead's. The optimum size and form of a lifeboat became the subject of long discussion. Overly large boats were impossible to pull in a heavy sea, and the consensus was that a boat of any more than 26ft was unfeasible. 'The size increasing the difficulty of pulling to windward in even a fresh breeze and consequently rendering her useless in a gale to go to windward, in which direction lifeboats are almost invariably required to act.'[12] They read reports from Lord Exmouth on trials of a boat designed by Pellew Plenty that was supposedly impossible to capsize. Plenty was summoned to present his model to the committee. At 18ft long and broad of beam, it was manoeuvrable in a heavy sea, and Plenty promised that if he received an order for two boats they could be ready in a matter of weeks, the committee were not entirely satisfied with his original design and insisted on alterations to the prototype. The airtight compartments in the base should be filled with cork; there should be two additional plug holes in the bottom for drainage and the seats for the rowers should be set lower in the boat, they stipulated.

There were also copious designs for life-saving apparatus to assess. Among them were plans for a mortar rocket; a kite for the same purpose, designed by Captain Dansey; and a life preserver, 'being a ship's water cask with appendages', submitted by Thomas Grant.

Hillary was not present at all of the meetings, although he attended when he could and kept in touch by a steady stream of correspondence at other times. The design of lifeboats fascinated him and early the following year he too would join the ranks of hopeful petitioners, submitting a detailed proposal for a steam lifeboat capable of travelling further distances in heavy weather than boats dependent solely on wind and manpower.

Nothing came of this idea, but he was honoured when at the annual general meeting of March 1825, a year after the institution's foundation, his place as 'original projector of the Shipwreck Institution' was formally recognised with the presentation of a gold medallion. Presumably to defuse further conflict, Captain Manby was also warmly praised and decorated. 'Mr Wilson entered into a high eulogium of Captain Manby's apparatus, which he considered very superior to boats. The Institution were particularly bound to support Captain Manby's plan, on account not only of its intrinsic merit, but the inventor's noble disinterestedness. Persons supplying boats reaped benefit from their employ but Captain Manby derived none from the use of his apparatus',[13] declared the *Times*, conveniently forgetting that Manby had been the recipient of more than one generous government grant for his invention.

If Hillary was in any way irked at the attention given to Manby, he avoided being drawn into further argument. He was able to be magnanimous; a year after the foundation of the Institution, he felt he had redeemed himself for his earlier transgressions. His sister Mary confirmed his vindication, demonstrating her pride in her brother's feat with an emotional poem, entitled 'Lines addressed to the members of the Royal National Institution for the Preservation of Life from Shipwreck, on their First Anniversary Meeting in 1825'. The descriptions of shipwreck must have been based on Hillary's accounts:[14]

> And thou, my Brother! On whose bounteous heart
> First fell the spark, that can such hopes impart;
> Great was the power, which led thee 'midst the storm,
> To see stern Danger in its direst form!

'Twas not the wrath of Heaven which bade thee know
And share such scenes of agonising woe;
No! 'twas His hand, whom winds and waves obey,
Which drew the forth to show the appointed way;
To bid Philanthropy's bright flame expand,
And pour new glories o'er thy native land!

He was happy too that financially the institution was prospering. After a year, £9,706 had been donated; enough money to pay for ten lifeboat stations to be established. It was a promising start, although many more would be needed before the coastline of Britain was as safe as he wanted it to be.

A new lifeboat was already being built for Douglas, where one of the first ten local branches had been established under his supervision. One lifeboat was not enough, however. As Hillary saw it, the Isle of Man was unique in terms of its geographic and economic importance and needed more. In June 1824, he had written to the central committee and the elders of Trinity House, who supervised the running of the lighthouses around Britain's coast, and had advised the committee where the lifeboat stations were most needed. Hillary wanted a further five lifeboats for the Isle of Man and put forward a powerful argument for the demand: 'With a population of only 40,000 – it possesses a coast of nearly eighty miles, the whole of which is of the most dangerous description', he wrote. He drew the committee's attention to the poverty of the island, pointing out that most of the ships that found themselves in difficulty off shore 'do not belong to the place – they are those employed in the coal trade from Cumberland to Dublin – those of Liverpool bound to the north – of Scotland to and from the South – and the whole coasting trade of the east of Ireland'.[15]

He made the request conscious that it was much to ask. 'I am but too well aware of the limited state of our finances in the present infancy of the Institution not to feel that it would be impossible to devote the requisite finds to establish six complete lifeboats',[16] he confessed. Nevertheless, he urged, local supporters might 'secure as large funds as might be practicable, both by way of donations and annual subscriptions'. The claim, however well meant, was not entirely candid. He knew that money would always be a stumbling block on the island but, typically ignoring inconvenient financial realities, he skirted the issue, suggesting that boats could be built in Douglas to reduce their cost. Glibly he assured the committee that although the island was short of financial resources, it had an abundance of human ones. 'I am persuaded that if supplied with the requisite means there would not be found a want of ... hardy boats' crews.' A year later, during the worst storm he had ever witnessed, the truth of his claim would be called into question.

Notes

1 A. Fothergill, *Essay on the Preservation of Shipwrecked Mariners, in Answer to the Prize Questions Proposed by the Royal Humane Society.*

2 Robert Kelly, *For Those in Peril* (1979) p. 36.

3 Simon Taylor Papers, George Hibbert to Simon Taylor, reel 17, f82, 8 September 1808.

4 RNLI Minute Books, 4 February 1824.

5 The original date of 24 February was changed because there was a meeting of East India Company directors on the same day. RNLI Minute Book, 16 February 1824.

6 *Morning Chronicle*, 5 March 1824.

7 Ibid.

8 A.J. Dawson, *Britain's Life-boats* (1923), p. 53.

9 RNLI Minute Books, 10 July 1824.

10 RNLI Minute Books, 26 May 1824.

11 *Ipswich Journal*, 28 November 1807.

12 RNLI Minute Books, 11 August 1824.

13 *The Times*, Friday 11 March 1825.

14 Mrs Henry Rolls, *The Kaleidoscope or Literary and Scientific Mirror* (1825) p. 353.

15 RNLI Archive, WH to Central Committee, 6 June 1824.

16 RNLI Archive, WH to Simon Cook, 22 June 1824.

7

The *City of Glasgow*

'Tis Night's most awful hour, her solemn noon!
Veil'd is each guiding star; the o'er clouded moon
Just gives at times a sudden dubious light
That heightens all the terrors of the night;
High heave the billows with tremendous roar,
Then burst in foam upon the craggy shore;
Whilst rolling thunder rends the darksome skies.

'Lines on the first anniversary of the Royal Institution for the Preservation of
Life from Shipwreck', Mrs Henry Rolls (*née* Hillary), 1825

Captain Carlyle, Master of the *City of Glasgow*, a 300-ton wooden paddle steamer, had no notion of the ordeal he would face when, soon after midday on Tuesday 18 October 1825, he set sail from the port of Greenock en route to Liverpool. The wind was fresh as he emerged from the shelter of the port with sixty-two passengers on board, but an hour later hazy sunshine dissolved into heavy clouds and a stiffening wind blew up a swell that put an uncomfortable strain on the steamer's engines. Carlyle was still several hours from Liverpool when the situation deteriorated further and one of the *City of Glasgow*'s over-taxed engines coughed, spluttered and died.

Early sea-going paddle steamers were equipped with sails as well as engines, but even so, they were heavily built craft and with only one paddle wheel functioning, Carlyle knew his ship was critically underpowered in such a sea. Rethinking his plans, he remembered that in a north-westerly wind, there would be shelter on the east coast of the Isle of Man, at Douglas. There, he decided, he would undertake repairs in the safety of the bay before carrying on. He reached Douglas at about 4 p.m. and, having anchored safely, ordered the ship's broken engine to be dismantled. Part of it was found to be too badly damaged to be mended by the crew and was sent ashore; other repairs were undertaken on board.

So far so good. But later that night, around 11p.m., the wind shifted unexpectedly to the east and 'in an instant,' according to the newspapers, had increased to gale force. With steepening waves rolling into the bay, the *City of Glasgow's* mooring began to strain and drag, exposing her to the risk of being swept onto the rocks at the far side of the bay. On board repairs were now complete, and Carlyle, was still waiting for the missing engine part to arrive from the town, had prudently ordered the boilers to keep up steam. With a failing anchor and foam-marbled waves looking increasingly menacing, he now feared waiting any longer would be foolhardy. He decided to ride out the storm at sea, returning to anchorage to finish the repairs once the conditions had calmed.

Conscious that one working engine would be no match for the tempest now blowing, he ordered the sails to be reefed and raised, presumably intending to beat across wind and out of the bay. But no sooner had The *City of Glasgow* begun to haul up her anchor chain than the wind overpowered her and she found herself 'tailing ashore... dragging her anchor broadside to the sea, thumping heavily astern, her rudder unshipped and the sea breaking over'.[1] Realising his predicament and his proximity to the harbour mouth, Carlyle manoeuvred the ship stern on to the sea, praying that with the force of the breakers and wind he would be able to sail her into the harbour. Under any conditions, navigation of this nature, in the dead of night, would have been onerous. With one overburdened engine, storm-battered sails and a funnelling sea it was too much to ask. The steamer was hurtled by the surging swell towards the headland and, an instant later, 'verged over the dangerous reef, called half-tide rocks at the harbour entrance',[2] where she came to an ominous standstill.

In the moonless sky Hillary could not have seen the *City of Glasgow* heading for the prong-like rocks, or listing inelegantly as they speared her. Nor could he have seen the foaming surf spewing over her bridge, or her terrified passengers, without the comfort of lifejackets, flayed by wind and rain, huddled on deck, certain they were about to drown at any moment. But, having seen the steamer come into the bay the previous afternoon, he was alert to the danger she faced from the moment the wind shifted and foresaw the predicament of those on board. It was for just such emergencies his institution had been founded.

Intending to muster a crew and launch the new lifeboat, he hurried to the quay. It was nearly midnight, but storms always drew people to the harbour, especially those who one way or another, legally or illegally, made a living from the sea. There were groups of boatmen about, most of them taking shelter from the storm in the town's taverns. Mustering his persuasive powers, Hillary pleaded eloquently, imploring them to join him and go to the aid of the stricken ship. But the response he met dismayed him. No one was willing to offer assistance to the steamer. According to the *Morning Post*, Hillary did not give in easily, continuing to counter their indifference, 'offer(ing) £20 to any of the boats that would go out and take a line to her'. But his rallying arguments and usual persuasive skill failed him. The men were unmoved, excusing themselves with mutterings that 'such was the sea at the mouth of the harbour'[3] a rescue would be impossible.

Later reports would damningly suggest that the reason for their apathy had as much to do with the alcohol they had drunk as the danger they faced. Adding to the fiasco, the new lifeboat, built to withstand just such extreme seas, was beached in an inaccessible spot and 'could not be brought into use from the situation in which she was thus placed'.[4] Hillary would afterwards unconvincingly explain that this difficulty was owing to 'the suddenness of the tempest and state of the tide'.[5] In truth, although he was infuriated and disconcerted by the lack of willing hands, he did what he always did when practical considerations conflicted his intentions – refused to be deterred. He sent word to rouse his volunteer crew from their beds and searched for an alternative rescue boat close to hand. The crew, at least, lived up to his expectations, stumbling bleary-eyed down to the harbour. These 'six brave fellows stimulated by his gallant example'[6] included men who were to become regulars on his life-saving missions: Isaac Vondy the coxswain, Thomas Kewn and James Kelly among them. By then Hillary had also secured a rescue vessel: the *Nestor*, a 'common harbour or fishing boat nearest at hand'.[7]

We can only imagine what it felt like to be one of the six men, rowing the diminutive *Nestor* towards the open sea where the violent storm raged. Since they were venturing out in the middle of the night, they must have heard the breakers beating the rocks and whipping across the harbour wall like a warning before they could see them. Their only source of illumination would have been an oil lamp or two; little help with the wind-lashed spray blinding and drenching them to the core. The closer they drew to the narrow harbour entrance the more difficult would have been their progress. The walls channelled the swell, transforming each wave into a malevolent wall of water, propelling them back like storm-tossed flotsam. Yet somehow they managed to hold their nerve and force their way through, then manoeuvre the *Nestor* across current towards the stranded steamer.

When Hillary reached the *City of Glasgow*, she was listing on her port side, one huge paddle wheel crushed against the rocky ledge, a splintered gash ripped along her hull with breakers exploding over her. He made out the outlines of passengers huddled on deck; women and children crying and praying for help, while according to the newspapers, one man – an artist – had perched himself perilously at the bow and was busily recording the scene.

Both Hillary and Carlyle knew that with so many passengers on board it would be impossible to evacuate them in a small single lifeboat without numerous trips – an unfeasible demand to make of six men in this vicious sea. Instead, Carlyle bellowed above the wind, asking the *Nestor* to take a hawser to the pier head. His hope was that with sufficient manpower they might somehow manage to haul the steamer off the rocks and back across the entrance. If they succeeded thus far, the waves would do the rest and transport her into harbour.

With no other obvious course, Hillary agreed. Catching the line Carlyle threw, he heaved it on board and with the added burden of the heavy rope dragging in the sea, the *Nestor* lurched her way with the rolling surf powering her along to the sanctuary of the harbour. By now the storm had reached hurricane force – at the end of the quay immense waves pounded over the outer wall, sluicing its surface with such ferocity that even to set foot on it was perilous. Ignoring the danger, Hillary and his men heaved the hawser to the pier head, drawing it as close as possible to the steamer and securing it to a capstan. Their example inspired others to abandon their earlier reluctance to help and follow. And so in the screaming wind, with sea water swilling around their feet, a team of men grabbed the line and yanked it taut, mustering every effort to pull the steamer free. The driving onshore wind and now ebbing tide made the task an impossible one. The *City of Glasgow* shifted slightly but remained impaled on the rocks, the roar of the surf muffling the terrified passengers' cries. The hawser had steadied her, but she remained vulnerable, likely to break up at any minute.

Hillary was not prepared to relinquish the passengers to their fate. The only way left to save them, he now decided, was to return to the ship in the rescue boat and evacuate her. Summoning his crew back to the *Nestor*, he explained what they must all have understood. Others were now willing to volunteer their services, and a second fishing boat, the *True Blue*, was launched. They rowed out in convoy, the *True Blue* following some distance behind the *Nestor*. Again Hillary's exhausted crew braved waves and wind, managing to manoeuvre themselves to the leeside of the steamer, where her hull offered protection from the onslaught of the surf.

Hillary and Carlyle knew that in such a small boat, the numbers he carried would have to be limited. They made no allowances for the reaction of the panicked passengers. As soon as the *Nestor* drew alongside they streamed on board, ignoring Carlyle's instructions to wait. Only when the *Nestor* was grossly overloaded with fifteen passengers was Carlyle able to stem the exodus. He and Hillary bluntly told those on board the small boat that by overburdening her, everyone's lives were endangered. But the passengers were beyond reason and no one would disembark. Uneasily Hillary decided he would head for the closest shore. If he made it he would debark them there, then return for more.

They did not get far before calamity struck. As the *Nestor* shoved off and rounded the *City of Glasgow*'s hull, a breaker smashed against the steamer's side. The ship pitched and crashed down against the lifeboat. The passengers cowering inside her were shaken but unharmed, but the *Nestor*'s gunwales were smashed and her rudder dislodged. With oars that were unusable, too many passengers on board and no rudder, there was now nothing Hillary could do to control her. In an instant the *Nestor* was sucked away from the ship by a racing ebb tide, lurching and rolling alarmingly with the incoming breakers. The petrified passengers must now have grasped the reality of their predicament – they had exchanged one stricken vessel for another even more fragile one. Moments later Hillary's worst fears were realised as a cresting wave swamped the *Nestor*. Overflowing with water, she heeled over and capsized, hurling her human cargo into the sea.

They were only yards from the shore, but drowning was the most probable outcome. Like most men and women of the early nineteenth century, Hillary could not swim, and nor in all probability could the majority of the other occupants of the boat. Miraculously, however, he found himself picked up by a breaker and washed ashore in the surf. Dazed and battered by rocks, he recovered his senses and charged back to scour the waves for more survivors. He spotted a body floating in the water, hauled it out, then returned to search again. Three times he went back, each time retrieving a casualty who would recover from the ordeal. Meanwhile the *True Blue* had been joined by a third boat, *Dart*, and these followed the *Nestor*, drawing alongside the steamer, loading passengers on board, and shuttling them to the shore.

By 5 a.m. some fifty passengers had been landed safely or dragged from the sea and were led along the rocks to a nearby army barracks for shelter. No one had drowned. Hillary was still worried for the safety of the few who remained on board – one passenger, Captain Carlyle and members of his crew. He rowed out to the steamer for a third time, offering to take them ashore in the *Dart*. The passenger climbed gratefully on board but Carlyle and his crew refused. Carlyle thought the weather was now lifting and was reluctant to abandon a ship launched only two years earlier and costing £50,000 to the predations of Manx plunderers and the capricious waves. It was a brave call, and in the event a correct one. As unexpectedly as it had blown up, the wind subsided, leaving the *City of Glasgow* holed in three places, having sustained much damage elsewhere, but still intact and repairable. A week later, Hillary reported, the ship was 'filled inside with empty corks and had as many as possible lashed outside and by these means was floated off the rocks into the harbour where she now remains in a very ruinous state'.[8]

Over the days that followed, there was general agreement that to have accomplished the rescue without any loss of life was little short of miraculous. Without Hillary's intervention events would have turned out very differently. One grateful passenger, R. S. Core of Liverpool, writing a brief letter to the *Manx Advertiser* the following day, 20 October 1825, summed up the prevailing mood:

> We struck on a rock at half past eleven and remained in the most perilous situation till 5 this morning. I write this principally to say no blame can be implanted to Captain Carlyle, nor can too much praise be given to Sir William Hillary, who himself came in a boat when no boatmen would stir to rescue the suffering passengers, who in that situation were exposed, every moment expecting our last until 5 o'clock this morning. I can scarcely hold my pen.

Captain Carlyle added his voice to the many singing Hillary's praises: 'I take the earliest opportunity of publically expressing my heart-felt thanks to the very numerous body of persons … to Sir William Hillary and the boat's crew who took the first hawser on shore, I am under providence indebted for the ultimate safety of the vessel'.[9] The press was also quick to latch on to the story. Heroism at sea provided rare respite from the commonplace anguish of death at sea, and a story containing both drama and a happy ending was one readers would relish.

From Hillary's point of view, the attention was welcome. He was shrewd enough to understand the importance of the press's backing when it came to attracting wider support for his institution. With more publicity, more donations would follow. Thus, in The *Examiner*, he was heartened to read, 'Sir William Hillary is the worthy Baronet who has recently founded an Institution for the preservation of life and property from shipwreck – an Institution that was particularly wanted in a maritime country with a dangerous coast … it appears that Hillary is as fearless and active as he is considerate and benevolent'.[10]

But there were risks as well as rewards to intense press interest. Over the following days a less savoury side to the story emerged. 'Almost all the hobblers were intoxicated, and … the upsetting of Sir William Hillary's boat and much of the confusion and danger which occurred is attributable to that source alone',[11] claimed *The Times* and *Manx Rising Sun*. The papers went on to reveal that some boatmen had refused to let passengers board their lifeboats unless they paid for the service. Whatever the truth of this, Hillary was aghast that a story of feel-good heroism should be sullied in this manner. The report emblazoned across the pages of *The Times* – a paper that most of his important patrons read – would be immensely damaging to his cause, threatening the very survival of the nascent institution. He wrote a forthright rebuttal:

> The boatmen of this place have, on many previous occasions of wreck con-
> ducted themselves with much bravery and have rendered important services in
> the preservation of life. I leave it to your own judgment whether a perseverance
> in such efforts can be expected from men who find the bitterest opprobrium
> the return they indiscriminately receive, after exposing their own lives to immi-
> nent peril for the rescue of others …

For the most part, he said, the men had behaved well:

> I have a pleasure and a pride in stating that they volunteered their assistance
> deliberately, and perfectly sober and through the whole of the night conducted
> themselves with the greatest order, coolness and judgement, neither stipulating
> any conditions previous to their services nor demanding any reward whatever
> afterwards … this was not the conduct of interested or intoxicated men.

There was an element of truth in the adverse reports, but, he claimed, they were grossly exaggerated. 'A very small number, who formed one boats' crew, … I hear conducted themselves much as you have described (but which I did not witness) …The venal error of three or four intoxicated men was first magnified to an almost incredible extent, and then unjustly attribute to the whole body of the boatmen',[12] he wrote, rebuking the press for misinforming their readers. It was a risky stance – one that could have backfired disastrously, but in the event paid off. Nobody wanted to contradict a national hero and, as he had hoped, the critics were silenced.

Behind the closed doors of the Shipwreck Institution, however, the *City of Glasgow*'s story continued to stoke dilemma and debate. The central committee believed the seamen involved in the rescue were eligible for salvage money from the steam ship company and that this would spare them the expense of paying rewards from their limited funds. Hillary disagreed, vehemently arguing that to encourage such a claim would be detrimental to the institution's reputation, especially given the recent furore. The institution should reward the men – this was one of its founding principles:

> The brave fellows who exerted themselves … have not received any recompense
> beyond a very few pounds. Anxious as I am that they should experience the
> bounty of the institution I will refrain from attempting to give any opinion of

my own, beyond remarking that from this class in life, most of them being poor
men with families, a pecuniary recompense would doubtless be preferable to
any other.[13]

Outwardly the Committee refused to be swayed. 'They consider[ed] it would
benefit rather than injure the cause of the institution were the boatmen to make
such a claim, and succeed in establishing it; and as he [Hillary] distinctly states,
that the vessel and every person on board were beyond all doubt preserved by
the first hawser being promptly brought on shore, they are of opinion the claim
for salvage should be made'.[14] Yet despite this rebuttal, Hillary somehow won the
battle. Two months later £25 was sent to J. Quirk, chief magistrate of Douglas, to
be distributed among the fifteen boatmen who helped save the passengers. Along
with the payment came a formal message from the central committee, thanking
Hillary for his 'humane and intrepid conduct.'

He received the praise with dismay. He had expected to be awarded a gold
medal for his bravery and a letter of thanks seemed a poor substitute. Venting his
frustrations in an unusually direct letter to the institution, he reminded them he
too deserved proper recognition for his bravery and testily set out his case:

> I trust the committee will not think I too far presume on any services it happily
> was in my power to be instrumental in rendering, when I express the conviction
> I feel that they will readily admit I may, with justice, aspire to a gold medallion
> under the 2nd resolution of 4 March 1824, the medallion 'to those who rescue
> lives in cases of shipwreck', which I have not yet received but I hope I have
> fairly won.[15]

The fact he had already been awarded a gold medal as the institution's founder
only a few months earlier should not prevent his winning another, he maintained,
for otherwise, 'I should almost alone be disqualified and excluded from being a
candidate for the honour to which I might be entitled from my aid to a cause
I have so ardently pursued'.[16]

The letter, addressed to Thomas Edwards, secretary of the institution, was
despatched via his 'good friend' George Hibbert. Hillary must have felt that after
all that had passed between them, Hibbert, of all his supporters, would understand and back his demand. If so he had misjudged him. Neither Hibbert nor
any of the other committee members was remotely supportive. In meetings from
which Hillary was absent, all agreed that the earlier medal sufficed. Presenting
him with a second so soon would be a waste of money and detrimental to the
institution's reputation.

Did the stain of past misdemeanours linger implicitly in this response? Probably not. It seems more likely that the institution had gathered its own momentum and confidence and wanted to send home the message that Hillary could not expect it to be run as his private fiefdom. No one could deny his contribution or wished to humiliate him, but the committee struggled to decide how to respond to Hillary's demands. Thus, in the hope that silence rather than confrontation would convey the message that their decision was final, the secretary did not reply.

Two months came and went. By mid-February, with the third annual meeting fast approaching and still no reply, Hillary wrote again, pointedly enclosing a copy of his first letter. His tone was now openly aggrieved:

> It certainly is painful to me, that I should myself have thus to bring forwards for consideration what I would have hoped my colleagues of the committee would have spared me from having occasion to do – and I can yet only believe that they have inadvertently omitted voting me a gold medallion ... I will can-didly own to you I should feel much hurt, and I may add, many of my friends greatly surprised, were the case of the wreck of the *City of Glasgow* to appear in our next annual report without my name to the flattering testimonial of the gold medallion.[17]

He asked not only for a medal for himself but also one for Thomas Wilson, for 'his exertions in the formation of the institution and subsequently as its chair-man'.[18] This too, he reminded the committee, was a previous request that had been rudely ignored.

It would be easy to dismiss this outburst as evidence of inflated self-regard but we can also read it another way. The four long pages expose a candour, in contrast to Hillary's usual florid turn of phrase. Undoubtedly a medal mattered because the appeal he had made and the institution he had founded mattered. But perhaps something more personal also lay behind his need for the public endorsement of a medal. A desire for atonement had spurred his efforts from the outset, ever since he had heard the *Vigilant*'s distress call. His shame would be expunged if his crusading mission and the risks he took were acknowledged by the society that once condemned him.

So having laid his feelings bare, the letter was sealed and sent. Then there was nothing to be done but watch the sea and wait.

Notes

1 *Caledonian Mercury*, 3 November 1825.
2 Ibid.
3 *Morning Post*, 25 October 1825.
4 RNLI Archive, WH to Thomas Edwards, 3 November 1825.
5 Ibid.
6 *Caledonian Mercury*, 3 November 1825.
7 RNLI Archive, WH to Thomas Edwards, 3 November 1825.
8 Ibid.
9 *The Times*, 25 November 1825.
10 *Examiner*, 30 October 1825.
11 *The Times*, 25 November 1825.
12 Ibid.
13 RNLI Archive, WH to Thomas Edwards, 30 October 1825.
14 Minute Books, 30 November 1825.
15 RNLI Archive, WH to Thomas Edwards, 16 December 1825.
16 Ibid.
17 RNLI Archive, WH to Thomas Edwards, 14 February 1826.
18 Ibid.

Ingenious Inventions

I have recently seen a more general account of Mr Trengouse's plans for
forming communications between stranded vessels and the shore ... Many
of his suggestions for this important object appear to me capable of being
carried into full effect, and I am desirous that they should be tried in throwing
a line, both from vessels to the land and from land to the vessel. I think we
unfortunately have as frequent opportunities for this purpose in the Isle of
Man as on almost any other coast – we have also a very intelligent and zealous
captain of the artillery resident at Douglas, who would I am certain devote
every attention to the subject ...

Sir William Hillary to the Central Committee, 6 September 1824

The bravado backfired. Hillary's second outpouring, written in the expectation that it would be only a matter of time before George Hibbert, his
old acquaintance and business associate, would reverse the earlier decision, met no more success than his first. The response – when it eventually arrived
– was unbending. There would be no second medal, he was frostily informed.
Despite his disappointment, Hillary salvaged his dignity, grasping the moral high
ground and the last word on the matter. 'Similar documents to those transmit-
ted would have insured such a vote to <u>any</u> other gentlemen', he countered. He
refused to accept that it all boiled down to a question of money, pointing out,
'I have expended out of my slender means more than fifty times the cost of
that medal in promoting the objects of the institution and am daily expend-
ing more'.[1] But the bluster was without bite. He knew, in his heart of hearts,
the argument had gone on for long enough; it was time to channel his energies

elsewhere. Forced to choose between tinsel and substance – a medal or presiding over the establishment of lifeboat stations in Douglas – there was never a question of where his priorities lay. He would stay true to his cause and resign himself to the injustice. Besides, there was much else to preoccupy him.

Restless as ever, his mind brimmed with new plans. To ensure the island was adequately provided with lifesaving equipment, he had requested three sets of Manby's apparatus. He did not think the request unreasonable, 'when it is taken into consideration that the Isle of Man has an extent of nearly 80 miles of most dangerous coast in the centre of a stormy sea navigated by the numerous vessels of the three kingdoms'.[2] Time wasted might lead to unnecessary lives lost, he maintained, reminding Edwards of the *Racehorse*'s grim fate, 'which calamity might unquestionably have been averted had Captain Manby's apparatus been at hand'.[3]

There was logic to his argument. He believed Manby's apparatus would be straightforward to use. A gunpowder-fuelled mortar propelled a barbed shot with a line attached. The mortar, fired from the shore, carried the line tethered to a stricken vessel. Attached to this, a cradle carried shipwrecked mariners to the shore, without the need for lifeboats being launched. Manby bundled copious instructions in with his equipment when he despatched the order, but there were unexpected hurdles when the equipment was tested. It rapidly became clear that using the equipment was a perilous undertaking and any degree of accuracy needed much practice plus a sizeable quantity of good luck. The angle of trajectory and precise quantities of explosive necessary to reach a given target were hard to perfect. Variable weather conditions – gale force winds, angry seas, lashing rains – only added to the difficulties.

Undeterred, Hillary held lengthy experiments on the beach at Douglas. Firing a 24lb cannon ball attached to a rescue line, he gradually increased the quantities of explosive until the line reached 260 yards. He pronounced the results: 'very successful and the distances to which the line was carried I believe are fully equal to any which Capt Manby has published.'[4] In truth the trials were far from trouble-free and had moments of high drama. Pedestrians strolled on the beach to watch the antics, unaware of the danger of rockets misfiring. A boy digging for bait on the beach narrowly avoided being hit when one of the mortars exploded a few feet from him, pounding a huge crater in the shore, blowing him off his feet and spattering him in sand. He was lucky to survive – a 9-year-old child watching a similar experiment in Brighton was hit by a blast that fatally ruptured his carotid artery.[5]

Had Hillary revealed his tribulations more candidly they would not have surprised the London committee. Captain Foulerton, a stalwart member of the management, had drawn similar conclusions after his own investigations. At Yantlet Creek, on the Thames Estuary, one bitter January morning, Foulerton set off a rocket fired at an angle of 45 degrees, only to find it broke the carefully coiled line 'and took an eccentric motion along the shore', while another 'fell in the water about one third of the way from the shore'.[6]

Manby responded loftily to any lacklustre reports or hint of criticism, dispatching yet more instructions, including 'an illustrative essay on the use of the mortar apparatus published by him'.[7] Whatever the disappointments and glitches, the exchanges reveal little sign of any lingering resentment Manby might have felt towards Hillary. Perhaps his prickly temper had been soothed a year earlier by the award of a gold medal 'as a public testimony ... of the great utility of the Apparatus invented by him for saving lives from shipwreck'.[8]

Regardless of his own wrangles over medals, there is no evidence to suggest Hillary objected to his rival being pandered to in this way. If anything, the reverse was probably true. Manby might occasionally try to steal his thunder, but Hillary found it easy to smother any disgruntlement, reminding himself that Manby's high profile made his continuing support imperative to the institution's reputation.

Keeping Manby happy did not prevent Hillary or the central committee from considering competing developments. Among a deluge of designs in the field of life-saving equipment, one stood out from the rest. Henry Trengrouse, a Cornish inventor, claimed to have made some credible improvements on Manby's mortar. Instead of a mortar-fired ball, his idea (inspired in 1807, by witnessing the sinking of HMS *Anson* with the loss of 100 lives within a few yards of the shore) used a metal rod fired from a musket to transport the line through the air. The line was then attached to a hawser and moving chair that Trengrouse elegantly dubbed a *chaise roulante*. The system had two key advantages over Manby's. Firstly, since muskets were lighter and more easily portable than mortars, ships could carry the equipment on board and fire them to the shore (which was easier to achieve than the reverse – trying to hit a storm tossed vessel from the land). Secondly, the cost was far less.[9]

By the time he began to petition the Lifeboat Institution, Trengrouse had been battling, largely unsuccessfully, for recognition for several years. It had been a bitter struggle. The endorsements and the financial prizes that institutions such as the Admiralty, Trinity House and the Humane Society could bestow fuelled fevered competition among hard-pressed inventors and (notwithstanding their philanthropic aims) waspish criticisms of rivals' creations were commonplace. Trengrouse's design became mired in controversy when its originality was called into question and William Congreve claimed that the idea of a rocket-fired mortar was his. Matters came to a head in 1818, when the fiery Trengrouse defended himself robustly in front of an Admiralty board meeting. The weary chairman, Lt Gen John Ramsey, recorded that:

> Sir W. Congreve ... stated that Mr Trengrouse's flare is by no means original and further to consider two letters in the Naval Chronicle in 1809 and 1810. Mr Trengrouse having attended, those two letters were shewn to him as well as a rocket intended for the same purpose as his ... Mr Trengrouse declared ... that he commenced his original experiments in 1807 in consequence of the wreck of the Anson Frigate and that he bought rockets in February 1809.[10]

Trengrouse produced receipts and other evidence to back his claim. The Admiralty's qualms assuaged, they relented, showing their approval by recommending that Captain Ross and Captain Parry take a set of the apparatus on their polar expeditions. But this was small beer as far as Trengrouse was concerned. Manby still hogged the spotlight and had received £2,000 of government money for his research, while Trengrouse had nothing for his efforts. 'If Capt M(anby) had witnessed some experiments made at Porthleaven last week by Mr Trengrouse of Helston, I have no doubt but he would have been candid enough, readily to have acknowledged, the far superior excellency of Mr T's invention for the same purpose',[11] wrote one partisan Cornish spectator who chose, suspiciously, to remain anonymous.

Over the years that followed, despite his energetic attempts to turn things round, Trengrouse made little headway. By 1819, still three years before Hillary would put pen to paper on the subject of a shipwreck institution, he tried his luck with the Humane Society. Standing resolutely on the bank of the Serpentine in front of Hillary's erstwhile patron, the Duke of Sussex, 'and several persons of distinction', Trengrouse ignited his rockets and pulled men across the water in a chair, while others floated safely, thanks to another of his ingenious inventions: 'a life preserving spenser, formed of several pieces of cork, covered with linen, and so constructed as to give perfect facility to the motion of the arms'.[12] The Duke of Kent was sufficiently impressed to present the Emperor of Russia with a set of the equipment. The press looked on, writing lengthy panegyrics underlining Trengrouse's laudatory aims to the wider world.

From the journalist's point of view, saving lives at sea was never a contentious subject. Everyone sympathised because, irrespective of wealth or status, all comprehended the agony of losing a loved one at sea. 'We trust other maritime nations will follow the humane example of the emperor; for when we reflect on the thousands of our fellow men that have from time to time unavoidably perished through shipwreck the mind is deeply afflicted, who alas that has not

The *Wreck of the St George*: showing the dramatic scene in Douglas Bay on 30 November 1830 when the Royal Mail Packet Steamer was wrecked on Conister Rock. (Courtesy of Manx National Heritage)

Lifeboat in the Act of Saving Part of the Crew of a Ship Wrecked Near Tynemouth Castle, after W. Elmes, 1803. (Courtesy of RNLI Heritage Trust)

An early illustration showing the difficulties faced by crews launching lifeboats in heavy seas. (Courtesy of RNLI Heritage Trust) (ref 291)

Statue of Sir William Hillary on Douglas Head.

Sir William Hillary's tomb in the graveyard of St George's Church, Douglas.

The Tower of Refuge, as it appears today. The tower was built by Sir William on the dangerous Conister Rock to provide stranded mariners with shelter.

CONASTER ROCK, STORM COMING ON.
ISLE OF MAN.

Nineteenth-century view of the Tower of Refuge in stormy seas. (Courtesy of Manx National Heritage)

TOWER REFUGE, ISLE OF MAN

Nineteenth-century view of Sir William Hillary's Tower in calm weather. (Courtesy of Manx National Heritage)

Model of the lifeboat designed by William Plenty and commissioned by the Shipwreck Institution for many of their early lifeboat stations. (Courtesy of RNLI)

Captain Manby's mortar apparatus for throwing lines to stranded vessels. Sir William conducted perilous experiments using the equipment in Douglas Bay. (Courtesy of RNLI)

RNLI National Memorial by Sam Holland – the monument stands outside the RNLI headquarters in Poole; bearing tribute to the lives of lost rescuers, it is inscribed with Sir William Hillary's family motto *With Courage Nothing is Impossible*. (Courtesy of RNLI)

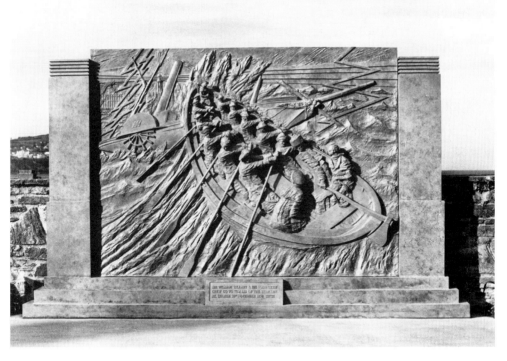

Memorial on the promenade of Douglas showing Sir William going to the aid of the stricken *St George* in 1830. (Courtesy of RNLI)

RNLI silver medallion showing Sir William Hillary in profile. (Courtesy of RNLI)

DOUGLAS, ISLE OF MAN.

Nineteenth-century engraving showing Douglas Bay from Fort Anne. The treacherous entrance to the harbour can be seen in the foreground. (Courtesy of Manx National Heritage)

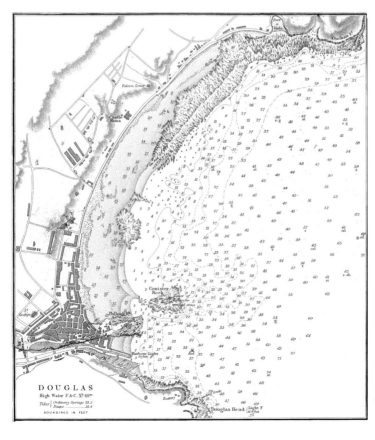

Chart showing Douglas Bay and Conister Rock. (Courtesy of Manx National Heritage)

BAY OF DOUGLAS & TOWER OF REFUGE
FROM FORT ANNE.

Douglas Bay and the Tower of Refuge from Fort Anne. (Courtesy of Manx National Heritage)

VIEW of FORT ANNE, near DOUGLAS, ISLE of MAN.
Drawn by George Eyre Brooks, Land Surveyor, 28, Old Bond St.

View of Sir William Hillary's home, Fort Anne, overlooking Douglas Bay. (Courtesy of Manx National Heritage)

DOUGLAS, ISLE of MAN,
from the Hill, near Fort Anne.

Panoramic view showing Fort Anne and Douglas Bay. (Courtesy of Manx National Heritage)

Portrait of Sir William Hillary. (Courtesy of RNLI Heritage Trust)

Wash drawing of the wreck of the *City of Glasgow*, on 19 October 1825, by Edward Price. The artist was a passenger on the paddle steamer and made this drawing the day after he was rescued. (Courtesy of Manx National Heritage)

had some dear relative or friend snatched suddenly from them through the over-whelming element, within, perhaps a few hundred yards of their native shore',[13] the *Morning Post* proclaimed, voicing the great concern of the age.

The Russian Emperor was among the spectators and presented Trengrouse with a diamond ring for his efforts.[14] This was a welcome gesture but not much sop to Trengrouse's need for the official recognition and financial support that still eluded him. To add insult to injury, in 1825 he wrote to the newly formed Shipwreck Institution offering to bring his apparatus to show the committee, but heard nothing back. Disappointment hardened to bitterness when later the same year he travelled to London to lobby Parliament and again met little success. Then, one evening during his stay, a visitor presented himself. Sir William Hillary had come unannounced to discuss the matter. In his carefully written diary entry of the encounter, Trengrouse paints a vivid picture of Hillary's beguiling person-ality. 'He talked very freely and friendly. He said as he had been the chief founder of the Shipwreck Institution he thought he ought to be instrumental to bring my apparatus into use. Thought he should have four or five life spensers, a chain, travellers, lines, 4 dry rockets etc'.[15]

His relief was to prove short-lived. Despite Hillary's promises, nearly three months passed with little progress, and eventually, short of money and patience, Trengrouse decided to return to Helston. Before doing so he dispatched a tersely worded note to the institution to warn of his imminent departure and enclosing a letter from Hillary reiterating his empty promise of support. Fortunately for Trengrouse, Hillary was still in town. He received a response by return, instruct-ing him to send samples of his equipment to the Institution, together with a bill to cover his expenses. Two days later, at 11a.m., Hillary paid the irascible inventor a second visit and once again soothed him with his charm. '(He) Tarried with me till half past 12. He appeared to be very honest in his expressed intent on my behalf – told me how he had proceeded and that he was striving for govern-ment to compel all vessels to carry such apparatus as might be calculated to preserve lives etc, and this he said was the best way he could think of serving me',[16] a pacified Trengrouse afterwards recorded. As the conversation went on, Hillary let slip something of his own financial disappointments. 'He asked what I thought the apparatus I was preparing for him would cost. I said about £20 or £25 – he answered he expected the committee would expect it would rather exceed that sum. He much approved of my exertions, and hoped I should be remunerated – ministers ought to have settled an annuity on me, and on my family.'[17] Trengrouse was unaware that Hillary believed himself to be equally overlooked by those with patronage to dispense. The conversation ended affa-bly, with Hillary promising to send Trengrouse copies of his famous pamphlet.

This time he was as good as his word, returning 'in the evening with a packet containing a few copies of his publication', then sending Trengrouse a further thirty copies of the second edition fresh from the printer to distribute among the great and good of Cornwall. Trengrouse, now completely in Hillary's thrall, was much struck by what he read. 'This is quite in unison with my own ideas and bears a happy coincidence with my plan for organising the inhabitants upon the coast for systemising the management of shipwreck, and which led to a bill being brought in Parliament in June 1818, for the better preservation of shipwrecked property',[18] he wrote neatly in the margin. There are similarly complimentary remarks on many other pages.

Hillary, ever eager to please and patronise, kept his promise to promote Trengrouse's apparatus enthusiastically to the institution. 'I am very anxious to receive the supply of Mr Trengrouse's rockets ... we have several skilful officers here and we much wish to try their effects',[19] he urged secretary Thomas Edwards. The request was approved, although there were still doubts over the equipment's efficacy. After Captain Foulerton had given up with Manby's mortars on that wintery January morning, it had been the turn of Trengrouse's rockets to be tested. The results had been no more satisfactory. 'Five small rockets were fired according to the instructions ... but did not go any distance from the yacht, the line either breaking or gathering in little twisted heaps, none of them exceeding 100 yards', read his scathing report to the committee. Hillary's trials were less disappointing. 'From the precision of the shot thrown with the mortars and the portability of the rockets, and the speed with which they can be conveyed over the most rugged rocks – we trust that the combination of these invaluable inventions thus brought to perfection by two active and meritorious friends to our seamen, will in future prove a great and important addition to the measures adopted by lifeboats ... to avert, as far as possible the calamity of shipwreck on the wild and dangerous shores of our Island', he recorded.[20]

Even more pressing than the need for life-saving equipment was Hillary's demand for more lifeboats for stations around the Isle of Man coast. Thanks to his vociferous petitioning, two had been promised, on condition that the Isle of Man Association raise half the money to pay for them. These terms had been agreed by Hillary and the conditions met, but by July 1826 the boats still had not arrived. For a man whose natural inclinations were to act rather than wait patiently, the delay was a torture. The summer months, when the sea was calm, the packet boats arrived punctually and storms were scarce, were the time to test new boats and familiarise crews with their idiosyncrasies. As weeks dragged on, with still no sign of them, an infuriated Hillary fired off letters to London demanding to know when the new craft would come, as well as every detail of their specification and fitting out. 'As we shall not now have much time to spare in making our arrangements on this coast preparatory to winter, I am anxious, as soon as possible to receive any information which you may be able to afford me as to the most approved construction and the manner of fitting up the safety boats', he insisted.

In the London headquarters, Edwards and other members of the committee fielded his demands, trying to maintain a balance with the needs of numerous other stations and tackling an even more worrisome concern – the dwindling of subscriptions. The downturn was linked partly to a growing number of rival charities, but mainly to a wider financial malaise; the aftershocks of a financial crisis. A year earlier, a stock market crash had resulted in the collapse of seventy banks, among them the institution's bankers. Hillary was conscious of the gravity of the situation, inquiring anxiously, 'I was concerned to see by the papers that our bankers had been unfortunate. Pray what funds had we in their hands – are we likely to lose much?'[21] Any losses suffered by the institution are omitted in the minute books, but the impact of the financial crisis was significant. Hitherto wealthy subscribers found themselves in fraught economic circumstances. Subscriptions fell from £9,706 in the first year, to a little over £1,000 two years later. 'The accounts which we receive of the shock Commercial Credit has received and the general public distress are truly alarming',[22] Hillary sympathised, without making any noticeable alteration to his demands on the institution's finances.

To try to reverse the trend, committee members were despatched throughout the country to muster donations. Their targets included cities in Britain's industrial heartlands, including Manchester, where Captain Dansey, one of the most energetic canvassers, was sent:

> I have waited on several gentlemen who I understand to be persons of the description you point out; possessing both benevolent dispositions and great local influence. The subject was met by them with much approbation and earnestness, and they expressed a willingness to proceed to such measures as would be necessary for promoting extensive subscription. I have also called three editors of newspapers who have promised to notice the institution recommendatiorily [*sic*] in their publications. The gentlemen to whom I have spoken are Messrs Heywood, Markland, Dawson, D Grant, Grimshaw, Truhill, Hindley, and the editors of the *Courier*, *Chronicle* and *Guardian* Manchester papers.[23]

George Hibbert, Hillary's old business associate and one of the institution's key founders, had family connections in the city and, prompted by Dansey, wrote letters of introduction to his nephew in the banking community. 'I delivered Mr Hibbert's letter to Mr Markland ... and observed that it had a most striking effect upon his zeal and activity seemed redoubled by the stimulus',[24] Dansey optimistically reported.

On the Isle of Man, meanwhile, Hillary paced the quay at Douglas, making few allowances for financial reality. Behind his frustration, a selfless desire to prevent needless deaths had intertwined with personal ambition. He viewed society through a stratified lens; class and social status would always be of concern. Quite apart from appeasing his conscience, founding the National Shipwreck Institution and taking up the role of president of the Isle of Man's local branch brought a social prominence he enjoyed. He was proud of all he had achieved, yet he wanted more: to consolidate the gain by further philanthropic feats and to win the respect and acceptance of the notoriously reticent Manx community. Perhaps then, his ultimate dream – a government role and the establishment's endorsement – would be fulfilled.

First things first: having given his word that boats would soon arrive for Castletown and Peel, Hillary was conscious that delay might kindle distrust and turn flimsy respect to resentment. Beneath the islanders' amiability cultural tensions were obvious. Manx-born residents regarded incoming settlers with suspicion and termed them 'come-overs'. They had brought changes and imposed laws, and their ostentatious way of living conflicted with that of frugal islanders. Hillary was always a man who wanted to please as well as chase dreams. The desire to benefit the lives of Manx inhabitants and earn their affection weighed heavy on his shoulders.

A slender hope alleviated the strain. His indignation at the Committee's refusal to grant him a second gold medal had been softened thanks to his old ally, Prince Augustus, the Duke of Sussex. The Duke had presided over the institution's second annual dinner in London in July and during the evening intervened in the delicate matter. A bar in the form of a boat could be introduced to represent a secondary honour. This would neatly solve two problems, the Duke suggested diplomatically. Less costly to produce than a gold medal, a bar would be an economical means of providing regular rescuers with the recognition they deserved. Anxious not to offend their royal patron, Wilson and Hibbert hurriedly nodded their agreement and the rest of the committee followed suit.

Overjoyed at the news, Hillary responded:

The very kind and flattering manner in which you ... have informed me the Duke of Sussex condescended to mention my name has been ... most gratifying to my feelings ... the boat you mention his Royal Highness to have given ...

instead of second medallion appears to me exceedingly judicious in as much as it greatly reduces the expense and in every other respect is an equally honourable testimonial',[25]

The turnaround did more than bolster his pride, injecting new impetus to his philanthropic fervour. He would no longer limit his activities to lifeboats. He would find further ways to improve the lives of islanders. With shipwrecks at the forefront of his thoughts, inspiration struck him on one of his journeys to London. The idea was innovative, and intertwined with his preoccupation for safety at sea: the construction of a great harbour wall for Douglas Bay. Given the constant to and fro of trading vessels, the present harbour was clearly inadequate. The entrance was only 200ft wide, with a dangerous sand bar that made it inaccessible at low water. Vessels entering in a swell were often damaged, while larger vessels trying to set sail could find themselves wind-bound by easterlies and unable to get out for weeks on end. Shipping caught in bad weather in the Irish Sea frequently sought shelter in Douglas Bay, but in south-easterly winds, the bay provided little protection. Hillary envisaged overcoming these shortcomings by extending the breakwater 'boldly across the bay', to form 'a stupendous port'.[26] Built in two parts, one section would measure over 500 yards long and stretch from Douglas Head towards Conister; the other in the opposite direction from Conister towards the west. There would be an entrance wide enough between to allow the largest packets to enter. Such a structure would provide shelter from winds, regardless of their direction, and water deep enough for shipping of all sizes to enter safely, even at low tide. Thus, he hoped, countless disasters could be averted to the benefit of both islanders and all those caught in hostile seas.

Returning to Douglas, Hillary set about giving shape to his scheme. With customary verve, he set out on calm mornings to map the area in a small fishing boat. 'I ... surveyed the bay and took the soundings myself, and having written the few pages of explanation committed it to the press',[27] he proudly explained to the central committee. The finished plan, complete with maps showing the projected wall and the depths of the sea bed, was written up over the winter months and published in a pamphlet, grandly entitled *The National Importance of a Great Central Harbour for the Irish Sea*. Hillary paid for 500 copies to be printed, then promoted the scheme energetically, drawing on the useful connections he had made through the Shipwreck Institution. 'I have already sent it to his Majesty's ministers, and it is in progress, as you will see, to be laid before the public and other departments',[28] he told Edwards in the new year of 1827, before asking him to forward copies to Lloyd's and Trinity House. He composed a long letter to the Home Secretary Robert Peel, enclosing a dozen copies and explaining that he expected to make no personal gain from such a scheme: 'Though of late years I have much resided there, yet I neither possess property in that island, nor am directly or indirectly connected with its politics or local interests and ... am only actuated by a thorough conviction founded on a considerable experience of these seas and coasts'.[29]

The question of money was always a thorny one for him and he approached the cost of the scheme with circuitous logic:

> I have not attempted to offer any estimate of the probable expense of construct-
> ing such a harbour – no doubt it would be considerable, but I am persuaded
> that after minute investigation it will be found such a work could be affected
> in few situations at so small a cost - perhaps scarcely any could the requisite
> sum be expended on an object productive of such great immediate and lasting
> public good – which would give employment to hundreds whilst in its progress,
> and when completed furnish returns more than ample to secure its support for
> all time to come.[30]

By then the first of the long-awaited lifeboats had arrived and Hillary had hurriedly put her to the test in Castletown Bay. 'I am happy to report that in all weather we have found her a most superior sea boat, and for her size, capable of every service in the most violent storms',[31] he told Edwards, adding that he thought her on the small side and wished she had been built 24ft long rather than 20.

He was doubtless comparing the new vessel to the larger Douglas boat that had been built in Sunderland with money donated by Lloyd's and individual subscribers. This vessel had proved her worth on 20 September, when the brig *Leopard* of Workington, bound from Drogheda to Liverpool, with around fifteen passengers and crew as well as a cargo of sheep and cattle on board, had found herself in difficulty. '(She) drifted between two dangerous rocks and cast anchor from which she drove on shore in a tremendous surf to the north of the har-bour',[32] Hillary recorded. Poised for such a moment, he ordered the new boat to be launched. 'I instantly put off ... accompanied by Vondy and some of my old crew.' It was early morning, the visibility appalling, with a horizon blurred by low cloud and a ferocious wind howling across the bay, whipping spray into their eyes. Having battled their way to reach the *Leopard*, Hillary discovered that the pas-sengers and crew were too terrified to be induced to board the lifeboat. He did not lose his composure or try to force them, calmly ordering the crew to moor alongside the brig until conditions improved. For the next two hours they waited on the lifeboat, hunched and shivering, as the waves crashed over them. Only when the tide had ebbed and 'the danger to those on board ... had ceased' could the passengers be coaxed to disembark.

What pleased him most in all of this was the manner in which the lifeboat had withstood the stormy sea. Swamped by waves on numerous occasions, she had 'instantly emptied herself through the apertures in the bottom', and shown herself 'master of a sea in which no common boat could live'.[33] By contrast, if further evidence were needed, a harbour boat that had also tried to offer help had been engulfed by the surf and sank so rapidly that her crew had been forced to scramble on board the *Leopard* and join those they were trying to assist.

The *Leopard*'s story ended more happily than many: no lives were lost and, despite the damage she had sustained, she was repairable. As soon as the storm blew itself out and the tide was high, she was loaded with corks, floated off the beach and towed into the harbour for repair.[34] Not all vessels blown ashore in Douglas Bay escaped so lightly. In mid-December, in a south-easterly storm, the *Fancy*, a sloop from Liverpool on her way to Anglesey, rounded Douglas Head at low tide only to find herself blown off course. In his report of the incident to the central committee, Hillary vividly described the vessel's rapidly deteriorating predicament:

It being at that time low water, and within ten minutes ran on shore in a small creek to the part of the harbour upon a steep shingle beach surrounded with rocks and in a very heavy surf. Only a few boatmen were at that time on the pier and but one small boat afloat, nor was there time to launch others or collect more people before her dangerous situation required immediate assistance.[35]

The *Dart* – to which Hillary referred as being the only boat afloat – was a small harbour boat. With five men aboard she set off to rescue those on the stricken sloop. By the time she had ploughed her way through the waves and reached it, the tide was on the turn. Immense rolling breakers crashing over the *Fancy*'s hull tumbled her on the shingle as if she had no more substance than a pebble. Five petrified female passengers managed to scramble on board the *Dart*, which, according to Hillary, 'being unable to return to the harbour, through the breakers over the bar – made for another little creek still further to the east and landed them there'. The *Dart*'s crew attempted to return to rescue the remaining men but found the surf unbreachable and after several valiant efforts, were forced to retreat. By then the timbers of *Fancy*'s hull had been holed and, as rescuers looked on from the shore, the *Fancy*'s deck disappeared under the foaming surf and she seemed likely to break up at any moment. The men remaining aboard had only one means of saving themselves. Clutching a line hastily secured on shore by the *Dart*'s crew, they launched themselves off the semi-submerged vessel and hauled themselves through the waves. Half-drowned, chilled to the core, miraculously, all four made it to the shore and survived.

Hillary was not part of the *Fancy*'s rescue team, but witnessed some of the drama, as he later testified: 'Having come down to the pier immediately after the boat had put off and before she had reached the sloop I am enabled to vouch for the above facts. I immediately had the life boat launched and had her crew on board at the moment the people were rescued.'[36] He sympathised deeply with both rescuers and rescued. As President of the Manx Association of the Shipwreck Institution, and as he would do on numerous other occasions, his report to the central committee insisted that the *Dart*'s five brave crew members, all men of modest means, deserved to be financially rewarded for their efforts in saving the women's lives. Furthermore, the present plight of those rescued could not be ignored. The *Fancy*'s cargo was ruined, the vessel beyond repair. Worse still, her crew and passengers had lost all they possessed and were in desperately straitened circumstances: 'worn out with fatigue and ... being persons in a horrible situation in life, the little they had on board ruined by the salt water and without money'.[37]

Conscious that offering food, shelter and support to those saved from ship-wreck was one of the institution's founding principles, Hillary ensured provision was made for those left destitute. 'The Douglas committee have taken charge of their support whilst here out of their own funds and the agent of the ... steam packet has liberally directed them to have a free passage ... to Liverpool',[38] he reported, pointing out that by alleviating distress the institution was further 'impressing on the public mind (its) beneficial effects'.[39]

There was another reason for the zest with which he championed the plight of the impoverished Irish. Aside from his pamphlet promoting the harbour wall, he had published (and would continue to produce) lengthy papers on various wide-ranging subjects, including steam lifeboats, the difficulties of dealing with fire at sea, improvements in London's town planning and the benefits of establishing a school of navigation on the Isle of Man. The subject of Ireland was one that fascinated him. A year before the *Fancy*'s distressing misadventure he had published *A Sketch of Ireland in 1824: the sources of her evils considered and their remedies suggested*.

There were personal as well as ideological reasons for his interest, with Irish family connections on Emma's side. Mercantile links between Ireland and the Isle of Man added weight to the impoverished circumstances of many inhabitants. The country's history also captivated him. He had always been drawn to ancient civilisations and Ireland's Celtic past intertwined with that of the Isle of Man. To Hillary the Irish were 'the earliest civilised people of the west; certainly one of the first two to receive Christianity'. The country's recent history roused his indignation. He questioned why other countries had prospered while Ireland had lagged behind, concluding it was a consequence of British intervention. 'For six hundred years treated as a conquered people, alternately the prey of civil dissensions or

religious law.' He blamed, 'unequal laws, unequally administered. Agents and mid-
dlemen oppressing and impoverishing the people; the lower orders deplorably
neglected, uneducated and unemployed, while vast tracts of fertile land remain
uncultivated'.[40] The argument, remarkable for its time, in many ways anticipates
the strife engulfing Ireland for the next century and the distaste for colonialism
that prevails to this day.

The central committee may have shaken their heads at these radical views, but
the bravery of those involved in the rescue of the *Fancy* could not be contested
and Hillary's suggestion was acted on. In a small ceremony in the courthouse each
member of the crew was presented with a gold sovereign. He relished officiating
at the occasion: formalities of this kind reminded him of the pageantry and rituals
of the Knights of St John in Malta. He clung to the view that hierarchy gave an
organisation strength and that ceremonies reinforced their status and structure. In
the case of the *Fancy*, the awards Hillary presented to the rescuers demonstrated
public appreciation and boosted their sense of pride. This, he hoped, would make
them more willing to assist in the future – essential if the institution was to thrive.

His sense of occasion did not blind him to practical concerns. The rescues of
the *Fancy* and *Leopard* had highlighted two recurring obstacles: firstly, the difficulties of launching rescue boats at low tide; and secondly, the problem of reaching
ships in difficulty any distance from the station. To rectify matters he commissioned the building of 'two excellent carriages for our two life boats'. Drawn by
horses or men, the carriages enabled boats to be 'conveyed a considerable distance with great speed and ... when no other boat would stir'.[41] Money remained
an ongoing worry, although his schemes were rarely hindered by its scarcity for
long. Equipping two stations, building a new boathouse for the recently arrived
Castletown lifeboat, paying for two carriages, added to the costs of shelter and
food for the shipwrecked Irish, meant that this year the Manx Association had
expended 'a considerable sum' over and above the money raised on the island; a
shortfall the central committee would have to meet.

The deficit did not prevent him from petitioning for further equipment. Two
boats were not enough for the Isle of Man, he argued. 'The peculiarity of this
place, its separate legislature, its poverty, the great extent of dangerous coast and
small population and that nine wrecks out of ten which take place are strangers.
I feel the vast importance as soon as possible that we should have boats also at Peel
and Ramsey ... my wish is, if possible, to accomplish these points out of our own
funds or as much so as we can and I feel a great confidence in the disposition of
the parent institution to aid us in this most important measure – that no time may
be lost ...'[42] Thus, over the following months, he would place pressure on the central committee to show similar energy and commitment. When his conscience was

ruffled by the demands he made, the economies he suggested were angled to suit his cause. Pushing for yet more boats for the island, he boldly suggested:

> We have at present in Douglas some able ship and boat carpenters from Liverpool, employed in building some large merchant vessels, or small yachts. Wages are low – timber imported with scarcely any duty and the master builder has offered in his gratuitous services to draft and superintend two boats on a rather smaller scale, but upon the plan of the Sunderland boat we have here – and if the London committee will extend their bounty so far towards us as to contribute one hundred pounds in aid of these two boats we will undertake whatever more may be needful for their costs, boat houses etc.[43]

As a concession to the difficulties the Committee faced, he added, 'from the kind and handsome manner in which the committee have expressed their dispositions to contribute to our efforts, I hope they will not think that in this proposal we trespass too far upon them'.[44] He was delighted that the argument was convincing enough to win a grant of £50 for one boat. The vessel would prove her worth sooner than anyone expected.

Notes

1 RNLI Archive, WH to Thomas Edwards, 1 March 1826.
2 RNLI Archive, WH to Thomas Edwards, 28 May 1826.
3 Ibid.
4 RNLI Archive, WH to Thomas Edwards, 29 May 1826.
5 *Morning Chronicle*, 21 July 1826.
6 RNLI Minute Books, 3 January 1827.
7 RNLI Minute Books, 21 June 1826, p. 124.
8 RNLI Minute Books, 1825.
9 *Oxford Dictionary of National Biography*, Trengrouse, Henry.
10 Cornwall Records Office, DDX 498/8, Minutes of Admiralty Meeting, Woolwich, 24 March 1818.
11 *Royal Cornwall Gazette*, 22 June 1816.
12 *Morning Chronicle*, 8 August 1818.
13 *Morning Post*, 9 September 1819.
14 *Morning Post*, 10 April 1820.
15 Truro Record Office, DDx 498/52 journal, 30 May 1825.
16 Truro Record Office, DDx 498/3 journal, 25 August 1825.
17 Ibid.
18 Truro Record Office DDx 498/59 journal.
19 RNLI Archive, WH to Thomas Edwards, 29 May 1826.
20 *Royal Cornwall Gazette*, 21 April 1827.
21 RNLI Archive, WH to Thomas Edwards, 14 February 1826.

22 RNLI Archive, WH to Thomas Edwards, 1 March 1826.
23 National Maritime Museum MS, Dansey to Edwards, 1825.
24 National Maritime Museum MS, Dansey to Edwards, 10 July 1825.
25 RNLI Archive, WH to Thomas Edwards, 18 July 1826.
26 *Monas Herald*, 12 November 1845, letter from Hillary to harbour commissioners.
27 RNLI Archive, WH to Thomas Edwards, 21 February 1827.
28 RNLI Archive, WH to Thomas Edwards, 21 February 1827.
29 BL MS40390 f295, WH to Sir Robert Peel, 31 December 1826.
30 Ibid.
31 RNLI Archive, WH to Thomas Edwards, 3 October 1826.
32 Iibid.
33 Ibid.
34 WH to Thomas Edwards, 3 October 1826.
35 RNLI Archive, WH to Thomas Edwards, 15 December 1826.
36 Ibid.
37 Ibid.
38 Ibid.
39 Ibid.
40 Sir William Hillary, *A Sketch of Ireland in 1824: the sources of her evils considered and their remedies suggested.*
41 RNLI Archive, WH to Thomas Edwards, 14 March 1827.
42 RNLI Archive, WH to Thomas Edwards, 14 March 1827.
43 RNLI Archive, WH to Thomas Edwards, 28 May 1828.
44 RNLI Archive, WH to Thomas Edwards, 28 May 1828.

9

Family Bonds

(The committee) referred to the case of the *Förtroendet* wrecked in Douglas Bay Isle of Man laid before the Committee ... the committee view with peculiar gratification the continued zealous exertions of Sir William Hillary in the cause of humanity aided by those of his son Augustus William Hillary and ... have voted to Sir William the additional emblem (a boat) as an appendage to the gold medallion for a second signal service in the cause of the Institution, which additional emblem was approved by HRH the Duke of Sussex at the last anniversary dinner.

Shipwreck Institution Minute Books, 16 January 1828

On 10 December 1827, a blustery, bone-chilling day, Andrew Ackerman, skipper of the *Förtroendet* from Carlscrona, Sweden, was nearing the end of his voyage. He was sailing to Glasgow from Marseilles with a cargo of madder – a valuable root cultivated in the eastern Mediterranean and used in the dyeing industry to make a brilliant scarlet pigment. The *Förtroendet* was a 28-year-old three-masted wooden sailing barque[1] and Ackerman, a cautious skipper, had put into Derbyhaven, taking on four additional crewmen and a pilot familiar with the coastline of the Isle of Man to help him navigate through the notoriously perilous waters. Despite these precautions, as the wind stiffened to a southerly gale and the sea built up, the bay at Derbyhaven became too exposed for a safe overnight mooring. With the tide rising, Ackerman, doubtless at his pilot's suggestion, decided to set sail for the short journey to Douglas to seek shelter in the harbour, which was only accessible at high water.

Ackerman successfully navigated his way into Douglas Bay and headed for the harbour mouth. To accomplish the most difficult manoeuvre, entering the narrow entrance, he adjusted course to bring the bow round. As he did so the barque came broadside to the waves. Piling swell slapped her hull, cresting over her decks and causing her to toss and pitch alarmingly. The turbulent sea made holding a steady course almost impossible, and the narrowness of the harbour entrance only added to the peril of the manoeuvre. Realising he risked capsize or collision with the harbour wall at any minute, Ackerman turned the helm and overshot the harbour mouth. He skirted Conister Rock then, reaching what he believed was the relative safety of the centre of the bay, dropped anchor. The futility of his action was soon made clear. Exposed to the force of the wind and racing tide, the mooring failed and the barque drifted towards the rocks of Conister. With mounting urgency Ackerman ordered his crew to raise and lower the anchor once more. Again the mooring was no match against the current and wind, and the rocks of Conister drew closer.

Watching the deteriorating situation, Hillary's first thought was of Trengrouse's apparatus. The barque appeared to be close enough to the shore to attempt firing a line to her. If the plan worked they might be able to beach and save her without rescuers' lives being endangered.

Orders were hastily given and rockets were fired at the floundering vessel. But the difficulties of accurate marksmanship in gusting winds at a moving target were insurmountable and none of the shots reached her. With no time to spare, Hillary ordered the lifeboat to be launched. He took command, as so often before, directing the diminutive boat and his crew of twelve men through the foam-plumed swell. They were not alone in going to the *Förtroendet*'s aid. HMS *Swallow*, a Royal Navy cutter moored in the harbour, had also noticed the barque's predicament and launched an auxiliary vessel to help. Two other harbour boats, perhaps mindful of her lucrative cargo, were also ploughing through the swell towards her. None of the three were in time to prevent the impending disaster. As the *Förtroendet* drew close to the white water marking the reef, a large wave tossed her up and withdrew, leaving her impaled on the rocks. The impact shattered her rudder and ruptured her side; her hull began to fill with icy water.

In the lifeboat, mindful there was little time to spare, Hillary directed the crew towards the open sea. As they came in line with the *Förtroendet*, he yelled the instruction to drop an anchor to windward. Great tumbling waves now propelled the lifeboat towards the shore, while the oarsmen, with all the force they could muster, steered across them, towards the stricken barque. Miraculously, given the conditions, they were able to draw alongside her lee bow, close enough for passengers and crew to leap aboard – some even bringing with them what luggage they could carry. Seventeen were rescued in all; too many to transport with the lifeboat's crew of twelve. Hillary did not dissuade any of those frantically boarding, but having cast off and manoeuvred clear of the rocks, he assisted some to transfer to the *Swallow*'s rescue boat. Given the raging sea, this in itself was a perilous undertaking but was accomplished without mishap.

By the following day, the wind had died down sufficiently for the harbour boats to begin to salvage the valuable cargo. They did not have long to do so. Two days later the vessel succumbed to the relentless pounding of the waves. Her three fractured masts were swept away and then, finally, her broken hull disintegrated.

For Hillary, the shipwreck of the *Fortroendet* would always have a special significance. For the first time, his son, Augustus, had served among the lifeboat's crew. Since his separation from Frances, Hillary had only seen his children fleetingly and the long years had been painful for all of them. Augustus had come to the Isle of Man a few months earlier for an extended visit that gave Hillary the chance to rebuild his ties with his only son. He must have become conscious as he did so of the impact of his own misfortunes on his offspring's lives. To escape the scandalous disintegration of the marriage, as well as for financial reasons, Frances had taken the children to France for extended periods, relying on the protection of her father, Lewis Disney-Fytche. Their peripatetic childhood had shaped Hillary's children. The bond between the siblings was close and they would crave a stable home. 'I shall never agree to quit England … I am indifferent where I go to once at a distance from my family all places in this country are alike to me, but I will never <u>again</u> quit it',[2] Augustus's twin sister would later write, a fear of separation branded into her childhood memory as she too faced financial ruin.

Augustus was now a striking young man of 26, with an air of European sophistication. He spoke fluent French as well as being proficient in German and Italian, but beneath the gloss there were scars. At the age of 16 he had pursued a career in the army, serving as a cornet (5th commissioned cavalry officer) in the 6th Dragoon Guards and rising to the rank of Captain. The commission, a sought-after one, would have relied on connections to secure, and (like the vast majority of army commissions at the time), was purchased probably by his mother or grandfather. By the age of 24 he inherited several properties from his grandfather, resigned his post and returned to live with his mother in Paris. Here, to escape what he would later describe as 'the unfortunate embarrassment of his [Hillary's] affairs', he tried to earn a living, with limited success. Having somehow lost his inheritance, like his father he hoped to secure a position as a diplomat. 'I am not likely ever to possess sufficient means to live, as I have been brought up without resource, (turning) to my own industry for some additional income I have for the last three years been living entirely in Paris, and have occasionally travelled with some of the government's cousins from this country,'[3] he confided to Sir Robert Peel, in an unsuccessful letter seeking a post.

Augustus's role in the *Förtroendet's* rescue was gratefully noted, but the committee's initial response to reports of what had happened was one of open incredulity: 'in regard to the Douglas lifeboat, it appears there were 12 men went off in her beside himself [Hillary], his son and Lieutenant Robinson, and that they took on board 17 men from the vessel with great part of their luggage this surely could not be the life boat we supplied them with, or if so how could they possibly stow them away?'[4]

Verification in the form of an official record by J.R. Quirk, High Bailiff of Douglas, reassured the committee. 'They [the Committee] view with peculiar gratification the continued zealous exertions of Sir William Hillary in the cause of humanity, aided by those of his son', the minute book recorded. An unusually large number of rescuers had been involved, but, despite limited funds, all were to be generously rewarded. There was a sovereign for each of the crewmen – including the ten men from the *Swallow* – a total of £22 – a substantial amount given the Institution's depleted funds. In addition, in recognition of their valour, Augustus and the two other officers involved (one from the *Swallow*) were presented with silver medals. For Hillary there was the unparalleled honour of a gold bar. 'I request you will assure my friends of the central committee of the pleasure with which I have received, through you, the flattering expression of their gratification',[5] he wrote to his friend Thomas Edwards.

Augustus stayed on with Hillary longer than originally planned – into the following year. The extended stay was partly because he had yet to find gainful employment but also because he was enjoying himself. Through his father's connections he had met Susannah Christian-Curwen, the 19-year-old eldest daughter of the island's most eminent judge, Deemster Christian. What began as a casual introduction led to a deepening friendship and serious courtship. Hillary, who always appraised matters of lineage with a hawk-like eye, approved of Augustus's choice. The Christians had all the connections he could have wished for, the family having been members of the island's judicial elite since the fifteenth century. (One member of the family, Fletcher Christian, was the mutinous master's mate on the *Bounty*.) Susannah's father, John Christian, had been educated at Eton and Cambridge and held seats in both the British and Manx Parliaments, as well as being the leading member of the island's judiciary.

Importantly, along with family prestige there was money. As owners of estates and collieries in Cumberland, as well as Milntown, a grand residence on the island, the Christians were among the wealthiest inhabitants on the island. Deemster Christian had an annual income of more than £4,000, with £800 from his position as First Deemster. Should the couple marry, Hillary had every expectation Susannah's dowry would make up for Augustus's lack of fortune and employment.

Augustus's matrimonial hopes were interrupted the following spring, when his mother's deteriorating health forced him to return to England. Frances was living with her elder daughter Elizabeth, at Blackmore Priory, Ingatestone, Essex.[6] At the age of 18, Augustus's twin sister had married Christopher Richard Preston, a landowner and local magistrate ten years her senior. Despite his sizeable estate and a generous marriage settlement of £14,000[7] (supplied by her grandfather Lewis Disney-Fytche), Elizabeth's marriage had not been immune from continued financial worry. The family struggled to run their home and educate their children and like Hillary, would eventually leave Essex, moving to Jersey, to live and educate their sons more affordably.

Frances died on 9 August 1828, leaving most of her estate, including a £10,000 trust fund, her jewels, clothes, art, china, furniture and books, to her younger daughter Wilhelmina. Oddly, she makes no mention at all in her will of her only son, Augustus. It is tempting to read the omission as evidence of a rift between them, perhaps over his abandonment of his army career, the loss of his French property from his grandfather, or his determination to visit his father. Hillary, however, was far from forgotten. For maintaining the charade of being the errant husband and father to Wilhelmina (and in accordance with an agreement recorded in a codicil of her father's will), Frances bequeathed him the substantial sum of £15,000.[8]

To raise such a sum the Danbury estate would have to be sold, a transaction for which Hillary assumed immediate responsibility. Revisiting the estate after two decades of exile, he discovered little was as he remembered it. The house had been sporadically tenanted and left empty for long periods and the signs of neglect were all too obvious. Water had poured in through the roof, disfiguring the fabric of the building. The graciously appointed rooms where Hillary and Frances had once entertained eminent guests were now furnished with rubble and adorned by the scars of damp. Even he had to admit that in such a dilapidated state the building was uninhabitable and would realise far less than he had assumed. Only the land that went with it, including 300 acres of farms and ancient woodland, retained significant value – but the question was, how much?

Adding to the complexity, there was family opposition to the sale. Frances's sister, Sophia, still felt an attachment to the home she had lived in as a child and wanted it to remain in the family. She had the wherewithal to buy the estate – with a trust of £10,000 from her late father – but she had little notion how tricky Hillary could be when it came to reaching agreement in such matters.

Hillary's attitude to money had always been flawed. Either he was too careless or not careful enough and business dealings brought out the worst in his nature, frequently leading to decisions that were ill-advised and which ended in acrimony. The sale of Danbury was typical, creating disgruntlement that ran throughout the family and ultimately disappointed everyone's expectations. Negotiations to agree the price began soon after the funeral: 'You know perhaps that there is a place in this county belonging to Lady Hillary's family [the Fytches] called Danbury Park, on which stands a mansion house quite in ruin … In the confused state of the affairs of that part of our family this place must be sold; and my wife, who has been attached to it ever since she was born is very desirous it should be preserved from falling in the hands of strangers'.[9] John Disney (Sophia's husband) wrote to his solicitor, broaching an initial offer of £9,000 to be put before Frances's executors. The offer was turned down because Hillary wanted nearly four times as much, £42,000.

Unsurprisingly, given this huge discrepancy, months passed without any agreement being reached. Almost a year later, with no obvious progress made, the trustees organised an independent valuation – at Disney's expense. The process involved identifying, measuring and counting all the trees on the estate, and cost Disney £78 – an enormous sum at the time. 'The timber is not only very various in its sorts but also in the quality which makes it absolutely necessary to examine every tree before I can form my opinion of the whole', the surveyor Comyns Parker explained. Augustus visited him during the survey. 'We had a great deal of communication on the subject … and as it rained hard while he was there we retreated to the house which we looked over and all the offices – as the rain was pouring in through various parts of the house and most of the offices he appeared to yield to the propriety of only valuing the sum as old materials',[10] the surveyor recorded.

Still, Disney hoped that as a family member, Hillary would smile on his offer: 'Mr Parker has seen Mr Young is co-trustee for sale; and <u>he</u> (Young) seems to think it desirable that the estate should be kept in the family.'[11] His hopes were also raised because he had been told that 'if it were known amongst the <u>gentlemen</u> in this part of the world that I were looking to it, they would rather desist than encourage competition against me'.[12] But the deal was far from done, and Disney was distraught when the estate was valued at nearly £16,000 – far more than expected. Presuming Hillary to be as eager as he was to conclude the sale, and therefore open to further negotiation, Disney tried to whittle the sum down by £871, citing the poor state of the buildings and high value per acre put on the land.

Hillary knew it was in everyone's interests to resolve the matter. By now he had set his sights on Fort Anne, a grand castellated Regency mansion, perched on the hillside with panoramic views over Douglas Bay. But itching though he was to buy, he could not bring himself to compromise over Danbury's sale. When Disney asserted that '<u>My opinion is</u> that Mr Comyns Parker's valuation for the lot

£15,871 is excessive', he was riled and negotiations turned to a game of brink-manship. Disney begrudgingly raised his offer to £15,000: 'I will state to my wife and son that I they may give that price though I think it a high one.'[13] Still Hillary refused to budge, threatening to sell the estate at auction. 'We must do as the rest of the world – be content as it is, and if at all bid at the auction', retorted Disney, calling Hillary's bluff. Unswayed, and probably believing until the last that his price would be met, Hillary instructed the auctioneers Garroways to put the estate up for sale. By then, much to his chagrin, Fort Anne had been sold to another buyer.

The day of Danbury's sale became a moment of farce rather than triumph. Disney submitted a bid below the reserve price. No one else put in a more sat-isfactory offer. The estate failed to find a buyer. It would eventually be sold in 1830, not to Disney but to John Round, a local Tory MP, who immediately pulled down the crumbling old building and replaced it with a new mansion.

Danbury's disposal had proved more problematic than expected, but Frances's death allowed Hillary to resolve another worry – this time more smoothly. The legality of his second marriage had long troubled him. As we have seen, the con-trived divorce from Frances and his subsequent marriage to Emma had all taken place in Scotland, according to Scottish law, despite the fact that neither he nor Frances had ever lived there. At the time the discrepancy had been allowable because Scottish jurisdiction had been recognised on the Isle of Man. But since then there had been amendments to the legislature that cast doubt on the mar-riage's validity. Anxious to resolve the matter, on 25 May 1829, he and Emma were married for a second time. The ceremony took place on the Isle of Man at Kirk Braddan Church, on the outskirts of Douglas. The record, written by the Reverend Thomas Howard, reads:

> Sir William Hillary Bart of Douglas, late of Danbury Place in the County of Essex and Amelia or Emma Tobin, commonly known by the name of Amelia or Emma Hillary of this parish were re-married in this church by license … This marriage was first solemnised August 30th 1813 at Whithorn in Scotland by the Reverend C. Nicholson in the presence of competent witnesses and after banns had been duly proclaimed… and it is now solemnised strictly according to the laws of the Church of England as a corroboration of the former ceremony and to debar all doubt or dispute as to its legal validity.[14]

Augustus returned to the Isle of Man soon afterwards and announced his engage-ment to Susannah Christian. Hillary launched into further financial negotiations and created further upset, this time arguing with the Christian family over

Susannah's marriage settlement. Augustus had yet to find employment but marriage into an affluent family, Hillary hoped, might secure his future – as his had
done. The settlement the Deemster offered seems generous enough. His family
interest in the Ewanrigg estate and colliery in Cumbria would provide his future
son-in-law with a business interest to develop as well as an income. Unbeknown
to the Deemster, his wife had also promised the couple a further £50 a year. But
Hillary thought they should receive more and, reluctant to accept the initial offer,
haggled over the figures as if it were a business deal. The wedding took place on
13 September 1829, attended by the island's elite. Shortly before, an infuriated
Deemster recorded in his diary:

> Sir William Hillary came up to see me and we had a long conversation calm
> and proper, and Mrs Christian – to keep the peace – conceded much. Hillary
> named what we were to give and to my surprise he said that Mrs Christian had
> promised £50 in addition. I wrote instantly on his leaving to acquaint Susan
> that what I had engaged for I would faithfully adhere to but that Mrs Christian
> could not in justice to herself or to her daughter pay £50 out of her small
> means and that I would not agree to it.[15]

His financial preoccupations did not diminish Hillary's commitment to the
institution he had founded, or his willingness to put his own life at risk if necessary. The new lifeboat for Ramsey, built in Douglas to the same design as the
Sunderland boat, was nearing completion when an early opportunity arose to
put her to the test. At dawn on 14 January 1830, the sloop *Eclipse*, bound from
Liverpool to Glasgow, was caught in a heavy gale. By the time Hillary was called,
the tide was on the rise and the boat had been swept on to rocks in the centre of
Douglas Bay near Castle Mona. Four of the crew of seven clambered into a small
boat belonging to the sloop and clinging to a line secured to the shore, made it
through the breakers to safety. But the surf, swollen with the rising tide, was too
powerful to breach on a return trip to rescue the captain and two remaining crew.
Stranded on the sloop, which was by now filled with water from the sea 'beating
heavily over her', the three had little chance of survival without outside help. The
new lifeboat was still unfinished; the crucial airtight cases had yet to be installed.[16]
But Hillary, as ever supremely confident in his own strength and mastery of the
sea, decided now was the moment for a sea trial. He mustered his twelve crewmen, who dragged the lifeboat to the beach and, with each oar doubly manned,
propelled the boat through the surf. For nearly a mile they ploughed through the
waves, eventually manoeuvring their way to the lee bow of the *Eclipse*, where
the three stranded men managed to climb aboard. The danger was far from over.

North of Conister Rock, on their return journey they were exposed to the full might of the storm. A succession of waves swamped them, each one filling the boat to the thwarts, entering the space where the airtight casings would be fitted in the bow, and greatly increasing the danger of capsize. Half the crew stopped rowing and set to frantically bailing out the water, using the only equipment available – their hats. Afterwards, when they had made it back to dry land, the master of the *Eclipse* confessed 'that on shipping the sea, he twice thought they would immediately have gone down'.

Newspapers recorded the rescue as little short of miraculous, further testimony to Hillary's intrepid brand of philanthropy. 'They were several times in danger of perishing and it was the general opinion that no other boat could have lived in such a sea', recorded the *Liverpool Mercury* in an article entitled 'Meritorious Conduct'.[17] Reading the subsequent reports, the London committee agreed that 'the promptitude and zeal displayed by him on this occasion' deserved reward: another gold bar – his third award. As they presented it to him the committee must have wondered whether Hillary's close brush with drowning would deter him from actively participating in further audacious feats. He would, after all, shortly be celebrating his 60th birthday – surely it was time to live life less recklessly. Both on land and sea, he would soon show them how emphatically he disagreed.

Notes

1 Built in 1799; I am grateful to Adrian Corkhill for supplying this information.
2 Essex Records, D/DQ55/115, Elizabeth Mary Preston to Rankin, July 1832.
3 BL add ms 40382, Augustus Hillary to Sir Robert Peel, 5 November 1825.
4 RNLI Archive Minute Books.
5 RNLI Archive, WH to Thomas Edwards, 9 February 1828.
6 The house is also sometimes called Jericho House.
7 Law Times Reports (1870) vol. 21, 346, 20 November 1856.
8 National Archives, PRO B 11/1749.
9 Essex d/dqc/2/3, John Disney to Rankin, 11 December 1828.
10 Essex d/dqc/2/3, Comyns Parker to Rankin, 13 July 1829.
11 Essex d/dqc/2/3, John Disney to Rankin, 11 December 1828.
12 Ibid.
13 Essex d/dqc/2/3, Disney to Rankin, 2 August 1829.
14 Robert Kelly, *For those in Peril*, p. 59.
15 Ibid., p. 58.
16 *Manx Advertiser*, 19 January 1830.
17 *Liverpool Mercury*, 29 January 1830.

The Rescue of the *St George*

Sir William Hillary receiving speedy intimation of her danger proceeded to
the pier and immediately put off in the lifeboat … and after two hours of
persevering exertions and considerable danger, by which Sir William Hillary,
W. Corbett and two boatmen were washed overboard but were fortunately
recovered they succeeded in rescuing the whole of the crew of the <u>St George</u>
from their perilous situation …

Committee report, Shipwreck Institution Minute Books, 2 June 1830

L aunching the *Mona's Isle*, a new steamer built on the Isle of Man to run
between the island and Liverpool, was a cause for lively celebration in
Douglas. At Dixon's Hotel islanders gathered for a commemorative dinner
at which the toasts were loud and the speeches rousing. None of those assembled
needed reminding of the island's reliance on efficient links with Britain, nor the
fact that the regular steamship service, introduced by the St George Steam Packet
Company between Liverpool, Douglas and Glasgow in 1822, had become a
source of bitter controversy. Liverpool's domination of the route was a sore point
among islanders. 'The usurpation of a gang of strangers and adventurers who have
long assumed, as their exclusive right, to convey the Island mail and passengers, at
their own extravagant prices, in any of their crazy and rejected craft',[1] one newspaper proclaimed, voicing widespread anger at the inefficient and inordinate cost
of the inferior service. The issue was not merely a matter of commerce, but linked
with wider questions of Manx identity and independence. 'Liverpool … absorbs
all our earnings and all our wealth. We would, then, ask her in return, if she ought
not to be disgusted with the conduct of such a public company?' thundered the
Manx Sun, berating the substandard services to the island.

Fired with such sentiments, in 1829 a group of local businessmen formed the Manx Steamship Company and the following year a new, elegantly lined wooden paddle-steamer was launched. Built in Glasgow at a cost of £7,052 and fitted with state-of-the-art engines, the *Mona's Isle* was 110ft long, with a large red central funnel, the three-legged Isle of Man emblem proudly emblazoned on her paddle boxes and an elegant carved female figurehead at her prow. At her launch on 30 June cheers resounded and toasts were cheerfully drunk to 'the brightest star among the numerous steamers that traverse the Irish sea … (it is) crowned with the laurel of victory over Liverpool, whose best steamers will vainly pant in her rear to accompany her.'[2] 'Hear, hear!' agreed the diners, raising their glasses to sip their wine and congratulate themselves. With the *Mona's Isle*, links between Britain and Man were about to change.

She began to ply her trade with fares priced competitively: a luxuriously appointed first-class cabin cost 5s, a steerage fare 3s. Rivalry between the two companies intensified. To lure islanders back to their ships the Liverpool company introduced their flagship steamer, the *St George*, and slashed fares to undercut those of the *Mona's Isle*, confident this would speedily bankrupt their competitor. To their dismay, however, shareholders in the Manx Steamship Company responded not by giving in but by subsidising the *Mona's Isle* to match them. The press was drawn into the competition, reporting on speed and numbers of passengers – often with scant regard for accuracy. 'It would appear that the *Sophia Jane* [another Liverpool vessel] had beaten the *Mona's Isle* on Wednesday last, whereas the contrary was the fact, the *Mona's Isle* having left George's dock pier head three minutes after the *Sophia Jane*, but before getting to the Rock … they were alongside each other',[3] reported the clearly partisan *Manx Sun*, before going on to proudly note that there were upward of 200 passengers on board the Liverpool-bound *Mona's Isle*.

The battle took a darker turn as summer's breezes gave way to autumn gales. On the afternoon of 20 November, the blast of a horn marked the arrival of *Mona's Isle*, under the command of Captain Gill, closely followed by the answering claxon of the *St George*, captained by Lieutenant Tudor. Both vessels carried passengers and freight. The *St George*'s hold was also laden with sacks of mail for Douglas, since its parent company held the lucrative delivery contract.[4]

With an already blustery wind blowing in from the south-west, both masters knew the hazards of Douglas Bay should the wind veer round to the east. But neither wished to lose the race back to Liverpool the following morning. Entering the harbour would mean waiting for mid-morning's high water before leaving and both masters intended to leave at first light. Thus, having unloaded at the pier, both Gill and Tudor decided to anchor for the night in the bay, prudently ordering the engines to maintain steam in case the wind shifted.

Their precautions were well-judged. Before dawn, when the tide began to ebb, the wind came round to the south-east, blowing directly into the bay and increasing to storm-force intensity. In these deteriorating conditions the sea began to build, and by 5 a.m. the waves were savage enough to snap the *St George*'s chain cable. In the dark of night the steamer was rapidly swept towards two hidden but equally treacherous outcrops, the rock-latticed Conister and the nearby Pollock Rocks.

Seeing – or rather hearing – what was happening, Gill ordered the crew of the *Mona's Isle* to weigh anchor and steered his vessel out to sea. Here he would ride out the waves and biting winds until the tide rose and he could safely enter the sanctuary of the harbour. For the unfortunate Captain Tudor, with a crew of twenty-two on board, the escape route was less obvious. Even though the dark night would have made arriving at any accurate bearing impossible, he ordered the engines into reverse, praying he would avoid the rocks. But it was too little too late. Moments later the *St George* struck the reef half hidden by the stormy sea and gloom. Her ruptured hull began to fill with water. A handful of crew launched the only small boat aboard the steamer and tried to head for shore to raise the alarm. They had hardly cast off when they were caught by a huge breaker and their vessel turned turtle, hurling everyone into the water. Fortunately they were still close enough to the steamer for those on board to throw lines and help them clamber back on board, soaked to the skin, freezing, but alive.

Only a quarter of an hour after the ship struck, the water level inside had risen enough to make her list unsteadily forward. She came to rest at an alarming angle, bow pointing to land, broadside to what the newspapers would later gloomily identify as 'the most rugged part of that fatal rock, from which few vessels that once strike ever escape'.[5] Tudor understood that the battle had shifted: saving the lives of those on board rather than the ship was to be his priority. He acted decisively, ordering distress signals to be fired, knowing as he did so how slender was the chance of rescue in such a violent sea. Meanwhile, desperate for other means to save his men, he instructed them to cut down the foremast. His plan was that the mast might serve as a makeshift bridge by which the men could reach the relative safety of the postage-stamp islet at the centre of the rocks. If they could survive till first light (no certainty since in storms and high tides the islet was often entirely submerged), they might have a slim chance of rescue in the morning. But with the mast felled Tudor hesitated: the scheme now seemed too dangerous to try. One surge of the sea was all it would take for the mast to be swamped by swirling water. Even if the men could cling on, the fury of the waves would in all probability batter them to death on the rocks before they scrambled onto the islet. The perils of remaining on board seemed preferable to exposing his crew to such risk.

By then, unknown to Tudor, Hillary had been roused from his bed, notified of the ship's distress, and had responded. At the pier he was joined by the *St George's* company agent, Mr Corlett, and a well-practised crew: Isaac Vondy his stalwart coxswain, Lieutenant Robinson, an unemployed naval officer, and a further fourteen oarsmen, who now launched the large lifeboat. They were eighteen in all but although the distance from the harbour mouth to the stricken vessel was not great – barely half a mile – in such hostile seas extra manpower was essential and each oar was double-manned.

The lifeboat laboured through the storm, as Hillary devised a rescue plan. They would approach the *St George* from the windward side and, when in position, let the anchor go. The force of the gale would push them towards the beleaguered vessel, while the anchor would slow them enough to draw alongside. But theory was one thing, reality another. The flaws in the scheme became clear as soon as they closed on the vessel. The sea pounding against the trapped steamer crashed over her deck with such force it was obvious no anchor would be strong enough to withstand it. Should the lifeboat come alongside, she would be smashed against the steamer's hull before anyone could safely be taken on board.

The only alternative was to manoeuvre the lifeboat onto the leeward side, where the calmer water would allow the men on board to be safely disembarked. But to do so Hillary would have to navigate the lifeboat over the rocks that had already claimed the steamer. It was a perilous undertaking but Hillary's conviction held trepidation at bay. Not so Tudor: watching the lifeboat change direction, he grasped Hillary's intention and the attendant dangers. Appalled at the possibility that the rescuers' lives might be lost, he bellowed his objections above the gale, ordering Hillary to return to harbour. 'We had considered it our duty to warn you off, for, from the vessel having bilged, the severity of the gale, the position of the wind, and the time of tide, there did not appear to us (amongst the heavy breakers then rolling upon Conister) the slightest chance of escape for you',[6] he would later write.

Hillary heard him but refused to comply. Tudor's assessment was beside the point. Supreme faith in his own invincibility – more than equal to the gale lashing his cheeks – had set in. His certainty was not just in himself but in his men and in his equipment. Manby and Trengrouse's inventions, his unsinkable lifeboat, even the foundering steamer, symbolised a world in which he staunchly believed. Sixteen years of effort had been channelled to create an organisation to save men from predicaments such as this. His reputation had been forged in treacherous seas. To turn around now would be to admit the failure of progress and humanity, to allow his achievements to be washed away and leave his history to reclaim him. This was not something to be contemplated. And so he sat erect in his seat, ignoring Tudor's cries, and directed the crew to manoeuvre the lifeboat, stern first, into the narrow gap.

They inched themselves into the channel, floating over the rocks that gripped and pierced the steamer's hull. In the lee of the vessel, the sea grew smoother, though still swirling and eddying with such intensity that newspaper accounts later testified the lifeboat 'was in danger of being instantly demolished by the rolling sea'.[7] And as it turned out, Tudor's warning proved well-founded. With a sudden rush of swell the lifeboat was jettisoned against the steamer's side. In the collision, the rudder, thwarts and six of the ten oars were broken or lost, and several of her airtight cases were ruptured. Worse still, four men were swept overboard. Carried into the freezing foam were Mr Corlett, two crewmen, and with them the redoubtable Sir William Hillary.

Corlett and the two others swam back to the side of the lifeboat where the others heaved them back on board. Hillary, who had never learned to swim, could not follow. Instead, floundering helplessly in the water, he managed with difficulty to grab at a rope dangling from the side of the *St George*. By this means he was temporarily safe. He could tether himself to the rope and haul his head above water whenever a wave approached. Even so, everyone knew that in a cold winter sea a man of average build can only survive for a matter of minutes before his body temperature drops to the point where he loses consciousness and drowns. Hillary, like the others in the lifeboat, would have been wearing ankle-length oil skins and heavy boots – all of which weighed him down and made the task of staying afloat almost impossible. Realising the urgency of the situation, Lieutenant Robinson bravely scaled the side of the *St George* and edged his way along her listing deck, close to the point where Hillary struggled in the water. With Tudor's help, the lieutenant grabbed the rope holding Hillary and dragged him, 'considerably bruised and hurt' but alive, out of the sea and on board.

Hillary had been saved from a watery grave, but for how long? Under the onslaught of the waves, the groaning timbers of the *St George*'s hull suggested she was in imminent danger of disintegrating. The weather was too severe for other boats to set out from the harbour, while escape in the now damaged lifeboat seemed impossible. Quite apart from her severely battered and less than seaworthy state, she was hemmed in on the lee side by the mesh of rigging dangling from the felled mast and by an impassable barrier of storm-whipped waves. Adding to the wretched situation, the tide was now on the rise, and the sea increasingly fearsome. 'Every wave swept the decks of the *St George* and nearly buried the lifeboat',[8] the *Manx Sun* unflinchingly reported.

There was one tenuous hope: to clear the debris obstructing the lee side of the *St George*, and put their trust in the shattered lifeboat. She would not make it to harbour – even Hillary no longer disputed that – but she might keep them afloat for a short distance. The rising tide created a narrow channel of water between the rocks, leading to a small patch of sand. If they could reach it, they might scramble onto the island. There were twenty-two men on the *St George* and eighteen lifeboat men, a total of forty. Had the boat been in perfect condition they would not have attempted carrying such a load – in her damaged state the risk was far greater. Could she transport so many this short distance? The question was one none of them can have wanted to ask, let alone answer.

It took two hours and much risk to all involved for the snarled rigging of the fallen mast to be hacked away. The lee exit route cleared, the *St George*'s crew crammed themselves into the lifeboat alongside the lifeboat men and cast off. With so many on board, the boat sat dangerously low, waves spilling inside with even the smallest of movements. Half the men busied themselves bailing out with buckets taken from the ship. The rest manned the oars that hadn't been lost or broken and, following the directions of the coxswain, rowed with every effort towards the channel.

They had travelled only a short distance when the lifeboat's hull scraped on a low shelf of rock. The impact made her tilt and despite the men's bailing, icy seawater flooded over the side, making the boat heel and ship yet more water. Almost capsizing, clinging to ropes, trying desperately to steady her, the men bailed and rowed. Somehow they remained afloat long enough for the waves to push them 'broadside to the more sheltered side of the rock'.[9] Here the boat finally capsized, but in water calm enough for them to clamber onto the tiny island.

There was nothing to be done but wait, exhausted, chilled to the bone and exposed to the vicious wind and sea, until dawn broke and the tide dropped low enough for them to wade out towards the shore. When they were spotted, two harbour boats came to ferry them across the narrow channel to harbour. 'Thus through a merciful providence (were they) delivered from the awful situation in which they had been so long placed',[10] wrote an astonished journalist.

The loss of the *St George* brought a new mood to the contest for supremacy on the Liverpool Douglas route. It was little short of astounding that thanks to the efforts of Hillary and his men, 'the whole of the 40 – persons, with whom on board, this large and superior boat had surmounted such difficulties were landed without the loss of a single life', agreed the press.[11] Even Hillary was incredulous when he saw the battering the lifeboat had sustained: '(She was) shattered in almost every part', he wrote afterwards, cataloguing the damage to his friend Thomas Edwards in London: 'two planks in her bottom were stove, by which the great air tight case under her floor was filled – six out of ten copper tubes round her sides, under the thwarts were fractured by the violent shocks she received, and otherwise she was so much injured that it is miraculous how she brought us safe to land.'[12]

Despite her mangled state Hillary was confident the lifeboat could be swiftly repaired. The *St George* was less fortunate and in the days that followed she was totally destroyed by the sea. When this news reached the press, old grievances were temporarily forgotten. Formerly critical Manx newspapers, magnanimous in victory, offered condolences on the vessel's plight: 'Our feelings on the subject of the contest, in which she was engaged, are suspended on the present melancholy occasion, and we sincerely sympathise with Capt. Tudor and the other sufferers on board',[13] wrote the *Manx Sun*.

Even so, the opportunity to highlight the local company's now proven supremacy was irresistible. The paper went on to remind readers:

[the *Mona's Isle'*] was also anchored in the bay when the *St George*'s cable gave way and seeing her tail on the rocks, Captain Gill left his anchorage and stood out to sea, till the tide rose, when she returned, and entered the harbour about noon. The same night she took the mail and passengers on board, and departed for Liverpool, where she would convey the very painful intelligence to the St George Company'.[14]

One can only imagine how the directors of the company greeted the news, brought by their arch-rival, that their newest ship was lost. They would struggle on for another year, but in the end relinquish the Isle of Man route, leaving the Manx company to take over the lucrative mail contract and expand steadily. In its heyday the company carried up to 20,000 passengers a year, investing in further steamers, one of which made the journey to Liverpool in four hours and twenty minutes.[15] Meanwhile, in the streets and taverns of Douglas, expressions of triumph were less restrained and reverberated with the verses of a doggerel rhyme:

Cheer up, cheer up, my countrymen,
Come listen, and I'll tell
How Mona's Isle beat the St George
Of Liverpool the swell–
The famed John Bull,
The Great Mogul–
Of Liverpool the swell.

In self-defence this boat was built,
The Mona's Isle our pride
In splendid beauty now she plies
Unrivalled o'er the tide:
Be this our son,
God speed her long,
Huzza! our Island's Pride![16]

Two days after the rescue, Captain Tudor had recovered sufficiently from his ordeal to put pen to paper, writing a grateful letter to Hillary:

> I want words, Sir, to express to you what we then felt, and what we shall ever feel, for the noble and determined manner in which you persevered in coming to our assistance, after we had considered it our duty to warn you off ... there did not appear to us, amongst the heavy breakers then rolled upon Conister the slightest chance of escape for you, and which from the crippled state of the lifeboat when she afterwards left the wreck was so nearly proving the case.
>
> Trusting, Sir that you may long live to preside over an establishment your philanthropy gave birth to and in which your humanity has always placed you amongst the foremost and most active of its members.[17]

Bruised though he was from his experiences, Hillary read the letter with unfettered delight. He had fractured several ribs and his breast bone was badly crushed. The injuries had seriously incapacitated him, but robust health was something he had always enjoyed and he assumed it would only be a matter of time before he recovered his former strength. In any case, even before the scars faded he was hailed as a national hero, a role he embraced with gusto. Hillary had never shied from prominence, partly from an inherent sense of entitlement and partly from an awareness of how his celebrity helped cause. He understood that the story of the *St George* might be used to crank up the publicity machine, and that Tudor's letter, spelling out his gratitude, represented invaluable copy. Hillary transcribed and circulated it among friends in the press, where it was widely published: a reminder to the world at large not only of his personal bravery but of the institution he had founded.

In subtler ways too Hillary capitalised on his new stature. He corresponded authoritatively with the Admiralty, putting forwards suggestions to benefit the institution and those who helped it. He drew attention to the important role played by Lieutenant Robinson, an unemployed naval officer, in the *St George's* rescue, despatching press cuttings to the First Lord of the Admiralty, Sir James Graham, hinting that a post might be found for Robinson. Graham's response was encouraging.

'I have signified to the board my wish that (on public grounds) an opportunity may be found of employing him afloat in some of HM ships,'[18] he acquiesced.

In London, the central committee was as impressed as everyone else by Hillary's efforts both during and after the rescue and needed little prompting to do their bit in harnessing the public mood. Clearly it was important that all those involved were seen to be handsomely rewarded for their valour. After the rescue of the *City of Glasgow*, Hillary had felt slighted when the need for economy had prevented them awarding him a second gold medal, although he had been soothed by the subsequent gold bars they had given him for the rescues of the *Förtroendet* and the *Eclipse*. But the heroism he had displayed during the rescue of the *St George* was in a different league. This time he had no need to petition for recognition: 'The present case is of so high a cast that combining it with the circumstance of your being the origina-tor of the institution, they have considered it an occasion where they can, without fear of disapprobation, gratify their feelings by voting you a second "gold medal-lion"',[19] Thomas Edwards told him. They were confident that in presenting him with a second gold medal they would not open the floodgates to other demands: 'Your situation being so peculiar, that this vote cannot by possibly be considered a precedent; you will therefore stand, and most deservedly, possessed of the highest dis-tinctions of the institution.'[20] Lieutenant Robinson, who had plucked him from the waves, would be similarly rewarded, while Corlett and Vondy would be decorated with silver medals, and the crew would get twenty guineas to be shared among them. The money arrived, fortuitously, on Christmas Eve.

The committee's accolades not only soothed Hillary's aching bones, they pro-vided further fuel for the publicity machine he was still busily stoking. For weeks afterwards, newspapers remained hungry for follow-up material linked to the heroic story and this letter too found its way into their pages. Well into the fol-lowing year Hillary sustained his place in the public eye. He sent press cuttings to Viscount Exmouth, a naval hero with powerful connections, who responded with an effusive letter of congratulation:

My admiration of your zeal, activity and overwhelming humanity, in braving the danger of shipwreck yourself, ...when I reflect on your age and see with what promptitude, energy and perseverance you eagerly embrace the dangers which would have appalled the boldest heart of youth I feel lost in admiration, wonder and surprise and ask myself if your heart must not have received the noble impulse from divine inspiration.[21]

Again, Hillary treated this letter as a useful resource, proudly copying and dis-patching it to the London Committee: 'We have in his lordship most valuable and from his distinguished character, a most powerful friend – he is I understand in high favour with the king, and I am persuaded would, on all occasions most readily use every exertion in his power, to promote the honour and the prosperity of our institution',[22] he urged. The letter, safely preserved along with the others he had received, would be recopied in the years to come, whenever a reminder was needed of his formidable credentials or his crusading passion.

In a wider sense Hillary's savvy networking in the aftermath of the rescue of the *St George* was to have long-lasting repercussions. He elicited a new sense of pride in the institution, consolidating establishment backing from the Admiralty and elsewhere, securing the support of the press and, for the time being at least, recapturing skittish public interest. At the Manx Institution's annual dinner, held in September 1831, the 5th Annual Report of the parent institution announced that since the charity's inauguration, a total of 1,818 people had been saved from imminent peril – 372 in a single year – and singled Hillary out for praise.[23] Hillary was unable to attend the dinner in person – his injuries still made travel any distance too painful. He read reports in the press some days later with mixed feelings, flickers of satisfaction dampened by impatience.

Notes

1 *Manx Sun*, 24 August 1830.
2 Ibid.
3 Ibid.
4 Belcham, *A New History of the Isle of Man* vol. 5, p. 218.
5 *Manx Sun*, 23 November 1830.
6 Letter of thanks from Captain Tudor published in the *Manx Advertiser*, 23 November 1830.
7 Ibid.
8 *Manx Sun*, November 1830.
9 *Manx Advertiser*, 23 November 1830.
10 *Manx Advertiser*, 30 November 1830.
11 Ibid.
12 RNLI Archive Hillary to Edwards, 22 December 1830.
13 *Manx Sun*, 23 November 1830.
14 Ibid.
15 Belcham, *A New History*, p. 218.
16 A. W. Moore, *History of Isle of Man Steam Packet Co.* (1904), pp. 57–78.
17 Letter published in *Manx Advertiser*, 23 November 1830.
18 RNLI Archive, Hillary to Edwards, 16 February, 1831.
19 Letter published in *Manx Advertiser*, 28 December 1830.
20 Ibid.
21 RNLI Archive; copy by WH included in letter to Thomas Edwards, 16 February 1831.
22 Ibid.
23 *Manx Sun*, 27 September 1831.

11

The Tower of Refuge

One of the first objects of interest which meets our eye on entering the bay is the picturesque building ... called the Tower of Refuge; it was erected in the year 1831 on a small rock, about a quarter of a mile from the shore ... commonly named Conister, which being covered by the sea, at high water and spring tides, is a rock on which many a gallant vessel has been dashed to pieces during tempestuous weather. At length it entered into the mind of Sir William Hillary ... to erect a building upon the rock, in which the shipwrecked mariner might take refuge, and outlive the storm.

The Primitive Methodist Juvenile Magazine, 1866

Throughout the fanfare in the aftermath of the rescue of the *St George*, Hillary had tried to ignore a pressing worry. He had yet to recover his health and he detested being an invalid. Until now physical fitness, even in his sixtieth year, was something he had always enjoyed. But months after the rescue he was still laid up, feeling weak and breathless, with bruised ribs making movement uncomfortable and travelling in his carriage for any distance unbearable. Assuming he would heal eventually, he endured these discomforts. But the following year, when spring squalls followed on from winter's storms, worn down by continued pain, he again sought medical attention. He optimistically told Thomas Edwards:

For some time after my last letter to you, I continue rather to get worse than to improve from the hurts which I received at the wreck of the *St George*. But it having been found that one of my ribs just over the heart, was fractured, and other internal injuries received more than was at first apprehended, proper measures were pursued and with good nursing and avoiding every exertion I am once more, though slowly, recovering, and with the return of warmer weather hope to regain my usual good health.[1]

In fact his recovery would continue to be slow and he never fully regained the robustness he had enjoyed prior to his misadventure: 'I am still an invalid, from the effects of the hurts I received at the *St George* – often suffering much pain, entirely unable to bear the motion of a carriage, and within the last year have not been more than two miles from home',[2] he complained more than a year later.

Painful though his injuries were, they did not prevent him from returning to the sea when he was needed. 'Wednesday night last presented all the wild phenomena of a tornado. The wind blew with the utmost violence from every direction, accompanied with torrents of rain, thunder, and lightning', the newspapers dramatically reported in November 1831, almost a year after the wreck of the *St George*. When, at about 10 p.m., a 'vivid light' was seen near Conister Rock, Hillary was notified and without hesitation responded. Mustering a crew of four he slipped out from the harbour in a small boat and headed for the rock. It was a murky night, the sea sucked and swirled about the harbour entrance. They emerged into the full force of the storm, their eyes flailed with spray from foam-flecked waves. The island was not far away – a distance of barely a quarter of a mile – and they were rowing with a racing gale astern, sweeping them through the swell. Even so, with the waves slapping the sides of the boat, the shudder of timbers must have resurrected frightening memories of the rescue of the *St George*. Arriving at the place where they thought the light had been, they scoured the starless night. But there was nothing to be seen, only sea and rocks, no trace of any vessel. Did this mean a ship in distress had now sunk? Worriedly, heedless of the surging waves and hidden reef, Hillary ordered the crew to circle the tiny islet, calling out and scanning the dark for survivors. But still nothing; no trace of shipwrecked mariners, no vessel in distress. Hillary reluctantly ordered the lifeboat to turn back to harbour – no easy feat head on to massing waves and a gale now blowing them out to sea.

The false alarm – for so it must have been – did no harm to his reputation. He was still bathed in the heroism of the *St George* and even fruitless exertions were deemed worthy of report in the press: 'The laudable exertions of the worthy Baronet and his enterprising crew merit more than medals – the gratitude of every sailor, and the admiration and respect of society',[3] declared the admiring *Manx Sun*.

Yet ventures such as this were the exception rather than the rule. For most of the time, particularly during the long damp winter months, ill health wore him down and confined him to his home. To add to his physical woes, there was also the anguish of a family scandal to bear. Augustus, now living at his father-in-law Deemster John Christian's Milntown estate, became embroiled in an embarrassing transgression that threatened a jail sentence.[4] One morning in early September he had gone out with the Deemster, his steward Joseph Nixon and several others. The party were net fishing for salmon along the banks of Sulby river on the family estate, when they spotted another group of men illicitly trawling from the bank. Among them was Nicholas Boscow, a tenant farmer who claimed rights to trawl, a matter the Deemster strongly refuted.

What happened next would become the subject of many different accounts. According to Boscow, the Deemster shouted at them to stop fishing and when they refused, his party assaulted them. Augustus grabbed the net, the men clung on and they eventually cut the drag ropes to prevent him from taking it. An undignified scuffle followed, with Augustus wrestling one man to the ground and threatening him with a stick, and the Deemster ordering his steward, Nixon, to throw a 14-year-old boy in the water. Nixon grabbed the boy by the collar and seat of his trousers and dropped him head first into the river. The water was about 4ft deep; the boy disappeared, surfaced, and tried to climb back up the bank. As he did so someone in the Deemster's party shouted, 'seize him and throw him in again.' The boy evaded them and waded to the opposite bank to rejoin the rest of his party.

The next day Boscow made a formal complaint about the boy's treatment, claiming that 'in consequence of the conduct of the said John Christian, Augustus William Hillary, and Joseph Nixon ... Arthur was put in great bodily fear of them and he is apprehensive of future danger from their hands'.[5] Deemster Christian vehemently denied the accusation, although he offered financial compensation to settle the matter. But no agreement could be reached and in early October, the Deemster and his friends, including Augustus Hillary, were summoned to face an accusation of breach of the peace.

Hillary and the defence team recognised other agendas at work here. As an enforcer of the law, Christian had many enemies on the island – several of whom were now standing as prosecution witnesses against him. The discrepancies in their evidence underlined deep-rooted rifts between Manx factions. Christian was a member of the upper land-owning class, a man of the law who had wielded his authority over the witnesses against him. So, the defence claimed, the prosecution was a rascally conspiracy intended to stain the Deemster's reputation and remove him from the bench. Amid the wrangling Augustus's role became pivotal. The defence argued that as an upstanding officer and gentlemen, his testimony could be counted on as reliable. His part in the altercation was minor, and therefore, he should be removed from the petition and called as an independent witness.

Unfortunately for Augustus, the judge in charge of the case, Deemster Heywood, disagreed. He was an old acquaintance of Christian's, but he foresaw the dangers of judicial bias and wanted justice to be seen to be done. When the defence asked for Augustus to be dropped from the prosecution, the judge ominously remarked: 'indeed ... I think quite contrary. It has been proved here that Mr Hillary was in the whole affray – that he was present when the boy was thrown into the water – and that he had a scuffle with one of the party; and ... aiders or abettors are equally as indictable as the parties actually committing the offence'.[6] Refusing to clear Augustus, he placed all three defendants in custody for the duration of the hearing.

The legal arguments continued into the night, until a weary Heywood declared himself unable to make a judgment, 'in his present exhausted state'. He would take the documents home to reread them before reaching his decision.

Next morning, Heywood altered tack and declared he 'could not come to a satisfactory decision without hearing the evidence of Mr Hillary.' Augustus claimed the Deemster had *not* ordered the boy to be thrown in the water, although he refused to deny that *someone* in the party had done so and would not name the person concerned.

Heywood now drew the matter to its close. Augustus was struck from the petition and the Deemster acquitted: 'There was clearly no desire or disposition to violence on (his part)', all evidence to the contrary had been disproved, said Heywood, adding that he 'knew his character so well, from an acquaintance of many years, to be that of a cool, deliberate and reflecting man'.[7] Still, he went on, Deemster Christian was not without fault in the affair: when the order was given to throw the boy in the river, he had not prevented it. The Deemster's steward Nixon was dealt with less sympathetically. The case against him was proved; he was fined 40s and sentenced to two months' imprisonment in Castle Rushen.

For Hillary as well as for Augustus, the case had been humiliating and its resolution came as a profound relief. Hillary swiftly obliterated the unpleasantness with more enjoyable pursuits. Fort Anne, the mansion perched on Douglas Head, overlooking the bay, which he had tried and failed to buy during the difficult sale of Danbury, was on the market again, and this time he was in a position to buy it. The house had been built by Thomas Whaley, an Irish adventurer who, not unlike Hillary, had retired to Douglas 'in a hopeless condition of insolvency' to begin a new life. Whaley had opted for an extravagant architectural style with a dash of fantasy that chimed with Hillary's taste. The mansion's exterior was festooned with castellations and turrets, and mock ruins sprouted improbably from a tumbling green hillside setting. Inside there were the luxurious fittings Hillary had always loved: inlaid mahogany doors, sweeping staircases, Carrara marble fireplaces and stuccoed ceilings that conjured the opulent feel of an Italian palazzo. Islanders rolled their eyes and dubbed the mansion 'Whaley's Folly', but neo-gothic eccentricity combined with splashes of Italianate opulence created an eye-catching mix, and Hillary wanted the world to notice him: 'The principal apartments are large, arranged with great taste and judgment, for the accommodation of a family of distinction, and finished in the most substantial and superior style',[8] gushed one impressed visitor.

Having bought the house for a substantial £1,800, Hillary set about extensive renovations. He installed 'a warm and cold bath' and constructed a conservatory 60ft long, which he filled with orange trees and other exotic blooms. He had always regretted having to sell his art collection, but with Fort Anne as his home he re-established himself as a prominent patron, building a huge gallery which he filled with old masters. Outside Hillary's aims were equally grandiose. He bought up surrounding parcels of land with commanding views of the anchorage and entrance of the harbour, so that he eventually owned 6 acres extending nearly a quarter of a mile along the south side of Douglas Bay. Within the estate he laid out picturesque walks and shrubberies, 'a well-wooded and Romantic Glen and four walled and well stocked gardens', filled with roses, wall flowers, polyanthus, periwinkle marigold cowslip hydrangea myrtle, violets and pinks. 'Sir William Hillary seems indefatigable in beautifying that prominent ornament of our coast',[9] reported the newspapers, riveted by the endless improvements.

Among certain gossiping circles, however, Hillary's unconventional past and unusual domestic arrangements would always attract more interest than his home improvements or botanical brilliance: 'Sir William Hillary ... lives here on £300 per annum and Miss St John with him, and Lady H, and pays £100. Keep their carriage and here fine folks',[10] remarked Dorothy Wordsworth, during her visit in the summer of 1828. Miss St John and Hillary had known one another since his arrival in Douglas. Their friendship had endured throughout the years and after Hillary's marriage to Emma she joined them as a member of the household, and paid for the privilege of doing so.

Hillary's improvements at Fort Anne did not distract him from his involvement in the Shipwreck Institution. Conscious that royal endorsement was of paramount importance, he was delighted that the new king, William IV, would follow his brother George IV and become the Institution's patron. 'Our reports will now go forth as formerly under the <u>highest</u> sanction in the realm and any, even the smallest doubt on that subject, could not fail, in some quarters, to have been prejudicial', he enthused.[11] He remained alert to opportunities to boost the institution's funds. Skimming the London papers, he noticed a bequest of £100,000 left in trust by the Marquis of Cholmondley to be distributed by the Archbishop of Canterbury and Bishop of London for charitable purposes. Writing to Thomas Edwards, he suggested the committee approach the clergymen, both of whom were vice presidents of the institution, for a donation: 'I would willingly hope they will consider our cause as coming under the description of one of the most humane and charitable ... and by its happy effects already demonstrated, as one which has as powerful a claim upon the public patronage and support as any in the kingdom.'[12]

The animosity he had witnessed during his son's court case hadn't diminished his desire to serve the Manx islanders. Rather the reverse; recognising that heroics at sea were not the only way to win hearts, he would campaign for wider improvements. The most pressing, and ultimately successful, of his crusades was, however, sparked by the rescue of the *St George*. When stormy conditions coincided with high tides, particularly during spring and autumn equinoxes, breakers crashed over the thicket of black rocks circling the islet, swamped the tiny scrap of dry land in the middle and made the hazardous reef all but invisible. Conister had claimed numerous vessels and lives since Hillary had lived on the Isle of Man and during the night the *St George* foundered, when he had scrambled ashore to wait exposed and shivering for dawn, he had experienced what it felt like to be stranded, without shelter, exposed to the fury of a storm with no hope of rescue till morning. Confined by ill health, over the long weeks of the winter of 1830–31 he devised a scheme to help anyone caught in a similar predicament. He would build a tower on Conister. It would not be a lighthouse in the conventional sense; one was already planned for Douglas Head. Rather his idea was for a structure large enough to provide a warning marker for shipping and offer shelter from waves and weather to anyone unfortunate enough to find themselves marooned on the islet. In keeping with his reputation as patron of the arts, the building would be architecturally distinctive – a landmark symbolising his philanthropic efforts and refined taste.

Fired with new purpose, he approached the harbour commissioners and John Quane, the owner of the islet, for permission to proceed. When they readily agreed, he formed a subscription to raise the necessary funds and commissioned a local architect, John Welch, to design the building he envisaged – a miniature castle in his favourite medieval style. Welch created a triangular building with a large tower of 21ft diameter standing 40ft above the level of high water, flanked by octagonal turrets and hanging parapets. Inside, Hillary made sure that the tower's romantic appearance incorporated practical elements. A spiral staircase enabled shipwrecked survivors to find shelter safely above the waves, a bell provided them with the means to summon help, and a supply of bread would be stored for emergency sustenance. Ever conscious of the need for public support and still craving public approval, he explained his scheme to friends in the press, who obligingly wrote laudatory articles on the subject. The *Manx Sun* predicted that:

> (The Tower) will afford a probable asylum in the event of shipwreck on the rock; it may also be made available for a station for the life boat, and even as a residence for the boat keeper. To strange vessels it will also be a beacon to mark the nearly covered rocks at high water; and lastly it will be an object highly ornamental to the bay.[13]

By April 1832, Hillary had raised £155 – enough for the first stone to be laid on Easter Monday, which fell, appropriately enough, on St George's Day. Never one to let a chance of creating a memorable occasion slip by, he orchestrated a theatrical ceremony. The morning began inauspiciously with heavy rainfall threatening cancellation of the event. By noon, however, the skies began to clear, the pier filled with visitors and streamers floated from a forest of masts in the bay. On the pier, as if he were a monarch in a water pageant, Hillary descended the steps and took his seat in the lifeboat with Quane and Welch. They were rowed the short distance to the island, accompanied by another vessel on which a band played *Rule Britannia*. Out on the islet a cluster of dignitaries had already assembled, and as Hillary and his party disembarked, the audience formed an avenue, standing in respectful silence, while Quane formally donated the island to the Shipwreck Institution and handed Hillary a symbolic parchment roll. Hillary responded with a short speech of acceptance, before the Archdeacon gave a blessing and school children sang verses from psalm 107: '*They that go down to the sea in ships, that do business in great waters; these see the works of the lord and his wonders in the deep...*' Afterwards, just as the sun obligingly burst out from a dark cloud, Hillary, wielding a silver trowel, laid the foundation stone, a cannon was fired and the band struck up *Rule Britannia* again. Closing the ceremony, Hillary gave a further speech 'of some length' and, having toasted the tower with a glass of sherry, he and the dignitaries boarded their boats heading for a celebratory dinner in the Castle Mona Hotel. The masons who would build the tower were among the crowd watching the ceremony. They lingered on Conister after Hillary's departure, drinking to the project's success until dusk fell. Anxious that the day should be a memorable one for all concerned and as always eager to be liked, Hillary had supplied them with two barrels of ale to enjoy before they headed back to the harbour.

Building could only take place for a few hours either side of low tide when the weather was clement; even so, by June progress was well underway. Watching the tower grow on the rock gave Hillary a welcome distraction from the pain he still suffered in his ribs. He confided to Edwards:

> I am happy to acquaint you that our projected Tower of Refuge ... is now in progress, with every prospect of its being completed before another winter. This interesting object engages a good deal of my attention, so far as my health will admit, of which I am not able to give a more favourable account than when I last wrote – in addition to the other contusions I received at that wreck the right ventricle of the heart is ascertained to have been injured.[14]

His optimism seemed misplaced later that summer, when headway was stalled by the unwelcome arrival of cholera on the island. The epidemic had raged through Britain from the close of 1831, and would eventually kill 55,000 people. In May, when the disease reached Liverpool, the city erupted into riots, with people distrustful of the medical profession and town authorities, convinced that bodies of victims were being misappropriated for dissection.[15] Thomas Woods, a blacksmith of Douglas aged 24, was the first Manx inhabitant to succumb to the disease, in late June. The epidemic would claim the lives of eighty-four islanders, and in Douglas a large burial pit was dug in St George's Churchyard for the internment of bodies.

To try to curtail the spread of the disease the Manx authorities formed a Board of Health, whitewashing houses (believed to prevent the spread of infection), distributing lime to be spread over rubbish dumps, and fundraising for a cholera hospital. Hillary, a prominent participant in the efforts, was bewildered at what he perceived to be a general indifference to the dangers of the disease and the reluctance among the wealthier inhabitants to donate to the hospital. Unafraid of stirring things up, he declared loudly that 'it was strange ... to think of the apathy displayed by so many on such an awful visitation'.[16] He had discovered that £6 was the largest sum subscribed for the hospital and was aghast that individuals who owned immense property in the parish were so reluctant to contribute more.

By the time the epidemic died out, in October 1832, the tower on which he had lavished much time and energy was complete. Its final cost was £255 – more than anticipated, and £74 less than the funds raised by subscription. Never one to let money stand in the way of an idealistic project, Hillary had made up the shortfall from his own purse. The tower remains to this day, an arresting monument both to his taste for medieval fantasy and his philanthropic energy. Those who see it for the first time are still enchanted. '(It)… appears rising out of the water like a fairy palace from below … to defy the shocks of every sea that rages and every wind that blows …' wrote one visitor to the island, going on to explain the local superstition: 'Whenever a tempest rages the moaning of the spirits of those who have been lost here is heard from the shore; and in the moon of night pale corpses are seen to look over the battlements … pointing to their own watery graves.'[17] William Wordsworth may not have noticed the tower's phantoms, but he was struck by its imposing appearance when he sailed into Douglas Bay soon after its completion and paid tribute to its indomitable creator:

The feudal Keep, the bastions of Cohorn,
Even when they rose to cheek or to repel
Tides of aggressive war, oft served as well
Greedy ambition, armed to treat with scorn
Just limits; but yon Tower, whose smiles adorn
This perilous bay, stands clear of all offence;
Blest work it is of love and innocence,
A Tower of refuge built for the else forlorn.
Spare it, ye waves, and lift the mariner,
Struggling for life, into its saving arms!
Spare, too, the human helpers! Do they stir
'Mid your fierce shook like men afraid to die?
No; their dread service nerves the heart it warms,
And they are led by noble HILLARY.[18]

Notes

1 RNLI Archive, Hillary to Edwards, 15 March 1831.
2 RNLI Archive, Hillary to Edwards, 17 June 1834.
3 *Manx Sun*, 1 November 1831.
4 The following account is based on the newspaper reports of 4 October 1831 in the *Manx Sun* and 11 October 1831 in the *Manx Advertiser*.
5 *Manx Sun*, 4 October 1831.
6 *Manx Advertiser*, 11 October 1831.
7 Ibid.
8 *Manx Liberal*, 10 October 1840.
9 *Manx Advertiser*, 29 May 1832.
10 Dorothy Wordsworth, *Journal of a Tour in the Isle of Man*, 3 July 1828.
11 RNLI Archive, Hillary to Edwards, 8 April 1831.
12 Ibid., 15 March 1831.
13 *Manx Sun*, 10 April 1832.

14 RNLI Archive, Hillary to Edwards, 23 June 1832.

15 S. Burrell and G. Gill, 'The Liverpool cholera epidemic of 1832', jhmas.oxfordjournals.org.

16 *Manx Sun*, 21 August 1832.

17 *A Six Day Tour Through the Isle of Man by a Stranger*, 1836

18 William Wordsworth, 'On Entering Douglas Bay, Isle of Man', 1833.

12

The Last Rescue

Nothing daunted by the sufferings he had undergone, we find this gallant man,
now 63 years of age, foremost at the wrecks of the schooner *Mary* and the
brig *Erin* in 1831 and in the following year at the rescue of the *Parkfield*, a large
Liverpool ship, stranded in a SE gale in Douglas Bay, from which 54 men were
saved by the life-boat.

Lifeboat, volume 2, 1853

On the evening of 2 February 1833, the East Indiaman *Parkfield* set sail
from Douglas in the dwindling winter light. She was embarking on
her maiden voyage with sixty passengers and crew on board, and a
small crowd lingered on the Red Pier to wave her off. Long after she disappeared
into the darkness the ship remained impressed in their thoughts. She was the largest vessel ever built on the island, 500 tons register, and, thanks to her elegant lines,
widely agreed to be 'decidedly the most beautiful'. Her launch had taken place
only three weeks earlier – a memorable day that brought a festival air to the town.
Watched by hundreds of spectators, she had ceremoniously 'saluted the briny element in the finest style',[1] before being towed into the harbour by the *Mona's
Isle* for her final fitting. Now, under the command of Captain Wynder, aided by
a local pilot, her new sails unfurled and set, the *Parkfield* was leaving Douglas to
travel the oceans and bring prosperity to the island. First stop Liverpool, then
across the Atlantic to New Orleans.

Out on the Irish Sea the journey began uneventfully. The night fell, the sky was
clear with brisk northerly winds, and while the *Parkfield* made steady headway, in
the comfortable passengers' saloon the wine flowed and the party that had begun

in Douglas blithely continued. But, as Sir William Hillary knew only too well, the Irish Sea is a notoriously capricious stretch of water. Winds and seas change in an instant and without the benefit of shipping forecasts, even experienced mariners could be taken unawares. Two hours later, barely 10 miles out of Douglas, the wind suddenly shifted to a south-easterly and strengthened to storm force. With the wind came rains, torrents that lashed the boat's sails and pock-marked the surface of the gathering waves. As quickly as the weather closed in, so the passengers' sunny mood darkened. Feeling the uncomfortable lurch and roll of the boat and the unnerving vibration of wind-tautened sails, their anxiety grew. Then, to their dismay, there was a sudden crash.

The *Parkfield* was underladen. Intending to take on cargo at Liverpool, she carried a ballast of paving slabs. The terrifying sound, 'like a death knell – similar to that of her being crushed on the rocks,'[2] was the noise of stones that had worked themselves loose in the jolting of the storm and shifted to one side. The effect of their movement was swift and dramatic. With the weight now on one side, the *Parkfield* was unbalanced and almost unmanageable, 'bringing the ship at one time on her beam ends, with every appearance of her immediately going down.'[3] Adding to the captain's problems, '[her] new rigging and shrouds refused to run, and thus prevented the precautionary measure of placing the ship in good steerage way'.[4] Critics examining the reason for the sudden destabilisation of the ship would later surmise that the ballast was insufficient to maintain her stability in such a heavy sea, and the little there was had been badly stowed. 'The nature of her loose, round, smooth ballast without any material to render it compact, which 50 or 60 tons of the common sea sand would probably have done, was certainly inconsiderate',[5] the *Manx Sun* concluded.

In the wheel house tempers between the captain and pilot grew short, a situation not helped by the alcohol they had consumed during the departure celebrations. The details of the argument are not recorded but presumably centred on what course the ship should take. The pilot, conscious of the perils of sailing an unstable vessel into the famously treacherous Douglas Bay, may have thought it preferable to weather the storm at sea, while Wynder's instinct was to return to harbour and seek shelter. In any event, Wynder asserted his authority and prevailed. With difficulty the ship was turned about and set on her new course back to Douglas.

They were propelled by a storm force tail wind, in the middle of an impenetrable winter's night, on a boat that, regardless of the gale, was listing uncomfortably. We can imagine the scene in the saloon; passengers spilling their wine and reeling to save themselves from being hurled on the alarmingly angled cabin floor, while the downpour flogged the windows and great waves washed the deck outside. We can picture Wynder and the pilot in the wheel house in an atmosphere charged with apprehension. No one needed to be told of the dangers of being caught in a storm in a disabled vessel. Surrounded by sea miles from shore, they sensed that fate was reaching out for them.

But then, soon after midnight, when the light that marked Douglas Head was glimpsed, the passengers felt a scintilla of comfort – land, they fervently hoped, was within reach. Wynder, however, experienced no such relief. Accurately navigating his unstable ship in the dark with unpredictable gusting winds and malfunctioning rigging was impossible and, according to later reports, when he gave the order to go about, the *Parkfield* 'missed her stays' (failed to alter course). Minutes later, to the dismay of everyone on board, there was an alarming shudder as the keel struck the hidden spine of rocks extending from the north-east point of Conister. But the impact helped the floundering vessel, which unexpectedly turned about and sailed free. Had this not been the case, the newspapers later pessimistically opined, 'all on board must have perished'.

A few minutes later, having put some distance between his ship and the rock, and reaching what he believed to be the safety of the middle of the bay, Wynder gave the order to drop two anchors. By now the tide had turned to a racing ebb, while the south-easterly gale was still blowing strongly onshore. Under these conflicting forces, the swell turned choppy and tugged at the mooring with such insistence that both the anchor cables snapped. Once again the *Parkfield* was in grave danger – now of being swept stern foremost towards the Black Rocks, the reef that girdles the beach at the centre of Douglas Bay. Wynder could nothing more. Under the brooding silhouette of the Castle Mona, the much-feted East Indiaman was checked. Rammed against rocks, stranded by the ebbing tide, with her rudder broken off, she rolled in the waves, flailed by sea and stone until her hull could withstand no more and ruptured. Cold sea engulfed the vessel, filming the floors of the cabins, seeping over decks and cascading down walls, sending the already frightened passengers scuttling on deck in a state of utter panic. The damage to the vessel was severe: 'The whole of the larboard (port) bilge of the vessel stove in, and from every appearance it was thought she was rapidly going to pieces.'[6] Later accounts testify that the confusion was made worse by the fact that 'several on board – (both crew and passengers) were still in 'a shameful state of intoxication'.[7] Meanwhile Wynder, struggling to maintain some semblance of order, instructed his crew to fire distress flares and launch a boat to raise the alarm. The flares were spotted through the whirling storm by the Custom House officers on duty. They alerted builders from the shipyard where the *Parkfield* had been constructed and others with vested interests in the ship. Word was also sent to Sir William Hillary, 'who proceeded immediately to the pier'.[8]

He took control with his usual clear-headed authority. Having ascertained how many passengers were in need of rescue, he summoned enough crew to man two lifeboats. In the middle of the winter's night it took some time for them to arrive and since Hillary understood the importance of aid reaching a stricken vessel speedily, he dispatched the smaller boat first, following in the larger one as soon as the remaining men arrived.

The reef on which the *Parkfield* was stranded lay beyond Conister, a mile and a half from the spot where the lifeboats were launched. The crews rowed hard into the storm, withstanding cresting swell and unrelenting rain to reach their target. Clustered on her sea-swept deck, the *Parkfield's* passengers saw the boats approach and took comfort in the knowledge that help, under the commanding presence of Sir William Hillary, was at hand. In fact the danger was far from over. With the surf still crashing over the reef and tide still low, it was too dangerous to attempt evacuating those on board. The lifeboats would have to wait until the tide rose and water over the rocks was deeper. Only when the first streaks of dawn seeped over the horizon, did they safely float over the rocks and submerged deck to begin helping the passengers into the lifeboats.

Even then the lifeboat crews faced considerable peril. As the smaller boat, loaded with passengers, cast off to head back to the pier, a freak wave swamped the larger vessel. Hillary was directing operations as best he could when his lifeboat was tossed into the ship's side and almost swept over the gunwale. The lifeboat was badly damaged by the impact[9] but remained seaworthy enough to make it back to the pier with her load of passengers. Hillary was mercifully unscathed. Thus, barely twelve hours after they had embarked from the Red Pier full of hope and glory, the *Parkfield's* crew and passengers, freezing cold, wet through and traumatised by 'having been exposed during the whole of an inclement winter's night to much misery',[10] and their close brush with death, were landed safely back on the same spot.

With all lives spared, attention now turned to the vessel that had yet to be insured.[11] To lose such an expensive ship would be calamitous for her owners and anyone whose livelihoods were linked to theirs. Could she be saved? The only hope was to lighten her, wait for high water, then attempt to float her off the rocks, provided the sea didn't shatter her first. Later the same day, as soon as the storm had subsided, a steamship was dispatched to remove 'as much of the rigging and such as could be effected'. The mission was successfully accomplished: 'Most of the spars and rigging have been removed, and as she has swung a little round last night there are some hopes that by means of the powerful aid of two steamers, she may be saved',[12] declared the press. For once fortune smiled. Buoyed up with empty casks and harnessed to the two steamers, the *Parkfield* was successfully hauled clear and towed into the harbour. They had rescued her in the nick of time – the following morning strong southerly gales blew up which, according to the papers, 'would utterly have destroyed her'. Despite the grave damage the *Parkfield* had suffered, she was found to be repairable. Three months later she would leave Greenock for a voyage to Bombay and achieve fame for the fastest return voyage to India – managing the journey in a record-breaking seventy-eight days.

Hillary's account praising the bravery of his crew was quickly written up and dispatched to the London committee: 'They embarked with their usual promptitude and exerted themselves in the most praiseworthy manner',[13] he recorded. What he meant, but did not spell out in so many words, was that they deserved a handsome reward – more than the £10 they had been awarded by the owners of the vessel. There was lingering rancour among the crews who had assisted with the *St George* three years earlier that they had yet to be properly recompensed by the St George Company. The committee didn't quibble with his opinion. 'The difficulties attending the exertions of Sir William Hillary and the companions of his danger in their most laudable conduct, in thus hazarding their lives, in the dead of a winter's night, are above all praise',[14] declared Thomas Edwards in his formal letter to the Isle of Man District Association. So to loud cheers of approval, Hillary announced that twenty sovereigns would be shared among the crew: Isaac Vondy, the coxswain, was to be awarded a silver medal and £3; the twelve men who had made one journey were given £2 each; and those who had made two trips an extra ten shillings. Vondy, responding on behalf of his fellow crew members, declared 'they would be ready to assist in the lifeboats whenever similar distress might require it'.[15]

The coxswain's statement raised spirits and reassured Hillary – lifeboats depended on men who were willing to place their lives on the line; this was why rewards had to be made. But it was in every sense a speech made for public consumption – this would be Vondy's last venture to sea. Hillary knew and sympathised with the reasons for his subtle withdrawal, but he also deeply regretted them. Vondy and he were the same age and had attended thirteen wrecks together. The passing years had brought them close. Yet for all the rapport that came with facing death together so many times, Vondy had never once overstepped the mark. He always called Hillary 'your honour', a mark of respect that Hillary valued as much as his bravery. 'He had for nearly 60 years in one capacity or other followed a seafaring life, more than 20 years of which he had been a master of trading vessels but without saving anything ... a fine old man – in many respects much beyond his class in life ... always prompt in going with me, and set an excellent example of coolness and courage to the men',[16] he wrote fondly four years later, when Vondy died after a lingering illness.

Like Vondy (and perhaps because of him), Hillary had begun to question how long he could continue active service on the lifeboats. He told Thomas Edwards that he had managed to survive the *Parkfield*'s rescue 'without any apparent occurrence to myself of the injuries which I received at the *St George*, from which I have reasonable hope to believe I have recently begun to recover', but this was short of the truth. His old injuries still troubled him and would continue to do so. 'I have been suffering under the longest and most severe attack of any which I have experienced since my hurts at the wreck of *St George* in 1830, and from which I am only just recovering, if recovery it can be called which leaves me so weak that I continue almost confined to the house and nearly reduced to a skeleton',[17] he frequently complained. There were days when he recovered his strength, when his bones didn't ache, when the pains in his chest were less troublesome. The *Parkfield*'s rescue was presumably one such night, but still it had exposed his underlying weakness. Public approval had always mattered deeply to him, yet when the committee commended his efforts but did not award him a medal, for once he did not argue with the decision. After all, he reminded himself, he had won two gold medals and two bars, more than anyone else, and his place as the institution's founder could not be usurped. He no longer needed to prove his worth.

Besides, there were plenty of distractions. At the end of the month he presided over a dinner in honour of the Lieutenant Governor of the island – an evening of extravagance far removed from the rigours of the storm: 'The confectionery and dessert were beautiful and expensive – the champagne claret and other wines were excellent in quality and unlimited in quantity',[18] a local newspaper gushed. Hillary had no qualms about indulging himself in this way. He had always enjoyed living life in grand style, seeing it as a hallmark of his status. His charitable activities were another aspect of civilised character and social standing, and he loved to be seen demonstrating philanthropic largesse. He held annual dinners for the customs officers and harbour boatmen, who provided volunteer crews for the lifeboats. He joined other grandees such as Deemster Heywood (whose efforts on behalf of Augustus he would never forget) and James Quirk, the town's High Bailiff, in organising an annual concert at Mrs Dixon's Hotel to take advantage of the influx of well-to-do visitors and raise funds for various island charities. He was an active campaigner for better law enforcement on the island. Crime had become an increasing problem and he urged the Douglas authorities to keep its citizens safe: 'something immediate must be done to preserve the peace of the country during winter',[19] he argued, promoting the installation of a permanent and efficient police force in the town.

There was also still much to do at his new home, Fort Anne: 'There is no finer site in the Bay of Douglas for a gentleman's seat than Fort Anne, and none whose capabilities have been put to better account than this by its worthy occupant. Everything at Fort Anne has a classic air and elegance about it, which shows a mind imbued with the fine feeling of the ancient Greek and Roman in the palmiest day of their country's glory; in every trifling feature you discover its noble proprietor, the greatness and benevolence of whose character cannot, however, be duly appreciated by minds immeasurably below his own',[20] rhapsodised John Welch, the architect whom Hillary had commissioned to design the Tower of Refuge. Hillary lavished his time and energy on his garden. He exhibited exotic blooms, nurtured in his conservatory, in the local horticultural society's shows (of which he was vice president) and took delight in escorting visitors along paths that meandered through walled gardens, shrubberies and wooded glens to admire the colourful glories: 'On Christmas Day last the following flowers in full bloom were gathered in the grounds of Sir William Hillary Bart at Fort Anne', enthused the *Manx Sun*, going on to list more than three dozen plants flowering unseasonably early, including hydrangeas, lilacs, carnations and three sorts of geranium.

But compared with his lifeboat work, gardens and dinners and public speaking, however pleasurable and worthy, were only diversions. When the last toast was drunk and the guests departed, he surveyed the bay from the windows of Fort Anne and nostalgically recalled his involvement with the lifeboats. Of all the causes he had championed, the institution would always be dearest to his heart. He remained involved in the running of the Manx branch, but it wasn't enough; he bitterly missed the physical side of his role and longed for another taste of it.

His wish was fulfilled sooner than he expected. In February 1833, a day after a grand dinner over which he had presided, the island was struck with the most severe storms in more than a decade. Shipping ran into Douglas for shelter, only to find the open bay provided little respite from the easterly wind. The storm raged for hours and newspapers detailed, 'the reign of alarm, confusion and destruction of property which prevailed throughout the harbour: vessels breaking from their moorings – running foul of each other – and carrying away everything they came in contact with. In fact any person to have witnessed the awful scene might have imagined that the powers and ingenuity of men were placed in competition with the mighty elements'.[21]

In the harbour and bay of Douglas there was mayhem; the sea battered the quay until it partially collapsed. The brig *Eliza* broke loose from her moorings, colliding with the *Mona's Isle* and carrying away the steamer's foremast, top mast, bowsprit, stanchions and bulwarks, as well as her much admired figurehead. Further afield, there was human tragedy. The *Sarah*, a collier brig on her way from Whitehaven to Dublin, was caught in the gale, lost nearly all her sails and began to ship water. In the early hours of the morning she turned towards Douglas but was carried away by the tide, was swept leeward of the headland and struck the rocks. It was still dark when she foundered. With the surf crashing over the sinking ship, one crew member and the captain clambered along the bowsprit, lowered themselves onto the rocks and, despite being badly lacerated in the process, crawled their way to safety. The remaining six men, watching their ordeal, were too panicked to follow, and instead clambered into the rigging. The captain tried to convince the crew to descend and follow him, but in the middle of the conversation the masts were swept away, with the loss of all on board. The captain and surviving crew member then had to scale sheer cliffs in their exhausted state to find safety. Only one body was later found washed ashore, and next morning, when the storm had abated, Hillary set out in a lifeboat to search for survivors or bodies. His helpful role in the aftermath of the wreck was acknowledged by the local press, who noted: 'That old and tried friend of mariners ... was early upon the shore, where the melancholy event took place, with the crew and the small life-boat, and has since been humanely employed in providing for the wants of the survivors'. [22]

A pall fell over the island after the storm had died. The Manx papers reflected the general sense of shock with heart-rending stories of the aftermath. But the reports, however sad, belonged to an isolated world, one that was easily ignored elsewhere in the British Isles. With too many similarly tragic tales closer to hand, the *Parkfield*'s remarkable rescue and the calamities of the great storm that followed went largely unremarked. [23] Hillary was infuriated by the inattention. Since the institution's foundation, he had battled against the island's remoteness, making frequent visits to London and maintaining a stream of correspondence to keep his adopted home, as well as his cause, at the forefront of public consciousness. He understood that public sympathy was as fickle as the wind. Without the newspapers to remind them, the public would turn elsewhere and the institution, always short of money, would sink like a foundering vessel without trace.

Letting this happen without a fight was unthinkable and he battled to search out new avenues to promote the cause, badgering the central committee to do the same. What was the point of holding an annual dinner if it was not exploited as a publicity exercise? Impatiently, he cajoled Thomas Edwards:

It strikes me that some paragraphs in any of the leading papers, previous to the dinner, strongly calling the public attention to the great national importance of our institution and stating that the first Lord of the Admiralty was to be in the chair would in addition to the usual advertisements be of much use – and the procuring afterwards favourable and detailed reports ... might have a still further beneficial effect. For I have felt that the more the objects and the efforts of our Institution are known, the more numerous will become the friends of our cause.[24]

When of one of the most harrowing wrecks of the decade took place the following summer, he recognised an opportunity and seized it. The *Amphitrite* was a three-masted convict transport, en route from Woolwich to Sydney, New South Wales, with 108 women prisoners, twelve children and a crew of sixteen on board. On 30 August 1833 she was caught in a storm off the French coast and ran aground on sandbanks near Boulogne. The tide was ebbing and a local fishing vessel and pilot offered assistance, advising the master, Captain Hunter, to evacuate his passengers and abandon ship. Had he agreed, Hunter could have safely moved all on board to the shore, but, perhaps worried that the prisoners might escape, he refused to allow anyone to leave the ship, insisting the women prisoners remain incarcerated below decks. The crew did what they were supposed to do, remaining loyal to Hunter. But the *Amphitrite* was an old vessel and her timbers were in a state of serious disrepair. As the water began to rise, her keel remained stuck fast in the sand. Alarmed at the sound of shuddering wood and crashing waves, the women prisoners demolished the barricades confining them. Rushing out on the deck confirmed the gravity of their predicament and they begged the captain to send them ashore in the longboat. But Hunter, blind to the danger and stubborn to the last, refused to back down. Oblivious to their 'uttering the most piteous cries', he forced them to remain on board until the ship broke up. All the women and children prisoners were drowned. Of the crew, only three managed to swim to shore and survive.

The first newspaper reports of this tragedy let flow a cascade of public outrage that focussed on failings far beyond the behaviour of Hunter. The dead captain's inhumanity was nothing compared to the unjust penal system that allowed young offenders guilty of only minor offences to be sent away with hardened criminals, or the indifference shown by the British consul in Boulogne, who had made little effort to save those who were washed ashore and might have survived. The tragedy also brought old prejudices to the surface: according to one popular strand of thought humanity was linked to class. Those who had behaved badly demonstrated flaws endemic in a certain strata of society. Callousness, greed and over-officiousness went hand in hand with 'the lower middle classes.' By contrast, the upper and lower strata of society knew their place and remained untainted. Thus, the argument went on, the venal mentality 'has not prevailed to any great extent amongst those who constitute the strength or those who present the ornament of the country'. Nor, were the lower orders sullied by such cruelty: 'We have still bold boatmen ready to peril their own lives ... and we have noble and generous hearts to reward such gallantry – and when the opportunity offers to stimulate it by their example.'[25] In other words, Sir William Hillary and his lifeboat crews were the antithesis of the reprehensible Hunter and his acolytes – the humane facet of nineteenth-century society; men to be proud of, men who understood their place and their duty to society.

In fact the references to Hillary and his Lifeboat Institution were not unprompted. Having read the harrowing reports of the *Amphitrite*, Hillary had fired off numerous letters to the press: 'We have received the following letter from the excellent founder of the Royal National Institution for the Preservation of Life from Shipwreck',[26] announced the editor of the *Standard* (unbeknown to Hillary, none other than William Makepeace Thackeray). Hillary's missive, which Thackeray generously printed in full, is characteristically forthright, listing his achievements and efforts, including his success in bringing his institution to the attention of other maritime nations. 'I had also felt it a duty to transmit the same plans to the various naval owners of Europe and America. They have, on a great or lesser scale been adopted with marked success on the coasts of Holland, Denmark and Sweden ... such a cause only wants the fostering hand of power to insure its firm and speedy establishment in every quarter of the civilised world',[27] he proclaimed, enclosing a bundle of pamphlets in case there was any detail he had left out.

The friendly Thackeray went on to exceed Hillary's expectations, praising his efforts and even promoting the idea hitherto mooted with little success: that the institution deserved government support. 'The one object ... is to call upon the people and upon the government to reinforce the funds of the institution so as to render them really adequate to the probable demand ... let them only suppose what would have been the different fate of the unhappy passengers on board the *Amphitrite* ... had the means of their safety been at hand in the form of good stout lifeboats, and had motive been supplied even to the selfish.' This was stirring stuff, and, to Hillary's delight, it ended even more rousingly:

> Before taking leave of Sir William Hillary for the present, we must, in justice to the founder of the Royal National Institution, mention that he is one of those fine, generous, enthusiastic beings whom heaven sends, when, in mercy more than in justice, it is pleased to rekindle the dying embers of what is noble in our nature. Hillary is not a man to ask others to do that which he will not do himself. Not contented with giving his labour and his money to promote the humane object which he makes the business of his life, we find him, in the 6th report of the institution, risking life itself as freely as any common boatman in the same cause.[28]

Reading this in the comfort of Fort Anne, Hillary should have felt deeply gratified. Here was the endorsement for which he had hoped – a sign that, regardless
of whether or not he still manned the lifeboats, his place as founder of the institution and national hero was acknowledged. And yet like so many who are fired
to undertake feats of extraordinary bravery, old ghosts lingered. Still dogged by
a need to draw attention to his achievements, he felt impelled to cut out the
articles, copy them and send them to the local press and to his friend Thomas
Edwards. The covering letter coyly pretended that he was 'unwilling to call your
attention to them, had the same paper not also pledged in such a manner itself
that I cannot doubt but they would meet your wishes to request the attendance
of an able reporter on the occasion of the dinner'. It is questionable whether
Edwards or Hillary himself needed to be reminded of the hero he had become.

Notes

1   *Liverpool Mercury*, 18 January 1833.
2   *Manx Sun*, 5 February 1833.
3   RNLI Annual Report, Case 355, 1833, p. 26.
4   *Manx Sun*, 5 February 1833.
5   Ibid.
6   RNLI Annual Report, Case 355, 1833, p. 26.
7   *The Belfast Newsletter*, 19 February 1833.
8   RNLI Annual Report, Case 255, 1833, p. 26.
9   *The Standard*, 11 February 1833.
10 Ibid. p. 27.
11 Kelly p
12 *The Standard*, 11 February 1833.
13 RNLI Annual Report, p. 28.
14 Thomas Edwards to Alex Douglas, Hon. Secretary of the Isle of Man District
    Association, reprinted in *Manx Advertiser*, 26 March 1833.
15 RNLI Annual Report, p. 29.
16 RNLI Archive, Hillary to Edwards, 13 February 1837.
17 Ibid.
18 *Manx Advertiser*, 26 February 1833.
19 *Mona's Herald*, 12 September 1834.
20 John Welch, *A Six Day Tour of the Isle of Man*, 1836.
21 *Manx Sun* and *Manx Advertiser*, 26 March 1833.
22 *Manx Advertiser*, 26 February 1833.
23 I have only found records of the Belfast Newsletter recording the *Parkfield*'s story.
24 RNLI Archives, Hillary to Edwards, 28 February 1834.
25 *The Standard*, 19 September 1833.
26 *Manx Advertiser*, Sunday, 4 October 1833.
27 *The Standard*, 19 September 1833.
28 Ibid.

13

Duties and Desires

We have passed Age's icy caves,
And Manhood's dark and tossing waves,
And Youth's smooth ocean, smiling to betray:
Beyond the glassy gulfs we flee
Of shadow-peopled Infancy,
Through Death and Birth, to a diviner day;

Prometheus Unbound, Percy Bysshe Shelley

Six months before the tempestuous night that claimed the *Parkfield*, on a breezy August day, Hillary sat at in his desk in Fort Anne, dipped his pen in his inkwell and began to compose a letter to Lord Melbourne. Words usually came easily to him, but this was a matter of some delicacy that required careful thought. In a clear bold hand, he began with stilted formality:

> My Lord – I feel that I must trust to your Lordship's indulgence to excuse my taking the liberty of addressing you relative to the Lieutenant Governorship of this island, which situation I have reason to believe that the honourable Lieutenant Governor Smelt from his advanced age (though still fully equal to all his duties) would from his friendship to me be willing to relinquish, if permitted to do so in my favour.[1]

For all his stiffness, Hillary was writing from the heart. The world was changing – horizons broadening, a new king on the throne, sweeping reforms transforming the political landscape, scientific advances revolutionising industry. Even on the isolated Isle of Man, he could not escape the fact that a pivotal moment had been reached. In the Bay of Douglas, shining beneath his window like a sheet of hammered silver, steamers with summer visitors clustering on their decks, were overtaking the old East Indiamen that relied on favourable winds. In Britain new railways had begun to lace the country. Technological advances and breakthroughs in science and industry would always fascinate him. Like the philanthropic good causes he promoted, they symbolised the improvement of civilised society, and as such he embraced them. The subject of steam power had first drawn his attention 14 years earlier and when he reached his 69th year it would do so again in a pamphlet entitled *A Letter to the Shipping and Commercial Interests of Liverpool on Steam Life and Pilot Boats*. He would always maintain that steam engineering offered a solution to many of the problems of modern life. Through steam, stormy seas would be tamed and shipwrecks avoided. But in a way, Hillary's forward-thinking openness to the new machine age was underpinned by the conventions of his privileged eighteenth-century youth. His willingness to write about scientific subjects exemplified the confidence of an earlier age, when amateur gentlemen demonstrated their intellect by reading up on scientific subjects in *The Gentlemen's Magazine*, attending public demonstrations, then dabbling themselves.

Part of him also still clung to the previous century's view that class entitlement would open any door, make anything possible. As he saw it, belonging to the social elite imposed certain obligations: he felt a duty as well as a desire to be a leader of society. Ever since he had served as royal equerry he had hankered for an official post that would allow him to relive those heady days. There were financial as well as ideological motives for his ambitions. On the Isle of Man he lived the life of a grandee but his resources, stretched ever since he settled there, were inadequate for his needs. Expenditure on Fort Anne was never-ending; he was unable to resist buying works of art to fill his new gallery. He was subsidising Augustus in developing his colliery in Cumbria and there was an endless stream of local good causes that he could not refuse. Which brought him to the purpose of his letter – an application soliciting the most powerful job on the island.

Hillary had felt sympathy for his old friend Cornelius Smelt, the island's 84-year-old Lieutenant Governor, when he fell ill. But after twenty-eight years in office Smelt's retirement seemed inevitable and the impending vacancy presented a solution to Hillary's problems. The position came with a salary and political kudos. The Lieutenant Governor was the king's representative on the island, wielding real influence and authority within the island's governmental Parliament; furthermore he was styled 'Your Excellency', a title to which Hillary felt well suited.

Before applying for the post he approached Smelt on the subject. They had been friends for the past two decades and Smelt was encouraging, advising Hillary

to write to Lord Melbourne, the Home Secretary, requesting he recommend him
to the king. Hillary began his letter expressing praise for Smelt's attributes, before
moving on to explain awkwardly his own credentials for the role:

> The grounds on which I venture to aspire to this honour – these, I feel can only,
> in the first instance, be founded on any claims which I may hope I have on my
> country for such public services as it may happily have been in my power to
> render – and also, owing to my long residence in this island ... I have therefore
> on separate papers endeavoured as briefly as possible, to lay before your lordship,
> what the nature and the results of my endeavours to serve my sovereign and
> my country have been – consisting of the best years of my life, and much more
> than £20,000 zealously devoted in this cause, without receiving any remunera-
> tion whatsoever.

Having hinted at his disgruntlement, he felt it would strengthen his case to point
out his powerful connections:

> Of the extent of those military services, and of my ardent endeavours, both in that
> and my subsequent efforts on behalf of our Shipwrecked seamen, I may venture
> respectfully to refer your Lordship to the highly distinguished authority of His
> Royal Highness the Duke of Sussex, with whom I have had the honour to pass
> some years on the continent, from whom I have for more than 30 years received
> many marks of condescending kindness, and who, being fully cognizant of the
> circumstances I have stated to your Lordship, will I presume to indulge the hope,
> further extend his kindness to me ... I will further take the liberty of mentioning
> to your Lordship that I am and every have been entirely unconnected with the
> local politics and parties of this island – am not possessed of estates therein but am
> of an ancient English family and a baronet of the United Kingdom.[2]

To bolster his application Hillary compiled two further documents. The first,
entitled 'The formation of the First Essex Legion by Sir William Hillary Bart',
laid out his early achievements during the Napoleonic Wars:

> On the renewal of war with France in 1803 when the kingdom was seri-
> ously threatened with invasion I availed myself of considerable influence I had
> acquired upon an exposed and important part of the coast of Essex ... where
> a large force was deemed to be requisite ... in the formation and discipline of
> this large body of men I neither spared my exertions nor my fortune, devot-
> ing my whole time for many years to this service and incurring an individual

expenditure of more than twenty thousand pounds, beyond any allowances made by government.

In this document he returned yet again to the old story – and the same old unspoken grievance, that notwithstanding his baronetage, he deserved proper recognition for all he had sacrificed.

Then he went on to detail his proudest achievement – the real reason he felt qualified to apply for the Lieutenant Governorship. 'The Formation of the Royal National Institution for the Preservation of Life from Shipwreck by Sir William Hillary Bart' looked back to the early days of his institution, and his inspiration:

> Having in my early years resided much on the sea coast I acquired a strong bias for maritime affairs … afterward, in the course of my travels as a young man I made several voyages in which I witnessed several disastrous shipwrecks, more than once narrowly escaping when numbers around me perished.
>
> More recently, having made the Isle of Man my usual residence, my attention was forcibly called to this deeply interesting subject, by some appalling and fatal scenes of this nature, which have left an indelible impression on my mind, and I turned my attention to the combination of a general system, worthy of the most powerful of Maritime states.

Set out like this, as bare facts on a page, how safe it all sounded. How impossible to convey the horror of watching a ship foundering in a storm, of what it was like to witness men waiting to die, without hope; of his compunction to act, regardless of the danger to himself, to prevent it. And so, after paying lip service to royal patronage, the role of the central committee, and the admiration of other maritime states, he shed the baggage of protocol and allowed his passion to shine:

> Perhaps I may be permitted to add that I have ever, on the occasion of wrecks on these rugged coasts, used all the means in my power for the assistance of those in danger – often with much hazard to myself, and more than once with severe personal injuries from the effects of which I still continue to suffer, but accompanied by the gratifying feeling that I have from various wrecks, been aiding in the rescue of fully 200 persons from imminent peril.
>
> Such is the simple narrative of the rise and progress of an institution which there is now every reason to hope, will extend in beneficial effects to many distant nations and become the means of preservation from shipwreck to thousands yet unborn.[3]

He could say no more. Signing the letter and the statements, he bundled them together with a copy of Lord Braybrooke's kind letter congratulating him after the rescue of the *St George*, and posted them to the government offices at Whitehall.

What did the Home Secretary make of this odd package when it reached him a few days later? The obsequious tone and name dropping make uncomfortable reading. Even if we excuse his style as conforming to the conventions of the time, it is impossible to avoid elements of untruthfulness in its content. Hillary claimed to be without business interests or property on the island. Yet he had both – including (as we will see) a shareholding in an increasingly lucrative mine. To disguise his involvement he had registered the investments in the name of his wife Emma and their long-standing live-in companion, Sarah St John. But this was merely a convenient front – and many knew the truth. Yet the letter is not an attempt to hoodwink the establishment but a plea for its endorsement. If you overlook the disingenuity and toadying tone and read the last paragraphs, you glimpse the essence of the man. His account rings of a sincere desire to serve.

Whether or not Melbourne recognised any of this is uncertain. All we know is that the petition met with an unfavourable response. Hillary was briskly informed that there was currently no vacancy for the position of Lieutenant Governor. And even when Smelt died in November, less than three months later, Hillary failed to win the appointment. It went instead to John Ready, who had served a similar role on Prince Edward Island in the Canadian Territories, where he had success-fully oversaw a period of transformation and growth.[4]

Hillary may have flinched at the prospect, but under Ready, change in one form or another was assured. Outwardly he would keep pace, frequently cham-pioning reform and progress. But in truth he cherished the reassurance of old traditions and for this reason would strive to keep the memory of Smelt alive. Thus it was Hillary who organised a petition to have a monument erected to Smelt in Castletown, the island's capital and administrative centre, and who took charge of supervising the design. No other Lieutenant Governor has ever been remembered in this way. It was Hillary who insisted that the monument should be inspired by classical tradition: a tall column with a statue of Smelt on the top – shades of Hadrian's column. And it was also, characteristically, Hillary who failed to consider the costs of his scheme. The funds were insufficient for his grandiose design and instead of the statue the column was surmounted by a cheaper urn. Quickly dubbed 'the candlestick' by islanders, it still stands in Castletown today – a lasting monument not only to the achievements of Smelt, but also the imprac-tical ambitions of the man who wanted to replace him.

Disappointed political ambition strengthened Hillary's determination to con-tinue serving the lifeboat institution. After the *Parkfield* he acknowledged he was no longer strong enough to join the crew in active service but hoped his health would improve: 'I sometimes allow myself to think I may yet be reserved for one great effort more, on some future occasion of disastrous wreck on our shores',[5] he confided to Edwards. The opportunity to participate in a final rescue arrived in December 1836, when a violent storm blew up, forcing several vessels to head into Douglas for shelter. For days torrential rain had fallen on the island and the river Douglas, abnormally swollen with floodwater, cascaded into the sea at Douglas harbour, creating treacherous whirlpools that added to the hazards of fierce wind and waves. The adverse conditions continued until the small hours of the following day, by which time, Hillary told Thomas Edwards, 'an eddy wind shifting every moment, a strong land flood rushing down the river, meeting the sea breaking over the pier head, made the entrance of this always unsafe harbour, doubly perilous'.[6]

Among a cluster of ships seeking shelter in the harbour was *Sarah*,[7] a brig from Harrington. Hillary had watched her attempts to enter the harbour at the height of the terrifying storm, and recounted how 'The *Sarah* got into this vortex and not having a cable went to let go her anchor, was carried into a tremendous surf between the pier and some rugged rocks, placing her in so hazardous a situation, that for some time I almost despaired of the people being saved'.[8] Heedless of his fragile health and the menacing conditions, Hillary took immediate control:

On seeing these vessels approach I had gone down and got the lifeboat ready, but thinking that a rope communication best met the exigency I got the life lines and hawsers from our store and after some difficulty, having got one small rope on board, three strong hawsers were in succession got to land, and ultimately the vessel and eight or nine people saved – which could scarcely have been effected, had it not been for the prompt and zealous assistance of the masters and crews of the steam packets and other vessels then in port, with the boatmen, fishermen and every other class of persons, by whose powerful aid, this and two other vessels which followed were extricated from a situation most perilous to the vessels and all on board.[9]

Despite the urgency of the situation, Hillary was conscious enough of his frailty to direct operations from the shore, without setting out in the lifeboats. Even so he was now approaching his 67th birthday and standing in the raging storm, exposed to the elements, proved too much for him. 'This was my last personal service, if such I may call it – but the effort being far beyond my strength, and being drenched by the sea, and exposed in that state for some hours to the cold of a severe winter evening, it mainly contributed to that last attack from which I am beginning to recover',[10] he admitted to Thomas Edwards.

Without lifeboats or government office to harness his energies, and with money in short supply, Hillary embroiled himself in other activities. He was living in an age of speculation and had only to open a newspaper for his eye to be caught by advertisements for a multitude of opportunities: railways, fishing enterprises, retail and manufacturing companies all clamoured for investors. 'Speculative madness or gullibility never was at so high a pitch as at the present moment',[11] recorded the *Manx Sun*. Hillary was no businessman but he was drawn by the mood of the moment and his desire to project the image of a conspicuous but benign figure of authority. His retirement from active service would not prevent him from continuing to champion the Shipwreck Institution. High-profile business ventures could help with promotion, he claimed, overlooking his desire for money and relish of the limelight for its own sake too.

Perhaps business also satisfied other cravings. By now, after a decade of setting out to sea on stormy nights, confronting danger had become second nature. Having shed his oil skins for a quiet life, the thrill that came with the risk-taking, which made him feel alive, was lacking. Maybe, after out-facing death in such vividly physical ways, he no longer recognised peril in other guises. He had always been reckless where money matters were concerned and this hadn't changed with the passing years. So he plunged into financial enterprises – hazardous waters where no lifeboats could save him.

His appetite was whetted by an early success. In 1822, two years before the foundation of the Shipwreck Institution, he had a lucky break, investing in a disused lead mine at Laxey on the east coast of the island. He bought a £50 share, registered in his wife Emma's name, a pretence that may have been connected to outstanding debts, or to an innate desire for secrecy where money was concerned. As we have seen, he used a similar ruse to buy Fort Anne, registering it jointly in the names of Emma and Sarah St John rather than his own. But the minute books show his keen interest in the business of the mine. He regularly attended monthly meetings in person, even offering useful suggestions for improving efficiency and safety when called upon.

Almost immediately small deposits of lead were discovered. At first there was not enough to cover extraction costs, and Hillary and the other shareholders subsidised operations. Five years later a new deep seam was discovered, a waterwheel operated pumping system was installed and the mine became profitable. One local newspaper painted a picture that for the patient investors now looked extremely rosy:

They are now producing 150 to 500 tons of excellent lead ore per month, containing from ten to 80 ounces of silver in the ton of lead... In one of the mines is now to be seen one of the largest bodies of ore ever discovered in Great Britain ... The great Foxdale vein, running nearly east and west, upon which the principal mines are now working extends across the island from sea to sea ... The great Laxey vein running nearly north and south, contains copper ore, lead ore ... The great Brada copper vein ... near to the seashore, has been pronounced by several Cornish miners ... to be as strong as any lode ever discovered in Cornwall.[12]

For Hillary this was extremely good news. Since his first investment he had quietly increased his shareholding. From the early 1830s the mine provided generous dividends and shares bought for £50 were said to be worth up to £2,000. Emboldened by the unfamiliar feeling of prosperity and swept along by the prevailing speculation fever, he looked for investment opportunities elsewhere.

He joined the board of the newly founded Isle of Man Bank for Savings as its president. The bank's proclaimed mission was to encourage 'tradesmen, mechanics, servants, labourers and persons of a similar description as well as their children ... to deposit a portion of their earnings, however small'.[13] Here, on the face of it, was another example of Hillary's philanthropy – his position as president was a voluntary one and he stood to make no profit. The fact that he knew nothing about banking seems not to have hindered him, or those who appointed him. Perhaps his social prominence and naivety where money was concerned seemed advantageous. It comes as little surprise, however, that the 'tradesmen classes' were less enthusiastic about this scheme, particularly when the *Mona's Herald* published a critical report claiming the bank was insecure, and the venture quietly disappeared.

But the banking project led to other schemes. The island was beginning to enjoy a property boom and Hillary was drawn to the possibility of developing land that had once formed part of the estate of Castle Mona, known as Falcon Cliff: 'I was induced to purchase some beautifully situated property, part of the demesne of the late Duke of Atholl overlooking Douglas Bay, which held out the promise of making a very large return',[14] he later explained to his friend Sir Richard Broun. Hillary screened his involvement behind frontmen who included John Welch, the architect of the Tower of Refuge, and the bankers Wulff and Forbes (also investors in the Laxey Mine). With their help he devised a complex financial structure known as a tontine, whereby individuals bought shares in the property that on their death would revert to others in the group. The property was divided into 800 shares at £50 each and widely advertised in the press.[15] The *Manx Liberal*, which regarded the enterprise as a sort of private pension scheme:

It is a species of institution much wanted in the Isle of Man, by means of which gentlemen of small property, officers, or professional men, may be enabled, by small periodical payments for a few years, to secure to their families a gradually increasing income ... until it furnishes an important aid towards support in old age[16]

Meanwhile, ostensibly to improve the spiritual well-being of islanders, but in reality to provide additional bait to investors, Hillary offered part of the land on his 'beautiful rising ground adjoining Castle Mona Plantations'[17] for a new church and parsonage, feeding the story to the local newspapers:

In the United States of America when a site is chosen for a new town, the first building that is erected is a church as the greatest attraction for settlers. In like manner a new church on Sir William Hillary's ground would be the greatest encouragement to buildings on the beautiful adjoining spots[18]

Hillary had no difficulty in raising the funds he needed to set the deal in motion. With Fort Anne as security, his influential banker friends Wulff and Forbes readily advanced the necessary sum. The pair had been involved in banking on the island for more than a decade. Forbes was a member of the House of Keys, the Manx legislature, and seemed trustworthy and competent; Wulff had been one of the trustees of the Isle of Man Bank for Savings. With business links and position among the island's establishment, Hillary had no reason to doubt the bankers' probity or competence; thus, when they proposed a new venture to him, he listened.

In the aftermath of the banking collapse of 1825, the industry had been transformed by new regulation and joint stock banks capitalised by shareholders, usually better funded and regulated than privately owned banks, had proliferated. Wulff and Forbes' idea was to form a joint stock bank with direct links to Britain. Such an institution would benefit the Isle of Man, where present financial transactions with Britain incurred prohibitive commission costs. Elsewhere such schemes were enjoying significant success and producing generous dividends for shareholders, they assured Hillary.[19] To avoid a conflict of interests with their existing bank, Wulff and Forbes proposed to merge the two businesses, in return receiving 2,500 shares at a discounted rate.

The venture was endorsed by the island's establishment: four of the bank's directors were to be Forbes's fellow members of the House of Keys. The press also supported the enterprise. One reporter confidently advised:

The extraordinary amount of the dividends which have been paid by this bank and the astonishing rise of the shares in the market, have fully proved that joint stock banking companies are based on a solid and stable foundation, and are not to be shaken either by the prejudices of the ignorant, or by the interested opposition of private individuals. *In no one instance* has a joint banking company failed ... in no one instance has its capital been diminished; on the contrary all are in the highest state of prosperity[20]

And so, with an expectant fanfare, the Isle of Man Joint Stock Bank was launched: 'It is with pleasure we call the attention of our readers to the advertisement in the day's paper, of the liberal offer made by Messrs Wulff and Forbes of converting their present well-established bank into a joint stock one. The great advantages that must accrue to the island by its establishment are so evident, that we shall say nothing farther on the subject',[21] cheered the *Manx Sun*. Without much hesitation, Hillary bought £75 worth of shares in his own name, a further £50 on behalf of Sarah St John and £75 for his son. He also presided over a preliminary meeting to attract further investors and, to help the bank on its way, agreed to pay the money raised from the sale of shares in the Falcon's Cliff tontine into the bank. It is uncertain whether he understood that, in the event of any losses, he and his fellow shareholders would be liable. If so, he believed the possibility remote: 'I was congratulated by my friends on the certainty of [the bank's] success,'[22] he told Broun five years later.

The bank opened for business on 15 July 1836, with Edward Forbes as manager. The first year's annual report exceeded expectation. The bank announced substantial profits; shareholders would receive a dividend of five per cent. There appeared to be no bad debts; although the stoppage of the Ramsey Shipbuilding Yard had left a sum of over £1,500 outstanding, there was every hope this would soon be recovered. In the meantime, the directors reminded the shareholders, 'it is scarcely necessary for us to point out the immense advantages derived by the public from the establishment of this bank'.[23] The good news continued the following year. The bank would pay investors a dividend of six per cent, and still retain £3,000 in the surplus account in case of bad debts. Prudently, the directors announced, they were now taking extra care in making advances. Reading the reports, Hillary congratulated himself on his canny business acumen and good fortune.

Notes

1 PRO HO 98/77, Hillary to Viscount Melbourne, 16 August 1832.

2 Ibid.

3 Ibid.

4 Belchem, (ed.),, *A New History of the Isle of Man*, p. 26.

5 RNLI Archives, Hillary to Edwards, 13 February 1837.

6 Ibid.

7 The brig *Sarah* was coincidentally called by the same name as the vessel that had foundered in 1833, but was not the same ship.

8 RNLI Archives, Hillary to Edwards, 13 February 1837.

9 Ibid.

10 Ibid.

11 *Manx Sun*, 22 April 1836.

12 *Manx Herald*, 25 June 1836.

13 *Manx Herald*, 1 August 1834.

14 Archive of Order of St John, Hillary Letters, WH to Sir Richard Broun, 8 March 1841.

15 Kelly, *For those in Peril*, pp. 86-97; from late October 1837 advertising appeared over several months in the Manx papers including *Manx Advertiser, Mona's Herald* and *Manx Liberal*.

16 *Manx Liberal*, 21 October 1837.

17 *Manx Sun*, 10 June 1836.

18 Ibid.

19 *Manx Sun*, 1 April 1836.

20 Ibid.

21 *Manx Sun*, 6 May 1836.

22 Order of St John Archive, WH to Sir Richard Broun, 8 March 1841.

23 *Manx Herald*, 5 September 1843.

14

Disenchantment

Our island is at this moment much agitated by the endeavours of the whole
people to obtain redress of some obvious grievances – and though by no
means indifferent to their cause – I have succeeded in keeping this great
harbour and shipwreck cause, <u>entirely clear</u> of all party feeling for this question
both sides concur:

William Hillary to Thomas Edwards, 9 April 1845

In January 1837, Hillary stood in the council chamber of Douglas Corporation
and addressed a meeting of local inhabitants. Smoothly dispensing with the
usual formalities, his tone altered and he voiced 'an ardent desire that there
might be no discord in the proceedings ... this was not the time to settle disputes
between the master and crew while the vessel was sinking'.[1] Despite the metaphor, he was talking here not about shipwrecks, but of a political and financial
maelstrom threatening to engulf the island. Hitherto the Isle of Man had enjoyed
fiscal independence from Britain. Goods entering the island had to be imported
via British ports and were restricted by licence, but taxes on the island were lower
than those elsewhere in the United Kingdom. Now this was set to change: the
British government proposed radical changes to bring the island into line with
British duties: 'The governments of the country both Tory and Whig have long
been <u>resolved</u> to do away with the anomaly ... with the fullest conviction that the
measure would greatly benefit the nation at large and the island more especially',[2]
explained a Manx observer reporting from London.

Unconvinced by the British argument that the island would prosper as a result,
most of the island's inhabitants were in uproar. An apprehensive Governor Ready

warned the Home Secretary, Sir John Russell, that 'it is not saying too much the greatest alarm is felt by all classes in this Island on the proposed assimilation of duties'.[3] Hillary sided with the prevailing outcry. The Isle of Man provided 'a comfortable and happy retreat to many brave officers on small half pay, and to numerous worthy but reduced families'. If the cost of living rose they might feel forced to leave the island 'and seek their bread in foreign lands'.[4] The measures might also encourage a resurgence of the smuggling that had diminished since the eighteenth century. 'With an ungrateful soil and a strong climate, with a long winter and a short summer, how can the Isle of Man compete with the commerce of the surrounding shores?'[5] he demanded.

Hillary agreed to act as chairman of the meetings convened in Douglas to decide a course of action. It was after all an official role, even if it was unsalaried. The subject was an emotive one, but for the time being at least, his ability to rally public sentiment and authoritative manner contained overt dissension. He drew the first debate to a close, receiving 'the highest complimentary thanks for his urbanity, zeal and ability'.[6] Agreement had been reached: delegates representing each locality on the island were to be speedily elected. Hillary would assist a committee in compiling a petition of objection to be signed by islanders and presented by the delegates to Parliament in London.[7]

But the Isle of Man was made up of opposing factions jostling for supremacy. As the weeks went by, resentments surfaced which hindered the election of deputies, and Hillary became a target of criticism. To some his manner seemed overbearing, to others his motives questionable. 'A meeting is to be held tomorrow … unanimity is alas gone and I fully expect an unpleasant scene. Hillary is casting about. He may be a good chairman but his egotism mars the headpiece',[8] wrote one unimpressed committee member as meetings turned acrimonious.

Newspapers fanned the dissension, reporting every spat: 'A very unpleasant misunderstanding arose between Sir William Hillary and High Bailiff, James Quirk, in reference to the inconvenience and delay experienced', the *Manx Herald* recorded of a heated row that broke out between Hillary and Quirk. Feeling himself slighted by the High Bailiff's late arrival for a meeting, Hillary had loftily revealed his impatience. The argument that followed grew so bitter that a third party had to 'interpose and request as a favour that all recrimination should cease'.[9] Elsewhere, in the press, Hillary's role was called into question. Biased in favour of Douglas, and secretly in favour of political reform, some hostile reports claimed that he was an unsuitable spokesman for the general interests of the island.

Stung by such criticisms, Hillary used his platform as chairman of the Douglas Committee to counter the doubters with more than a dash of melodrama, proclaiming with characteristic gusto:

He feared not the scrutiny, but was ready to stand or fall by the rectitude of his acts ... he deprecated the idea of his being able to act for the promotion of Douglas alone. It was not the town of Douglas. It was the entire Isle of Man he had adopted as his home. His heart could not beat for one part of the island without the whole',[10]

His supporters applauded such rhetoric, but some in the audience remained unconvinced, and one meeting descended into mayhem that 'for a time assumed rather the appearance of a pot-house squabble'. Weeks dragged on with little progress. Unable to deny the problems he faced, he wrote to a friend admitting that 'illness and far more troublesome affairs than an invalid can well get through have occupied me incessantly .... Our last public meeting was from many causes, hail, snow and apathy'.[11] Even so, not everyone had deserted him. Among the liberal press he still had friends willing to spring to his defence. 'Hillary's character stands far beyond the reach of such a mendacious craven ... (his) name alone, from its never being heard but in connection with some effort for the good of his adopted home, is a heavy overmatch for the united combination of monopolists and license mongers, clique and keys',[12] lauded the *Manx Herald*, one of the newspapers that was always staunchly supportive.

Spurred on with such encouragement, Hillary urged John Bluett, a Douglas-based barrister, to travel ahead of the squabbling delegates to London and begin to lobby ministers for support. He coached Bluett carefully on what line to take with the British authorities:

Your first great object I hope will be to impress on the minds of ministers the utter injustice and paltry meanness of adding to the taxation of so poor a speck in the empire, which yet pays all its cost to government and yields them £16,000 a year surplus revenue of which they give us no account ... get them if possible to give up altogether the idea of new taxation ... stand firm to our cause, make all the friends you can and fight our battle manfully.[13]

Next, Hillary turned to the Shipwreck Institution for aid. The institution's secretary recorded:

Hillary says their little committee are under much alarm from the government having announced their intention to make several alterations in their fiscal and navy laws, and if they take such a turn to render an appeal to the House of Commons if necessary, he hopes such gentlemen on the committee as are members of Parliament would afford him their conscientious support.[14]

Although he had retired from active rescues, his influence within the committee remained strong and its members offered their support without hesitation: 'In reference to observations respecting the intended measures of government the deputy chairman of the committee, Mr George Palmer MP, will most willingly do everything in his power to assist his view',[15] the secretary of the institution assured him.

Fortified by allies in London as well as Douglas and ever the opportunist campaigner, Hillary capitalised on the political spotlight to resurrect another of his pet causes – the harbour wall at Douglas. 'If something must be done with our fiscal and navigation laws – and I suppose there must whether the island pleases or not ... at least part of such increased revenue should be expended for the good of the island – above all for my favourite plan of a refuge harbour in Douglas Bay',[16] he urged Bluett, bundling up copies of his pamphlets relating to the cause.

Hearteningly, the topic that had preoccupied him intermittently for the past eight years now seemed feasible to Lieutenant Governor Ready and Douglas's harbour commissioners. An updated version of his pamphlet, framed with approving editorial comments, appeared in the press:

> On the northern coast of Wales excepting Holyhead the whole of the coasts of Lancashire, Cumberland and southern Scotland as far as mull of Galloway – about 300 miles, there is not a single harbour which can give shelter to vessels in distress at low water or even half tide, yet within this range is Liverpool, the second largest port in Britain, at which more than 120,000 vessels arrive annually, besides the bustling ports of Lancaster, Whitehaven, Maryport and Workington, to which belong one third of the commercial navy of the whole empire. The value of these vessels and their cargoes is enormous – value of the lives on board is beyond all estimate.

As time passed, he sternly reminded his readership, more lives were being lost and more livelihoods ruined:

> In a single week in November 1834, besides thirteen persons who perished, vessels and their cargoes exceeding the value of £60,000 were lost ... all of which had passed Douglas Bay in search of shelter and where they would have found safety had the proposed asylum harbour existed ... and it is unquestionable that within ten years, property to an amount much beyond half a million has been sacrificed.

In case this wasn't emotive enough, he issued a further stark warning: 'every year of delay in providing the certain means of rescue from these dreadful calamities is attended with a responsibility too awful to be contemplated.'[17] With fresh impetus, the harbour authorities employed a second engineer (Sir John Rennie had previously carried out the task) to survey Douglas Bay, draw up plans, estimate construction costs and report to shipping grandees in Liverpool. Despite his enthusiasm, Hillary felt too ill to travel and therefore was unable to bolster the scheme with his presence. When the proposal was presented it became mired in logistical practicalities and again progress ground to a halt.

For the rest of his life the matter would rumble on, at times tantalisingly close to realisation, but always unresolved. In the interests of practicality he would change his design to an innovative and less costly floating structure made from wood, which he published in *A Report of Proceedings at a public meeting held at the Court House Douglas* (1842). This scheme drew energetic support from islanders as well as ministers in London. 'The state of the times, the public feeling and the views which government seem to have formed of the necessity of establishing fortified Harbours of Refuge on our most exposed coasts all seem to indicate that the moment is favourable ... I shall feel final success an ample compensation if I live to witness it ... I am most anxious to see it established as a great national principle',[18] Hillary would write to Thomas Edwards in 1845, hoping at last to see some action taken. It never was.

Meanwhile the political unease with Britain bubbled on. The fractious Manx delegates finally left the Isle of Man and assembled in London in May 1837. Their interview with Lord Russell was imminent when, in June that year, William IV died, throwing any chance of political reform into abeyance. The interlude did nothing to soothe tensions in the Isle of Man. Disharmony now shifted to the island's self-elected legislature, the House of Keys.[19] Hillary, who had always proclaimed political neutrality, tried to remain aloof from the debate, but was quietly drawn to side with the reformers who believed representatives should be openly elected. His high profile ensured that his tacit allegiance was given prominence, and members of the Keys now viewed him as an opponent. He would painfully learn they were dangerous adversaries to make.

The only respite in this divisive backdrop came with Queen Victoria's coronation on 28 June 1838. Spurred on by the patriotic fervour sweeping the nation, Hillary enthusiastically organised celebrations to mark the event in Douglas. His intention was to re-establish a sense of community spirit, heal old rifts and restore harmony. He spoke idealistically of his hope, 'to induce a spirit of loyalty in the inhabitants, which he hoped would extend over the whole of the island, and to all parties, because this was no party question'.[20] Douglas's buildings were decked with bunting, flags fluttered from the masts of ships in the harbour, bells were rung and cannon fired. A dinner of pea soup, roasted and boiled meat and plum pudding was dished out to the poor of the town, while at Castle Mona Hotel, Hillary presided over a banquet and entertainments for 200 invited guests of elevated standing.

Carried along by the new mood of nationalism, soon after the celebrations he published his most ambitious pamphlet yet. Entitled *The Naval Ascendancy of Britain*, it was a history of key naval engagements, a tribute to those who had served in them, as well as a polemic criticising the Admiralty's failure to sponsor new advances in steam-powered ships. He explained to his friend Broun that he had begun writing it several years earlier, hopeful that he might attract an eminent sponsor:'The manuscript lay by me, [I was] hoping that some leading officer would give the cause the sanction of their high names – but the present crisis has roused me ... I can only plead my motive to my countrymen as my excuse for coming forward at this momentous period'.[21]

The dawn of the new reign also heightened Hillary's attachment to the past. He made contact with the Knights of St John, the chivalric order that had impressed him nearly four decades earlier in Malta. Recently, a new branch of the order, or langue as it was known, had been formed in London, and new recruits with aristocratic connections were needed. The langue's aim was to raise £240,000 to buy arms and vessels for an expedition to restore the order in the Mediterranean. Hillary had little in the way of financial resources to aid this ambition, but needed no persuasion to help in other ways:'I bear a strong predilection to the knightly dignity of past days when based on an honourable and truly chivalric foundation',[22] he wrote, explaining his long-standing admiration for the order. In grandly convoluted style he argued that the Knights' principles chimed with those of his lifeboat cause and that the two might help one another:

> May I not venture to hope that this great and sacred cause of the shipwrecked of every nation, may open a field for the generous effort of an order renowned for ages by their exploits on the ocean as on the field and so much in accordance with their chivalric valour.[23]

In truth, it wasn't only the knights' ideology that resonated with him. He loved the associated bravura and romance, finding solace in their traditions, ceremonies and sense of brotherhood. In the changing, challenging new Victorian age, these were values he understood – even if in many ways the order's world was one of fantasy and escape. The knights attached great importance to their members' ancestry, a subject Hillary had always found fascinating, and he needed little encouragement to re-examine his family history, highlighting his illustrious lineage and weaving it to that of the order: 'It is singular that in the chancel of the church of Danbury in Essex there lay the effigies of three ... ancestors – cross-legged knights of the order in armour,'[4] he told the order's secretary Sir Richard Broun, in one of his many long letters.

Hillary's self-promotional skills and connections to royalty (which he unashamedly played up whenever possible) made him exactly the sort of enthusiastic new recruit that Sir Richard Broun needed and the two men became firm friends – despite the fact they probably never met one another. Hillary was elected a Lieutenant Turcopolier of the langue and, although too ill to travel to London, fulfilled Broun's expectations, nominating new members and helping to stimulate interest in the order. His old friend the Duke of Sussex was one of the first illustrious contacts he tried to recruit. 'I ... immediately wrote to HRH ... availing myself of that liberty he kindly allows me strongly to urge on his consideration all those arguments, which in my mind plead in favour of his acceding to our wishes, and which I thought would impress him favourably towards them,'[25] he told his new friend.

The duke was reluctant to join the langue, excusing himself on the grounds of ill health: 'I wish I could get amongst the English friends of my youth we might enlist a few stalwart kings to the good cause, I also hope the fine season may bring some of them here',[26] Hillary frustratedly complained. When he heard that the holy city-port of Acre was under Turkish control he was inspired to write a pamphlet suggesting[27] that the Holy Land should be preserved in Christian control. A year later he continued the argument with a second pamphlet, *An Address to the Knights of St John on the Christian Occupation of the Holy Land*. In it Hillary adopts a quasi-medieval tone, 'entreating my brother knights of every langue of our noble fraternity, cordially, strenuously, and energetically to unite in advancing this great and sacred undertaking',[28] in other words to join him in setting out on a new crusade. Unsurprisingly, the publication drew much attention to the order and Hillary, but nothing came of its impractical suggestions.

Notes

1   *Mona's Herald*, 24 January 1837.
2   Bluett Papers, 09566/2/5, Bluett to Hillary, March 1837.
3   Belchem (ed.), *A New History of the Isle of Man*, vol. 5, p. 32.
4   Ibid.
5   A Manx patriot, *Manx Quarterly*, 14 September 1914.
6   Ibid.
7   Observations on the proposed changes in the fiscal and navigation laws of the Isle of Man addressed to the delegates from that island to His Majesty's Government, Hillary 1837.

8 Bluett Papers, Lawrence Craigie to J. Bluett, 28 March 1837.

9 *Manx Herald*, 14 March 1837.

10 *Manx Liberal*, 15 April 1837.

11 Bluett Papers, 09566/1/18, 4 April 1837.

12 *Mona's Herald*, 30 May 1837.

13 Bluett Papers, 09566/1/14, 28 March 1837.

14 National Maritime Museum Archive, record of a letter from Hillary to London Committee, 1 March 1837.

15 Ibid.

16 Bluett Papers, 09566/1/19, WH to J. Bluett, 7 April 1837.

17 *Manx Herald*, 24 October 1835.

18 RNLI Archive, f.57, WH to Edwards, 9 April 1845.

19 Belchem (ed.), *New History of the Isle of Man*, vol. 5, pp. 36-42.

20 *Manx Sun*, 22 June 1838.

21 Order of St John Archive, WH to Sir R. Broun, 24 Sept 1838.

22 Order of St John Archive, WH to Sir R. Broun, 19 May 1838.

23 Order of St John Archive, WH to Sir R. Broun, 13 June 1838.

24 Ibid.

25 Order of St John Archive, WH to Sir R. Broun, 27 February 1839.

26 Order of St John Archive, WH to Sir R. Broun, 1 April 1839.

27 Suggestions for the Christian reoccupation of the Holy Land as a sovereign state by the Order of St John of Jerusalem.

28 T. Riley-Smith, *The Oxford Illustrated History of the Crusades*, p. 371.

15

The Final Maelstrom

Some years ago I was induced to purchase some beautifully situated property,
part of the demesne of the late Duke of Atholl overlooking Douglas Bay,
which held out the promise of making a very large return. I also took shares
in a joint stock bank then establishing here and as they were at first profuse in
their advances – in an ill hour I considerably extended my first instructions
and was congratulated by my friends on the certainty of their success. But the
prospect more recently became over clouded – the great pressure for the last
two years on the monetary affairs of the whole empire has in its consequences
still more heavily affected this island, property has become un-saleable even for
half its prior worth, and our bank, which was wretchedly conducted, become
themselves embarrassed …

Sir William Hillary to Sir Richard Broun, 8 March 1841

Hillary had always had a gift for reinvention and escape. He liked to portray himself as a loyal subject and member of the establishment, but his had been a chameleon life. He had swapped the life of a Liverpool merchant and left his Quaker family for the glamour of royal service. He had married 'up', joined the gentry – and then bought his way to royal notice and ennoblement. During his life on the Isle of Man he had erased the shame of bankruptcy and a failed marriage with selfless campaigning. Through the Shipwreck Institution he had been vindicated and become a heroic figure. And, in later years, as he variously speculated in mining, property and banking ventures, actively (if controversially) participated in of the island's political reform and championed the Order of St John, his respectable image was maintained. But his strength, political adroitness and good fortune were not limitless and, in the final decade of his life, avoiding the shoals of misfortune was to prove impossible.

An inkling of the difficulties that lay ahead came at the close of 1837, when it became clear that the development at Falcon Cliff would be less lucrative than he had hoped. The property boom had failed to materialise, many of the plots were unsold and the bank was pressing for repayments on outstanding loans. Rather than take the customary route of selling the property under duress and losing money, Hillary opted, with typical bravura, for a novel means of disposal – one that he gambled would be more profitable.

He organised a lottery. The land, divided into 100 plots, was the prize for the 1,800 tickets he would offer for sale, priced at £5 each. If all the tickets sold, he stood to make a fraction of the profit he had hoped for – but it would more than cover his costs. There was, he knew, a real risk that the tickets would fail to sell and his losses would be substantial. But, just like the danger he had often faced setting out to sea on stormy nights, it was a risk he ignored.

Tickets went on sale in May 1838, and were widely advertised in the press. The draw was scheduled for the end of the tourist season, in mid-September, to give both islanders and the holidaymakers who flocked to the island over the summer months ample opportunity to buy tickets. The strategy might have worked better had the summer not turned out to be a washout. As it was, persistent rains and gloomy skies meant the usual influx of holidaymakers did not materialise and tickets sales were disappointing. Nevertheless, as the date appointed for the draw grew closer there was a palpable sense of anticipation. 'The interest in this scheme increases in a ration scarcely to be expected', reported the *Mona's Herald* the day before the draw, detailing the equipment and procedures planned to ensure all was above board. Adding to the suspense, the paper also revealed that, 'Sir William Hillary intends after the sale of a certain number of tickets (and we believe that number is nearly approached) to suspend the remainder for sale and take the chances on his own shoulders'.[1]

The draw lasted for two days. 'The fever of expectation has now subsided into the ague of disappointment',[2] reported the *Manx Liberal* when it was all over. Hillary had not only raised nearly £6,000 from the sale of his tickets, which he duly paid into the bank to offset the loans, but had also profited by buying the unsold tickets and winning one of the more valuable lots.

The setbacks connected with his investment in the Joint Stock Bank could not be resolved so smoothly. Hillary, along with his fellow shareholders, had gradually become aware that Wulff and Forbes were not the irreproachable bankers they had portrayed themselves to be. Their previous banking enterprise had been saddled with bad debts that were now discovered to have been covertly absorbed into the Joint Stock Bank when the two merged. Added to this, a succession of improvident loans made since the new bank's formation had swallowed up the capital put up by shareholders – a fact hidden until the situation became too desperate to conceal. Discovering the bank's mismanagement, the press whipped up public fury. 'The swindle – for we can call it by no milder name was accomplished and the "prince of jugglers" (Forbes, who was the bank's manager) now entrusted with unlimited powers, placed in a more favourable position than ever to carry on his reckless speculations with the resources and credit of the bank',[3] stormed the *Manx Herald*.

Had the bank's manager and directors come clean, the failure would have been damaging but not catastrophic for its investors. But Forbes continued to dissemble, falsifying accounts and, contrary to the caution he claimed to advocate, continuing to advance unsecured loans for several more months. It would later transpire that tens of thousands of pounds of unsecured loans were advanced to various creditors – not least £10,000 to Don Carlos, a Spanish pretender, 'to support divine right despotism and the inquisition in Spain'.[4] Worse still, according to Hillary, the money raised from the lottery that he had paid into the bank also disappeared without ever being credited against his outstanding loans.[5]

When the unpalatable truth emerged, Forbes was dismissed and fled the island and a new manager was installed. Wulff also escaped justice, dying in 1840. Eventually, nearly £100,000 in bad debts would fall upon the shareholders, including the beleaguered Hillary, who was threatened with legal repercussions when he failed to pay his losses. Bitterly he told Broun:

> Our bank, which was wretchedly conducted, become themselves embarrassed and seek redress by turning round on all to whom they had before been so lavish in their advances, and in resentment that I resisted some most oppressive attempts to dictate unwarrantable exaction from me (when they were already amply received), and which I was in honour bound to resist – with the shortest possible notice; they took legal proceedings which by the laws of this island are most prompt and severe.[6]

Cornered by debts of over £3,500, and without any proof of the fraud perpetrated against him, Hillary could see little alternative but to put his beloved Fort Anne, which was still legally registered in the name of his mysterious and loyal companion Sarah St John, on the market. 'The principal apartments are large, arranged with great taste and judgment ... with mahogany doors and plate glass in the windows ... the entrance is through a conservatory nearly sixty feet long', read the advertisements that appeared in all the newspapers. But despite the evident attractions of the mansion, its six acres of land and extensive sea frontage, no buyer came forward at the price needed to repay the outstanding loans and debts. Fort Anne became blighted by whispers that he should never have paid £1,800 for the house in the first place, nor should the bank have advanced £3,500 against it.

Hillary's embarrassment was compounded when the bank refused to honour his cheques to tradesmen. With Fort Anne unsold, he needed to raise funds quickly and decided to sell his prized art collection. He put a brave face on his crumbling circumstances. Pretending he disposed of his collection willingly, he wrote to Broun, 'I am now actively engaged in disposing of my property as speedily as I can, so that as years advance upon me I fancy I have more leisure for those objects and pursuits more congenial to my mind and feelings'.[7] According to one account, he intended to auction his pictures in England but was prevented from doing so when an injunction was secretly taken out by his creditors and the pictures crated and loaded on a ship in the harbour were seized.[8] Meanwhile further light was shed on his dismal circumstances when a court hearing was told much of the collection legally belonged to Sarah St John and therefore was not his to sell. Hillary had used the artworks as security against loans she had advanced him in 1825 and had never repaid.[9] His shares in the Laxey Mine were also appropriated, and, even though he put on a show of resignation, there were times when the facade slipped and his frustrations became visible in his letters to Broun:

> I have sold property of mine of considerable value for less than half its worth, owing to the state of the times and the manner in which I have too much reason to believe they purposely conducted the sale, and all my efforts are for the present requisite to avert still further injuries, from a set of vindictive, low minded men, whom from my heart I despise, but who unhappily have the power and the will to wound and a malignant pleasure in oppressing their superiors.

Hillary knew that the actions taken against him had been endorsed or even prompted by a hostile cabal in the House of Keys. Occasionally, worn down by their actions, he persuaded himself that they had won the battle. But mostly he remained firm, telling himself that his ordeals were tests of his true metal, and that moral and social superiority were defences against the disarray:

> I shall weather the storm and think not ... I am cast down or subdued – my indignant feelings have supported and will support me through, and I trust that I am now taking such measures as may defeat their further march, though (not) I may say with joy, and now they scoff at me whose fathers I would have disdained and should have sat with the dogs of my flock. To the dispensation of

providence I hope that I know how, humbly to submit – but to the tyranny and aggression of man alone I never will bow.

Were this not the act of only a few, disavowed and execrated by all which is good and honourable in the community, I should feel disgusted at receiving such treatment as this, in a land whose honour and best interests I had so long and so greatly prompted. From the Governor, the Bishop and other high minded men, I have received the <u>most marked countenance and support</u> in these unexpected affairs.[10]

The treatment meted out to him was undeniably hurtful and profoundly shook his affection for his adopted home. In March 1841, he told Broun bitterly:

The link which so long bound me to these shores is severed – I shall wind up all my affairs here, as speedily as I can and then take my leave of them, perhaps forever – and in other lands, most probably in England and on the continent I shall find pursuits congenial to my mind and feelings and where they may have a wider range, than cramped up in this narrow sphere.[11]

Even so, the hostile conspiracy was not infallible. Somehow, he managed to save three dozen of the best pictures from the bailiff's clutches, ship them to England and sell them at auction in Manchester. The *Manchester Guardian* reported the 'valuable and choice collection of original paintings principally by ancient masters which lately formed part of the collection of Sir William Hillary, Bart at Fort Anne, Isle of Man and have been removed here for the convenience of sale'.

The pictures included highly regarded old masters: 'a landscape with figures by Salvador Rosa, a *Portrait of Jan Cornelius Silvius* by Rembrandt, *The Woman Taken in Adultery* by Poussin, *Christ after his Resurrection* by Carracci and the *Incredulity of St Thomas* by Murillo'.[12] For a man who prided himself on his patronage of the arts, the list is a revealing one – these are all works by European masters, the sort of things an observant young man would have seen eighteenth-century aristocrats buy on the grand tour. Times and fashions had changed since Hillary's formative youth in Italy and yet his taste had not. There is no sign here of the vogue for new British painters – no Turner, no Constable, no Landseer. The world of art as well as political privilege had left him stranded.

It was humiliating to lose the trappings of his world, but the reversal of fortune reinforced Hillary's commitment to the Shipwreck Institution. He reminded himself that his efforts were needed as much as ever. In the new Victorian age, charitable good works were much in vogue: 'We live in an age when humanity is in fashion', announced the *London Magazine*, as a social conscience began to be seen as much a sign of refinement as a smart new carriage. 'There are swarms of societies engaged in good works, societies for saving the life of drowning persons, for the ... advancement of science, for the protection of animals, for the suppression of vice',[13] noted Hippolyte Taine, a French scholar and visitor to mid-nineteenth-century London. In Hillary's opinion, it was hard to think of a subject more closely connected with everyone's lives than shipwreck. But the Royal Humane Society (founded in 1774 to resuscitate people who had drowned) and the Shipwrecked Mariner's Benevolent Society (which took care of people after rescue) overlapped in public consciousness and competition from these and other needy causes had stemmed the flow of money, leaving the institution chronically underfunded.

Burdened by financial worry and restricted by poor health, 'almost confined to the house and nearly reduced to a skeleton',[14] Hillary could easily have ignored the problem and left others to take up the baton, but to do so was as unthinkable as it had always been. 'My mental energies and my devotion to this great object of my pursuit remain unimpaired',[15] he assured his old friend. Once before the institution had saved him from scandal. Now, in fighting for its survival, he found purpose and, in some measure, shelter from his own sadly straitened circumstances.

The Central Committee were so hard pressed they failed to publish an annual report, let alone hold their usual annual dinner, and were unable to maintain regional stations without drawing on their invested capital. On the Isle of Man, subscriptions to fund the four lifeboats had dwindled to dangerously low figures. Hillary had donated more than £100 for repairs and maintenance but, facing bankruptcy as he was, this could not continue. Fearing that the island's stations would be forced to close, on 1 November 1838 he wrote to the Home Secretary, Lord Russell, asking for financial aid. He argued forcefully that the island was a unique case; the four stations in Douglas, Ramsey, Peel and Castletown gave assistance to shipping that was mostly not based on the Isle of Man. The island's resources could not be expected to meet these costs indefinitely: 'our efforts, our expenditure are all employed not for insular purposes alone, but for the benefit of the shipping and that state aid should be provided.' Russell responded curtly and without sympathy. 'Similar institutions are left to private benevolence.'[16] The Isle of Man was no different from anywhere else.

Despite the chilly retort, the institution's funding crisis was temporarily alleviated by an unexpected tragedy. At dawn on 7 September 1838 William Darling, keeper of the Longstone Lighthouse on the Farne Islands, off the Northumbrian coast, was woken by his 22-year-old daughter Grace. A storm had blown up overnight, and Grace had spotted the outline of the paddle steamship *Forfarshire* wrecked on a nearby rocky island and now apparently broken in two. Using the lighthouse telescope, Darling scanned the distance for survivors. To begin with he saw none, but as light improved he picked out the outlines of what appeared to be three or four people clambering on the rock. Assuming the weather was too bad for the lifeboat to be launched from the station at Seahouses, Grace and her father launched the lighthouse's coble (a 24ft open boat) and set out. They rowed a circuitous route of over a mile to avoid exposing themselves to the worst of the mountainous sea and raging wind. On reaching the rock they found nine survivors – eight men and one woman. Of the sixty-two people on board the *Forfarshire*, everyone else had drowned. Nine passengers was too many for the diminutive coble to carry in one trip, and Darling and his daughter decided they would have to make two journeys, Grace remaining on the lighthouse to look after the rescued passengers while her father and three men went back for the rest. The lifeboat from Seahouses reached the island later that day, but the storm remained so severe that it would be three days before it was able to take the survivors back to the mainland.

When the story of Grace's role in the rescue reached the newspapers she was feted as the embodiment of ideal Victorian womanhood and became a national heroine. Subscriptions were raised for her (Queen Victoria sent £50), artists and poets were inspired by her and medals were awarded to her by both the Humane Society and the Shipwreck Institution. There was a further unexpected consequence of the public interest in the story. As the subject of shipwrecks was brought so powerfully to the forefront of public attention, donations to the Shipwreck Institution flooded in, more than ten-fold from the previous year, to £1,276. Even today Grace's renown lives on, eclipsing Hillary, and she is widely believed to have founded the institution.

The upturn in the institution's fortunes was short-lived, and three years later the situation had again become desperate. Rejoining the fray, Hillary sent his earlier correspondence with Russell to the newspapers. If he had learned anything over the years, it was the importance of galvanising the press's support:

> I speak not for myself; it is a cause to which from every impulse of my mind and every sense of duty, I have devoted my best, as well as my declining years – in which I have suffered many severe personal injuries … other nations have taken higher views of this subject: the enlightened kings of Holland – of Denmark – of Sweden, and other sovereigns, have deigned to express to me their most flattering approbation – they have adopted this cause as their own … but in the greatest, the most powerful empire on the globe, after mature deliberation, the government have declared, that the preservation of the very supporters of her

ocean throne shall be left, in the last extremity of peril, to the spontaneous aid
of a benevolent people. Is this my Lord, the final resolve?[17]

To underline the importance of his cause, he added an account of the rescue
of the *St George* and a copy of Lord Exmouth's admiring letter, pointing out an
obvious injustice: since the foundation of the Isle of Man branch alone, more
than 500 lives had been saved from vessels unconnected to the Isle of Man, by
boats mainly funded and manned by the impoverished island community.

The press seized on the story, backing his argument, and a flurry of editorials
condemned Russell as much for 'a coldness peculiar to his Lordship' as for his
rejection of the plea for government funding. This was exactly the response for
which Hillary had hoped. Press criticism and comment outweighed the blow of
Russell's refusal. By ensuring the institution remained in the news, even without
government help it would cling to life.

In months overshadowed with financial worry and ill health, Hillary was
also kept busy by the resurrection of the old debate over fiscal integration with
Britain. Asked to represent the island in discussions, despite his frailty, he did not
turn down the invitation. In a letter to Broun, flattered, but conscious of the
complexities of his role, he wrote:

> I have again been called into action by the crisis which is at hand in the position
> of this island with the British government. My situation in the discharge of this
> office was from circumstance delicate and difficult – many of those for and with
> whom I have to act approach more to the democratic class, whilst I am regarded
> in this island as aristocratic ... but the people have rights and privileges which
> have long been either neglected or withheld, and abuses have crept in which
> have roused the public energies.[18]

His delicate path was smoothed by the intervention of Dr John Bowring. The
MP for Bolton promoted the island's interests, advocating free trade, and eventually succeeded in pushing through reforms that were broadly seen as beneficial.
When the controversy was resolved in 1844 Bowring visited the Isle of Man, and
was given a hero's welcome. He modestly played down his part in the changes,
instead reminding islanders of Hillary's efforts on their behalf with a public accolade: 'You bore the burthen and the heat of the day; however we must mutually
congratulate one another at the gathering in of the harvest.'[19]

Hillary savoured the compliment because, temporarily at least, his pressing concern connected to the bank had lifted. 'Since their books and papers have been
placed in the hands of a receiver some most extraordinary and disgraceful cor-

respondence have come to light, and strong hopes are entertained that William's Deacon etc [the London clearing house] demand will be overthrown and if so the community will be relieved from heavy responsibility', he told Broun. He was hopeful that there might be some proof of the misappropriation of his money – although he admitted, 'as you may suppose these recent pursuits have called for more effort than my half renovated constitution was equal to'.[20]

His health had deteriorated as a result of a serious fall: one night at Fort Anne he slipped on the stairs on his way to bed, 'and was precipitated backward with much force'. Hillary was unconscious when he was discovered and remained so for some time. A hastily summoned doctor testified to the severity of his injuries. He had suffered 'several severe contusions and bruises on the head and other parts of his person … and remained some time insensible', announced the press, going on to reassure readers that 'though still very weak' he was out of bed and on the road to recovery.[21]

The financial respite was predictably short-lived. An enquiry found there was no evidence that Forbes had embezzled his lottery money and by 1845, Hillary was once again besieged by demands to pay losses which he had no resources to meet. The liabilities overshadowed not only his own life, but those of the people closest to him. He had registered shares in the bank in the names of Emma, Sarah St John and his son Augustus, who had been developing his colliery in Cockermouth. Augustus was declared bankrupt – an event widely and humiliatingly featured in the newspapers. Meanwhile, Sarah St John, his long-standing friend and companion, aged only 53, fell gravely ill. The newspaper announcement of her death in April 1845 tells us only that she died 'at Fort Anne the residence of Sir William Hillary Baronet and after a protracted illness, in the 53rd year of her age, deeply regretted'.[22] We do not know to what extent, if any, her illness was connected to the strain of her financial circumstances, but it is hard not to believe there was some connection.

What is beyond question is that Sarah St John's untimely death added profound personal sorrow and further complication to Hillary's life. Until now Fort Anne had to some extent been protected from his creditors by being officially registered in Sarah's name. Before illness overwhelmed her she had tried to protect Hillary, naming him the executor of her will but making Emma her beneficiary and leaving her Fort Anne 'for her life and separate use and free from the routroul of her present and future husband and not subject or liable to his debts or engagements.'[23] Presumably they all three knew the measure would provide only limited protection: Emma was also a shareholder in the doomed bank – but the claims against her were probably substantially less than those against Hillary after the debacle of the missing Falcon's Cliff money. However, Sarah's careful actions proved futile – and a worse calamity was to follow. Soon after Sarah's death, Emma fell seriously ill.

Hillary's second marriage had been one of profound happiness and the prospect of losing Emma on top of everything else he faced was unbearable. Miserably he told Broun of the 'severe domestic afflictions which have in succession come upon me ... my mind has been so much distressed ... Thank God my dearest wife has for the last two days been a little better, but I feel too truly that her situation is still most critical and I am too much absorbed in this overwhelming evil to be able to give my mind to other subjects'.[24]

His worst fears were realised the following day, when Emma relapsed and died shortly afterwards, according to a newspaper report, from an illness, 'borne with exemplary fortitude'[25] An inconsolable Hillary buried her in St George's Churchyard, in a vault to the right of the main entrance. The inscription bears testimony to his utter devastation:

> Within this vault repose the remains of Emma, Lady Hillary, the youngest child of Patrick Tobin ... and the dearly lamented wife of the Hon William Hillary Baronet. To him who has survived the affectionate and devoted partner of his life, her loss is irreparable. The remembrance of her many virtues inspires him with the firm belief that through the Divine mercy there is awarded to her a peace and an everlasting resting-place, which he humbly hopes to be permitted to share with her beyond the grave. She departed this life at Fort Anne on 20th June, 1845, aged 62 years.

Without Emma to defend him, the circling creditors closed in. After months of legal wrangling, Hillary's claim to have been the victim of fraudulent practice was dismissed. He was forced to move out of Fort Anne and the house was sold at a suspiciously low price to a developer who would convert it into a luxury hotel. For Hillary, who had lavished so much effort and money on the property, this must have been a galling moment, but he maintained a dignified front and some months later told Broun he had moved to 'a small but very gentlemanly house beautifully situated with fine prospects over our bay'. The house was at Woodville, ironically one, the residences built as part of the ill-fated Falcon Cliff development that had marked the beginning of his financial undoing.

But behind the courageous carapace, the shock of it all had taken its toll: 'Since my removal from Fort Anne I have been more than usually unwell and have suffered much in body and mind from the harness of both',[26] he revealed. In these dark times, his connection with the Knights of St John and the Shipwreck Institution were all that was left: 'Our illustrious fraternity, the welfare of which (and of the shipwreck cause) find the warmest place that is left in my almost desolate heart,' he told Broun sadly. Even so, as the anniversary of Emma's death approached, his sense of purpose seemed to fade and grief overwhelmed him:

> This is a moment when I feel most bitterly my irretrievable lost. Saturday the 20th will be the first anniversary of that severe dispensation of the Divine will which has thrown the darkest cloud over all my earthly hopes. Alas my dear friend, my mind is of that cast that my dearest affections are rooted there forever and the grim return of that fatal day revives if possible every recollection of the past <u>still more strongly in my … recollection.</u>[27]

He would live for six more sorrowful months, without writing any more letters to his old friend. Then, in the first week of the new year of 1847, as the winter winds blew into the bay and milky waves pounded the rocks wreathing the Tower of Refuge, his formidable strength finally weakened. He died peacefully, confident that he would be reunited with Emma. His friend, J. J. Rogers, wrote to Broun on the following day:

> I regret exceedingly to inform you of the death of our old and respected friend Sir William Hillary, which took place (in his 78th year) and an early hour yesterday morning. His mind was previously quite resigned and at peace. He has indeed left us for a brighter better life, but we have to deplore the loss of one of the highest minded philanthropists that ever dwelt upon our shores.[28]

He was buried ten days later,[29] as he had wished, alongside his beloved Emma, in the vault he had built for her. Curiously, however, there was almost no mention of his funeral in the press, nor was his name inscribed alongside Emma's on the tomb. Whether this omission was connected to Hillary's impoverished circumstances, or to shelter him from his dangerous enemies – perhaps a means of protecting the body from seizure by creditors until relatives paid his outstanding debts – or whether, in the absence of any close family remaining on the island, it was an accidental oversight, remains open to speculation.

Augustus, named as his beneficiary and executor, inherited his title, and could surely have done something to commemorate his father's final resting place, but he did not. Nor did his wife's powerful relatives, the Christians, or Emma's family, the Tobins. After his bankruptcy Sir Augustus (as he was now) avoided the Isle of Man and divided his time between London and France. When in London he would occasionally attend meetings of the Shipwreck Institution, although his role was not an active one as his father's had been. Five years later, having dabbled in various business ventures, including insurance and railway companies, his financial difficulties overtook him and he was declared an 'outlaw' in the press – doubtless as a result of unpaid debts.[30] He outlived his father by only seven years, dying in 1854. His widow seems to have been more conscious of Hillary's legacy than he was. Two decades after her father-in-law's death she presented the institution with the portrait of Hillary that still hangs in the RNLI headquarters.[31]

Whatever the reasons for his unmarked grave, Hillary's passing was not devoid of tribute. Those who relied on the sea to earn their living – the herring fishermen, the crews on sailing vessels, the skippers of harbour boats, the sailors and masters of the new paddle steamers – would always hold him in high regard. To them he was 'the mariner's friend': he had battled on their behalf to make their perilous lives safer, and his reduced circumstances were no reason to forget him. According to one newspaper account, as news of Hillary's death spread, every ship in Douglas harbour displayed its flag at half-mast.[32] Another journalist said his funeral procession was followed by crowds 'who had witnessed his heroism and self-devotion in saving the life of the shipwrecked mariner'.[33]

Obituaries in the Manx and British press spoke of Hillary as 'a man not less distinguished for his great philanthropy than for his unceasing endeavours to promote the honour and welfare of his country'. Even the London papers noted that he had personally been responsible for saving the lives of some 500 people (the figure is open to debate) and, with characteristic Victorian loftiness, implied that his illustrious lineage was somehow connected to his extraordinary valour: 'he was sprung of a family than which there are few of higher antiquity',[34] the *Chronicle* explained. The *Morning Post*, singled out his writing as further proof of his elevated stature, and thought it: 'remarkable for the great elegance, perspicuity and force'.[35] Both in London and on the Isle of Man, there was general agreement that of all his feats, one stood apart: 'his indefatigable exertion in alone originating, and by the distinguished patronage bestowed upon him subsequently, in establishing the Royal National Institution for the Preservation of Life from Shipwreck'. Oddly, few of the writers mentioned his personal efforts in saving lives, or the fact that his four gold awards (two medals and two bars) were unmatched by anyone else. His record would remain until the twentieth century, when Henry Blogg of Cromer was awarded three gold medals and four silver.

Only one commentator went further and acknowledged the political enmity he had confronted in his later years. The *Mona's Herald* saw Hillary's persecution by a cabal of the island's conservative elite as a further badge of heroism:

> The most illustrious benefactors of mankind who have adorned the annals of history have received but a poor reward from the hands of their contemporaries

... it is therefore, almost a matter of course, that the powers that be, will rise up against a reformer – make his name hateful to community, as far as detraction can accomplish it; shut him out from the pale of good society to the utmost of their power, and caution everyone against his influence.

Here was the amiable, the benevolent, the philanthropic Sir William Hillary, who alas! is no more ... he came to the island more than thirty years ago, in the fullness of his intellectual strength, and during this long period, has faithfully and disinterestedly devoted his brilliant energies to the good of the people of this island, as their generous benefactor and friend ... But alas ... he mingled in his enlarged schemes of philanthropy sentiments of political reform – he thought the people ought to be represented in their legislature ... that they should not remain serfs and slaves ... this was enough – the ban of proscription placed upon him by the clique, has been marked – he suffered as a reformer ... when the sunlight of truth shall beam on posterity, virtuous actions will meet their reward, the name of Sir William Hillary will be cherished and loved.[36]

It would be many decades before this optimistic prediction was fulfilled. There was no mention made of his passing in the minute books of the central committee and five years passed before the institution agreed to provide Douglas with a new lifeboat named 'in memory of the distinguished services of the late Sir William Hillary, Bart, who was the projector of the Shipwreck Institution and who personally assisted at the saving of 305 lives of persons shipwrecked in Douglas Bay'.[37] Occasional efforts by members of the local lifeboat society were made to identify Hillary's final resting place, but for more than seventy years his tomb was left to fall into disrepair, unnamed. When the General Secretary of the RNLI visited the Isle of Man in 1920, he was mortified to discover the founder's resting place crumbling and overgrown with weeds. With long overdue determination he made swift arrangements for the installation of a marble memorial slab and for the tomb to be repaired. The first inscription on his tomb credited Hillary with having helped save 305 lives, although after a public outcry this figure was amended to read 509.[38]

Yet if his grave and name were long forgotten, his pioneering efforts on behalf of stranded sailors were not. In the years immediately following his death, the Shipwreck Institution teetered on, sometimes seeming on the brink of foundering from lack of funds, but sustained by public concern and the sporadic efforts of writers such as Charles Dickens, who wrote of the lifeboat men of Goodwin Sands:

These are among the bravest and most skilful mariners that exist. Let a gale rise and swell into a storm; let a sea run that might appal the stoutest heart that ever beat ... these men spring up with an activity so dauntless, so valiant and heroic, that the world cannot surpass it.[39]

Four years after Hillary's death, in 1851, the institution reached a turning point. It was now under the presidency of the Duke of Northumberland, and the aptly titled Sailor Duke tried to reawaken public involvement with a competition and prize of 100 guineas for a new lifeboat design. Fifty of the best models were exhibited at the Great Exhibition in Hyde Park. The winning entry was a self-righting boat with twelve oars and a sail designed by James Beeching of Yarmouth. The competition went some way to recapturing media attention but did not adequately repair the institution's desperate finances. Donations became so scarce that the committee were only able to fulfil their 'sacred mission of saving poor creatures from perishing when shipwrecked on our coasts' by a continued drain on its small funded capital.[40]

Realising the need for radical action, the Duke secured a government subsidy of £2,000 and at this point Hillary's Royal National Shipwreck Institution was rechristened the Royal National Lifeboat Institution. The government grants helped with the installation of new stations and with the maintenance of existing ones, but fifteen years later, the Duke had steered the institution so well that this help was no longer needed. Ever since, the RNLI has maintained political independence and relies, as it did in Hillary's day, solely on private donations.

What of the legacy of the man himself? Hillary's life and career echoed the ideologies of his age. His was a world of rapid change in which status still mattered but the rules and priorities of society were evolving. In this unregulated, shifting world, banks and boats could founder in an instant, however invulnerable they appeared. It was a confident world, where leadership and good deeds were seen as signs of civilisation, a world where a charismatic young man instilled with romantic idealism, steely determination and a splash of self-interest could stir things up and make things happen.

There may be no easy answers as to why Hillary's name has never been mythologised as many other nineteenth-century pioneers have been, but historical oversight does not render his existence or his achievement less significant. As an island race, the sea will always be indivisible from British identity. It is no longer our only highway to the wider world; technology has greatly tamed the waves, but it remains a crucial mode of transport and there are still times when systems fail and nature fights back. It is for this reason that, even today, a sturdy link traverses the currents of time and anchors Hillary to us, and his institution, the RNLI, maintains its hold on the nation's heart.

Notes

1 *Mona's Herald*, 11 September 1838.
2 *Manx Liberal*, 22 September 1838.
3 *Manx Herald*, 5 September 1843.
4 Ibid.
5 Kelly, *Those in Peril*
6 Order of St John Archive, WH to Sir R. Broun, 8 March 1841.
7 Order of St John Archive, WH to Sir R. Broun, 30 July 1841.
8 According to Kelly (pp. 104-05) the paintings were seized whilst on board the sloop *Gazelle* en route to Liverpool.
9 *Mona's Herald*, 19 January 1841.
10 Order of St John Archive, WH to Sir R. Broun, 8 March 1841.
11 Ibid.
12 *Manchester Guardian*, 14 August 1841.
13 Quoted by Gertrude Himmelfarb in 'The age of philanthropy', the Wilson quarterly, 1976.
14 Ibid.
15 Ibid.
16 Appeal to Lord John Russell, 15 January 1842.
17 Ibid.
18 Order of St John Archive, WH to Sir R. Broun,15 April 1844.
19 *Manx Sun*, 10 August 1844.
20 Order of St John Archive, WH to Sir R. Broun, 15 April 1844.
21 *Morning Post, Mona's Herald, Standard*, 16 December 1843.
22 *Manx Liberal*, 19 April 1845.
23 Kelly, *Those in Peril*, p. 134.
24 Order of St John Archive, WH to Sir R. Broun, 19 June 1845.
25 *Mona's Herald*, 25 June 1845.
26 Order of St John Archive, 28 March 1846.
27 Order of St John Archive, WH to Sir R. Broun, 18 June 1846.
28 Order of St John Archive, J.J. Rogers to Sir R. Broun, 6 January 1847.
29 S. Norris, *Manx Memories*, p. 53.
30 *Standard*, 1 January 1854.
31 RNLI Archive minute books, V, 6 June 1867, p. 100.
32 *Manx Liberal*, 9 January 1847.
33 *Manx Quarterly*, 5 November, 1908, p. 501.
34 *Morning Chronicle*, 9 January 1847.
35 *Morning Post*, 11 January 1847 – The *Morning Chronicle* and *Gentleman's Magazine* also included tributes.
36 *Monas Herald*, 20 January 1847.
37 RNLI Archive; minute book R, 22 July 1852, pp. 24–5.
38 Unpublished Report in the RNLI archive compiled by Dennis J. Horgan, 1987, p. 201.
39 Charles Dickens, *Household Words*, quoted in O. Warner, *The Lifeboat Service*, (1974) p. 21.
40 *The Standard*, 8 December 1854.

Epilogue

I believe I am the only person alive who has received personal recollections
and descriptions, from those who knew him, of Sir William Hillary, the
founder of the Royal National Lifeboat Institution ... Call it hero-worship
if you like, but the fate of this great public benefactor during his life and
the neglect of his memory after death, is strange and remarkable – so full of
extraordinary mystery and tragedy and coincidence that it contains all the
essentials for a drama, or the subject of an epic poem.

Manx Memories and Movements: A Journalist's Recollections, Samuel Norris, 1938

When I visited Douglas I did so without expectations – I had never
been to the Isle of Man before, and went there for the purpose of
researching this book, to consult archives and library records, the
slivers of fact with which to piece together Hillary's story. I timed my visit badly –
it was Tynwald week and the library within the Manx Museum was closed when
I had expected it to be open, but I had booked my tickets and, reluctant to alter
my plans, I decided I would kill the hours until the archives were open by seeking
out the remaining traces of Hillary's life within the town.

I did not have far to look. Arriving at my hotel I was shown into a room with
a picture window overlooking the bay. I had seen many images of the Tower of
Refuge but nothing had prepared me for the reality of the crenulated building
that sprouts like a Hollywood fantasy from the jagged black mound off shore.
I stood transfixed. Much in the panorama laid out before me bore comparison to
Hillary's day. Gulls zigzagged and screamed in the grey-washed sky as they have
always done; the wind still tufted the pewter sea with white peaks. But much

had also changed. The twenty-first-century landscape of Douglas is not the awe-inspiring natural wilderness admired by Wordsworth and patrolled by Hillary. The bay has been transformed into a sturdily built esplanade, busy with traffic and shops and hotels with large lettering touting panoramic sea views like mine. There are a lot of banks – the island is still a financial haven, but in the opposite sense from Hillary's day. Now it is wealthy people who run there to shelter themselves rather than impoverished gentlemen in reduced circumstances.

All this urbanisation has had the effect of shrinking the natural landscape, making it seem smaller and safer. On the calm day I arrived, the sand glistened with the receding tide. People strolled across the beach and waded out to the fearsome Conister Rock that has claimed many ships and lives.

But if Hillary's name has been swept away in the ebb and flow of British history, in Douglas at least he is commemorated. On the sea front, opposite his tower, there are manicured gardens with a plaque depicting his valiant rescue of the *St George* and an inscription outlining the story. Follow the winding streets beyond the seafront, up the hill behind and you come to St George's Churchyard where his grave lies. These days it is conspicuously surrounded by freshly painted railings and carefully maintained. Each year, on the anniversary of his death, a memorial service is held here. The island's dignitaries assemble with members of the RNLI, suitably seafaring hymns are sung and a wreath in the form of an anchor is laid on his grave. From what I have learned of his character, Hillary would be pleased, I think, to be remembered in such a way.

But my strongest sense of the thread that connects Hillary to the present day, comes not here, but when I retrace my steps, walk around the bay, cross the harbour bridge, and take the road that leads up the headland. I walk past the stark white stuccoed edifice that has been rebuilt on the site of his beloved Fort Anne, past houses that cluster where once his gardens bloomed, to an area of rough grassland beyond. Here stands his statue: larger than life size, and like the man himself clad in ankle-length oil skins and heftyy boots. The statue's surface has been muted by inclement wind and rain to shades of mottled verdigris. His face is craggy and heavy-featured. I gaze at him staring intently over my head and out to sea. He seems to be poised, as if searching for someone to rescue, ready to jump into a lifeboat and set off through the surf. In a way this is no illusion. He is ready, because down below, invisible in a sturdy boathouse, the modern Douglas lifeboat sits ready on its ramp. The vessel is named for him – *Sir William Hillary* – and, as the man himself once did, it awaits the next call.

Bibliography

Manuscript Sources

Archive of the Order of St John: Hillary Letters.

British Library: add MS 38379: ad 40390; ad 40382;.

Cornwall Records Office: DDX498/52; DDx498/31; DDx498/59.

Essex Records Office: D/DQC/2/3; D/DQ55/115; D/dop/D/Drh f25/12; D/ Dmy/15m50/84/12.

Library of the Society of Friends, London: MS vol. 338f193; TEMP MSS 745/ HR3/p11.

London Metropolitan Archives: acc 76/1098b.

Manx National Heritage Library and Archives: MS00414C; MS 01245A; MS02331C; MD10075; MS09909; MS02341; MS 9566/1-4; Bluett Papers, Correspondence between W.H. and John Bluett; Minute Book of Committee of Kirk Lonan Mining Association 1822–28; Minute Book of Proprietors of the Laxey Mining Company/Laxey Mining Association 1829–48.

National Archives: Letters of Sir William Hamilton 1798–99; Slave Compensation Records T71/1215 and T71/1381, St James; Will of Isaac Lascelles Wynne, PRO B 11/1916; Will of Hannah Hillary, online; PRO B 11/1749. .

National Maritime Museum Archive: MSS 85/040.

RNLI Archive: Sir William Hillary, Letters addressed to the Shipwreck Institution 1824–45; Minutes of the Committee of the Royal National Institution for the Preservation of Life from Shipwreck; Letters accepting or declining office 1824.

Senate House: Simon Taylor Papers, reel 17.

Published Sources

British Newspapers and Journals

The Belfast Newsletter
Caledonian Mercury
Examiner
The Gentleman's Magazine

Jacksons Oxford Journal
Leeds Mercury
The Liverpool Mercury
Manchester Guardian
Morning Chronicle
The Morning Post
The Observer
Royal Cornwall Gazette
St James's Chronicle
The Standard
The Times
True Briton
The World

Manx Newspapers and Journals

Manx Advertiser
Manx Herald
Mona's Herald
Manx Liberal
Manx Quarterly
Manx Sun

Other Published Sources

Annual Reports of the Royal National Institution for the Preservation of Life from Shipwreck, 1824, 1831.

Baines, Thomas, *History of the Commerce and Town of Liverpool*, vol. I.

Belchem, John, *A New History of the Isle of Man, The Modern Period*, vol. V (2000).

Boardman, James, *Liverpool Table Talk A Hundred Years Ago* (1882).

Booth, Christopher C., *Quakers of Countersett, Presidential Address* (2005).

Bridges, G. W., *Annals of Jamaica* (1828).

Butler, Pierce, *The Letters of Pierce Butler 1790–1794* (2007).

Cameron, Ian, *Riders of the Storm, The Story of the Royal National Lifeboat Institution* (2009).

Carrington, Selwyn H.H., *The Sugar Industry and the Abolition of the Slave Trade* (2002).

Corkhill, Adrian, *Shipwrecks of the Isle of Man* (2001).

Dallas, Robert Charles, *The History of the Maroons* (1803).

D'Arblay, Madame, *The Journals and Letters of Fanny Burney*, ed. Joyce Hemlow (1972–84).

Dawson, Major A.J., *Britain's Lifeboats – The story of a Century of Heroic Service* (1923).

Debrett's Baronetage of England.

Elliot-Drake, Lady (ed.), *Lady Knight's Letters from France and Italy, 1776-1795* (1905).

Fothergill, A., Essay on the preservation of shipwrecked mariners, in answer to the prize questions proposed by the Royal Humane Society (1794).

Gell, William, *The Hero King, an Epic Poem* (1907).

Gillen, Mollie, *The Royal Duke* (1976).

Gore's Liverpool Directory, containing an alphabetical list of the merchants, tradesmen and principal inhabitants of the town of Liverpool, 1781, 1790-1818

Greathead, Henry, *Report of the Evidence and other proceedings in Parliament respecting the Invention of the Life-boat* (1804).

Himmelfarb, Gertrude, 'The Age of Philanthropy', *The Wilson Quarterly* (1976).

'The Wreck of the St George in Douglas Bay', *Journal of the Manx Museum*, vol. V (1941).

Kelly, Robert, *List of Vessels wrecked on the Coast of the Isle of Man from 1822–1841* (1842).

Kelly, Robert, *For Those in Peril* (1979).

Kelly, Robert, *Sir William Hillary and the Isle of Man Lifeboat Stations* (1994).

Hillary, William, *An Appeal to the British Nation on the Humanity and Policy of Forming a National Institution for the Preservation of lives and Property from Shipwreck* (1823).

Hillary, William, *A Plan for the Construction of a Steam Lifeboat* (1824).

Hillary, William, *Suggestions for the Improvement and Embellishment of the Metropolis* (1824).

Hillary, William, *A Sketch of Ireland in 1824: the sources of her evils considered and their remedies suggested* (1825).

Hillary, William, *The National Importance of a Great Central Harbour for the Irish Sea...* (1836).

Hillary, William, *Observations on the Proposed Changes in the Fiscal and Navigation Laws of the Isle of Man...* (1837).

Hillary, William, *The Naval Ascendancy of Britain* (1838).

Hillary, William, *A Letter to the Shipping and Commercial Interests of Liverpool on Steam Life and Pilot Boats* (1839).

Hillary, William, *A Letter to the Rt Hon Lord John Russell, Secretary of State for the Home Department...* (1842).

Hillary, William, *Great Central Harbour of Refuge for the Irish Sea, Douglas Bay, Isle of Man by means of Floating Breakwaters* (1842).

Hillary, William, *Suggestions for the Christian Occupation of the Holy Land as a Sovereign State by the Order of St John of Jerusalem* (1841).

Hillary, William, *Decree for the Foundation of the restored Order of St John of Jerusalem in Italy.*

Hopkirk, Mary, *Danbury Historical Notes* (1945).

Ingamells, John, *A Dictionary of British and Irish Travellers in Italy 1701–1800* (1997).

Langford, Mary Jones, *Fairest Isle – History of Jamaica Friends* (1998).

Laurens, Henry, *Papers of Henry Laurens 1759–1763* (Hamer, 1972).

Lukin, Lionel, *The Invention, Principles of Construction and Uses of Unimmergible Boat* (1806).

Moore, A.W., *History of the Isle of Man Steam Packet Co.* (1904).

Morrit, John B.S. (ed.) *The Letters of, G.E. Marindin* (1914).

Mortimer, Theo, '175 Years of the Royal National Lifeboat Institution', *Dublin Historical Record* (1999).

Norris, Samuel, *Manx Memories and Movements* (1938).

Owen, David, *English Philanthropy 1660–1960* (1965).

Oxford Dictionary of National Biography (online edition): William Hillary, Lionel Lukin, Captain George Manby, Mary Rolls, John Rushout; Henry Trengrouse.

Philip, Mark, *Resisting Napoleon* (2006).

Porter, Roy, *English Society in the 18th Century*.

Ralfe, Pilcher G., 'Manx Banking', *The Scottish Banker's Magazine* (1917).

Riley-Smith, Jonathan, *Hospitallers, the History of the Order of St John* (1999).

Rolls, Mrs Henry, *The Kaleidoscope or Literary and Scientific Mirror* (1825).

Scarffe, Andrew, *The Great Laxey Mine* (2004).

Scott, Walter, *Letters of 1821–1823* (1934).

Shee, George, *Sir William Hillary founder of the Institution* (1921).

Shore, Charles John, *Sketches of the Coasts and Islands of Scotland and of the Isle of Man* (1836).

Stenning, E.H., *Portrait of the Isle of Man* (1958).

Sheridan, R. B., 'Simon Taylor, Sugar Tycoon of Jamaica, 1740-1813', *Agricultural History*, vol. 45, (October, 1971).

Taylor, Patricia, *Thomas Blaikie (1751–1838): the Capability Brown of France* (2001).

The Laws of Jamaica 1681–1759 (1802).

The Oxford Illustrated History of the Crusades (2001).

Warner, Oliver, *A History of the Royal National Life-boat Institution 1824–1974* (1974).

Welch, John, *A Six Day Tour through the Isle of Man* (1836).

Whitworth Porter, Major, *A History of the Knights of Malta* (1858).

Wood, G. W, 'A Manx Patriot, An Account of his Writings', *Manx Quarterly* (14 September 1914).

Wordsworth Dorothy, *Journal of a Visit to the Isle of Man* (1828).

Philip Wright (ed.), *Lady Nugent's Journal of her Residence in Jamaica from 1801–1805* (1966).

Wynne, Elizabeth (ed.), *The Diaries of Anne Freemantle, vol. II 1794–1798)* (1937).

Index

If you enjoyed this book, you may also be interested in…

The Lifeboats Story

EDWARD WAKE-WALKER

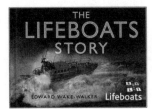

The RNLI is one of the best known maritime rescue organizations in the world. It receives no financial support from the British government and is supported entirely by public donations. Edward Wake-Walker, the RNLI's former director of public relations, tells the story of the Institution from it's beginnings during the reign of Queen Victoria, to the hi-tech rescue maritime organisation it has become in the twenty-first century.

978 0 7509 4858 6

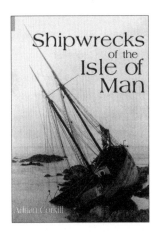

Shipwrecks of the Isle of Man

ADRIAN CORKILL

This book looks at a selection of 85 wreck sites around the Isle of Man (wrecks far from the shore or too deep for the sports diver are excluded). Each entry gives an extensive description of the wreck site with any special features for a diver to note. A detailed account of the history of each shipwreck (together with photographs, diagrams or newspaper headlines, where available) is also provided, along with technical data on each vessel as she existed prior to her loss. A separate section gives valuable information for the diver on how to access sites etc. Several maps of the location of the wrecks sites can be included.

978 0 7524 2698 3

Visit our website and discover thousands of other History Press books.

www.thehistorypress.co.uk